SHANE VICTORINO

SHANE VICTORINO

The Flyin' Hawaiian

Alan Maimon

TRIUMPH
BOOKS

The Library of Congress has catalogued the previous edition as follows:

Maimon, Alan.
  Shane Victorino : the flyin Hawaiian / Alan Maimon.
    p. cm.
  ISBN 978-1-60078-542-9
  1. Victorino, Shane. 2. Baseball players—United States—Biography. I. Title.
  GV865.V53M35 2011
  796.357092—dc22
  [B]
                        2010044886

This book is available in quantity at special discounts for your group or organization. For further information, contact:

  Triumph Books LLC
  814 North Franklin
  Chicago, Illinois 60610
  (312) 337-0747
  www.triumphbooks.com

Printed in U.S.A.
ISBN: 978-1-60078-941-0
Design by Patricia Frey
All photos courtesy of Shane Victorino unless otherwise indicated
Title page photo courtesy of AP Images

To my parents

"Sports do not build character. They reveal it."

—John Wooden

CONTENTS

PREFACE

Few players have had as eventful a few years as Shane Victorino. And the 2013 season represented another memorable chapter in the Flyin' Hawaiian's improbable baseball journey.

At a time when some baseball observers felt Victorino's skills were on the decline, he bounced back to enjoy the finest season of his career. In his first season with the Boston Red Sox, he helped the team celebrate its first World Series–clinching victory at Fenway Park since 1918. A beloved figure in Philadelphia for years, Victorino quickly achieved legendary status in Beantown with his postseason heroics, which included a game-winning grand slam in the American League Championship Series clincher against the Detroit Tigers.

The first edition of this book chronicled the personal and professional battles that Shane waged on his way to becoming the first Maui native ever to appear in a Fall Classic. Throughout childhood and into adulthood, Victorino has worked to control his attention deficit hyperactivity disorder. Following the publication of his biography, Victorino signed on as a national spokesman for ADHD, raising awareness of a disorder that affects millions of Americans.

A multisport athlete in high school, Victorino experienced a career's worth of hard times in the Los Angeles Dodgers organization before entering into a sustained period of prosperity with the Phillies. His banner year with the Red Sox in 2013 reaffirmed his status as one of the most compelling players in the game.

"I've faced obstacles my whole life," Victorino said. "I came from a place that didn't produce a lot of major leaguers, and I wasn't a big guy. But I've always worked hard. And I will continue to do that as long as I put on a jersey and get to play the game I love."

SHANE VICTORINO

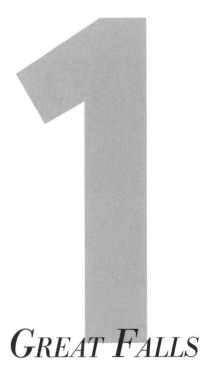

1

GREAT FALLS

IT MUST HAVE BEEN A RECORD FOR THE GREATEST AMOUNT OF candy ever dumped on a motel room bed in Medicine Hat, Alberta, Canada.

Shane Victorino, fresh off a marathon flight from Maui and a five-hour drive through the outer reaches of Montana, had barely exchanged hellos with his roommate, Dave Detienne, when the seemingly endless stream of confections started flowing from Victorino's backpack.

The introduction to the newest member of the rookie league Great Falls Dodgers left Detienne slack-jawed. "It was my second year playing for Great Falls," Detienne said. "They told me I was going to get the new guy from Hawaii as my roommate. I was, like, 'Okay, that's fine.' Well, we're on the road in Medicine Hat when he joins the team and he comes running into the motel room all loud and hyper, and immediately starts dumping out all this candy. And he's just talking a mile a minute. 'Hi, I'm Shane. How's it going? Where you from?' He had his mouth full of candy and he asked me if I wanted to eat some candy, too. He was really kind of freaking out. I'm thinking to myself, *Wow, this guy really has some energy. Maybe he's on a sugar high or something.*"

The role high-fructose corn syrup played in the commotion was open to debate, but that the 18-year-old from Maui was excited to be in Medicine Hat, or anywhere else he had to go to play professional baseball, was beyond dispute.

Victorino had spent the previous weeks deliberating his future and professional goals, weighty subjects for any 18-year-old, and especially for Victorino, who had always lived for the moment. The soul-searching led to this first stop, north of the border to a Canadian town known more for slap shots than stolen bases.

On June 2, 1999, a few weeks before Victorino met his Great Falls teammates in Medicine Hat, the Dodgers made him their sixth-round pick, the 194th overall selection, in that year's Major League Baseball draft. Leading up to that day, Victorino had publicly stated he would sign a professional baseball contract if he got drafted in the top eight rounds. But based on what scouts were telling him, it appeared he might go closer to the 12th round. If that turned out to be true, he was leaning toward attending college. The University of Hawaii was prepared to offer him at least a partial baseball scholarship. And he was also being courted by soccer programs at the University of California, Berkeley, and Hawaii Pacific University.

The drama increased on draft day. Within hours of his selection by the Dodgers, University of Hawaii football coach June Jones, who had followed Victorino since his hiring by Hawaii a year and a half earlier, phoned Victorino's home to extend him a full baseball and football scholarship. Jones wanted Victorino to catch passes in his high-octane offense in the fall and star on the diamond for the Rainbow Warriors in the spring. The offer was tempting to Victorino for two reasons: it would allow him to stay close to home, and it would allow him to play two of the four sports he starred in at St. Anthony High School in Maui. In addition to baseball, football, and soccer, he also ran track.

On draft day, Victorino's hometown paper, *The Maui News*, which had named him its male athlete of the year a week earlier, pressed him about his plans. "I honestly don't know right at this moment," Victorino responded. "I don't know much about the Dodgers and their farm system. I just have to sit down and figure everything out."

For Victorino, playing the games had always been the easy part. Sports came naturally to him and, because of his problems with hyperactivity, had in some ways been a savior. Everyone in Maui marveled at his development as an athlete.

"When I first knew him, he was the little kid in the park running around like crazy, going from group to group," said Craig Okita, who was Victorino's assistant baseball coach at St. Anthony. "In high school, he showed he had so much raw talent. He was the best hitter I've seen in high school at that age."

Though he adored all the sports he played, Victorino decided his preferred future was on the baseball diamond. His mother wanted him to get a college education. But a few days after the draft, he inked a contract with the Dodgers while sitting at the dining room table of his family's Wailuku home.

"There were choices for me to make, and my family and I talked about the different options," Victorino said. "My mom was very big on education. I told her that college will be there for me later, but I didn't know if I'd have the chance again to get drafted and play minor league ball. It took a lot of thinking, but with the longevity and the opportunities baseball presented, we felt like it was best suited for who I was. And it was just an exciting opportunity."

In choosing baseball, Victorino followed his heart, but for years, he would periodically question the decision. During particularly frustrating moments in the minor leagues, he felt tempted to pick up the phone to see if June Jones' offer of a football scholarship was still on the table.

The contract with the Dodgers came with a $115,000 signing bonus. As a member of the rookie league team, he would earn $650 per month and play alongside most of the organization's 1999 high school draftees. His instructions were to report to Great Falls of the Pioneer League's North Division immediately, but due to a lingering dental problem, he could not depart for Montana right away. A procedure to remove his impacted wisdom teeth required about 10 days of recovery time.

When he was ready to travel, about 75 well-wishers gathered at Kahului Airport to say goodbye to Victorino, who sported a pair of white pants, a white ballcap, and a shirt that was somewhere between teal and turquoise. Mike Victorino Jr., Shane's older brother, recalled the scene at the gate of the airport: "I was crying. I remember he was sobbing, too. Everyone was very emotional. Seeing him go away was like seeing a boy become a man."

Shane had eight hours of flying time to mentally prepare himself for the enormous challenge that lay ahead. Born and raised on the island paradise of Maui, *ohana*, or family, was immensely important to him. But on that June day in 1999 when he joined his minor league team, he left loved ones behind to embark on his climb up the professional baseball ladder. As he devoured fistfuls of sweets in the motel in Medicine Hat, he and his new teammates stood on the bottom rung of the ladder. There was no sugar-coating that reality.

SHANE VICTORINO'S EVOLUTION FROM SCRAPPY all-around athlete to serious baseball prospect happened quickly—and with a degree of luck. Yes, major league scouts flocked to Hawaii during his senior year of high school but not necessarily to get a look at him. The object of their desire was a talented pitcher from Honolulu named Jerome Williams, who in his senior year at Waipahu High School boasted an 8–1 record with a microscopic 0.12 ERA. Williams wound up as a first-round selection of the San Francisco Giants in the 1999 draft, taken 155 picks before the Dodgers chose Victorino.

While scouts were in the "neighborhood" of islands looking at Williams, a growing number decided to check out the 5'9", 170-pound dynamo from Maui who was putting up big numbers of his own at St. Anthony High School. Hawaiian scout Eric Tokunaga, who worked for the Kansas City Royals at the time, was one of the first baseball emissaries to take real notice of Victorino. Tokunaga got a good glimpse of him at a high school tournament on the island of Kauai in the early spring of 1999.

"He stole five bases, got down the line in less than four seconds, and came in as a relief pitcher and threw 86 miles per hour," said Tokunaga, a standout shortstop in the late 1970s and early 1980s at the University of Hawaii. "He did a lot of stuff that day that I hadn't seen on a baseball field. It was clear to me he was a different player from everybody else. But I think the other scouts didn't see that because he wasn't big in stature, and he wasn't hitting the ball very hard."

When the Royals worked out Victorino on Hawaii's Big Island, Tokunaga looked on as Victorino smoked the ball all over the field with a wooden bat. He approached Shane's dad, Mike Victorino Sr., who was watching from the stands. Tokunaga introduced himself and told the elder Victorino he thought his son had a possible future in Major League Baseball. In fact, Tokunaga told him, he had the potential to be the next Rickey Henderson, baseball's all-time stolen base king who also had racked up more than 3,000 hits during a Hall of Fame career.

"What? You're kidding me, right?" was Mike Victorino's surprised response.

His astonishment did not signify a lack of confidence in his son's athletic ability. Rather, it was suggestive of a sports culture on the Hawaiian islands that was less pressure-filled than on the mainland. Kids played sports for enjoyment, not to groom themselves for professional careers. Mike's sons were no exception.

"I knew Shane had abilities, but when I heard what Eric was saying, I thought, *Come on! Don't blow too much smoke here*," Mike Victorino said.

When Tokunaga started phoning the Victorino home a few times a week during Shane's senior season, his mother, Joycelyn, did not know what to make of it. Who was this man calling her son and asking how his baseball season was going? Why did he care so much about a high school baseball player?

"She was really upset, because she thought I was harassing her son," Tokunaga said. "She didn't know who I was or what I was doing."

Joycelyn Victorino's standoffishness was in contrast to an otherwise sunny disposition. But she felt it was important to keep her son grounded, and she wanted to maintain parental control. "I was mad at Eric," she said. "I told him I didn't appreciate him calling and talking to my son, putting all these things in his head when there was a chance nothing would come to fruition. I told him, 'You build up his big hopes, and then maybe he has a great fall. If you call our house, you respect us as parents. You talk to us first, and we'll give you permission to talk to Shane.'"

Fred Engh, the founder of the National Alliance for Youth Sports and author of *Why Johnny Hates Sports*, a book that casts a critical eye on parental over-involvement in youth athletics, believes Joycelyn Victorino's reaction to the calls was fully justified. "Mrs. Victorino is a rare exception today," Engh says. "If all parents were like her, then the world of organized sports for children would be much different, and better, today. Today's parents would give up a lot to have a child as gifted and talented as Shane, and they will go to unbelievable lengths to try to make it happen."

As someone paid to deliver his bosses the best possible talent, Tokunaga was just doing his job. But he heeded Joycelyn's wishes and began going through her and her husband first before talking to Shane. Thanks to his glowing reports to the home office about the kid from Maui, the Royals sent Steve Flores, the organization's senior scout responsible for vetting prospects, to check out Victorino's game.

When Flores, a so-called national crosschecker, came to Hawaii to look at Tokunaga's potential draftees, he asked to see Victorino take batting practice and run the 60-yard dash. But he also requested to watch him play in a soccer game near Waikiki. During the game, a dog ran on the field, disrupting play for several minutes. The referees and some of the players tried to chase the animal off, to no avail. Then Victorino sprang into action, taking off after the dog, catching him, and shooing him away, allowing play to continue.

Later that day, Shane did his formal workout for the scouts. After batting practice, Flores appeared ready to shut things down for the day.

"When do you want him to run the 60?" Tokunaga asked.

"We don't need to run him," his colleague replied. "The kid can catch a dog."

With Flores on board, the Royals set their sights on Victorino as a draft pick. And they likely would have gotten him if not for the impressive showing Victorino made during a last-minute tryout for another major league team, one that had never seen him play in high school.

With the encouragement of Tokunaga, who had by then earned the trust of the Victorino family and become an unofficial adviser to them, Shane flew to Los Angeles less than a week before the draft to take part in an open workout sponsored by the Dodgers. Decked out in all yellow, the colors of his high school, he made an impression on everyone before he even picked up a bat or glove. And when he hit three home runs at Dodger Stadium and outran everyone else at the camp—including future college football and NFL star Troy Polamalu, a multisport athlete in Oregon—Victorino immediately landed himself another strong suitor.

On draft day 1999, future major leaguers like Josh Hamilton, Josh Beckett, Barry Zito, and Ben Sheets got snapped up in the first round. Later in the draft, the Dodgers and Royals became engaged in a game of chicken over Victorino.

Tokunaga recalled the sequence of events that led to Victorino going to the Dodgers: "Before the draft, the Royals called me and told me to ask Shane how much he would sign for, because they were thinking of drafting him in the sixth or seventh round. During the draft, I called his mom, who told me he would sign for $100,000. Well, 15 minutes later, Shane calls me and says the Dodgers just drafted him in the sixth round. Oh my goodness, talk about being pissed off! We just missed getting him."

Gracious in defeat, Tokunaga sent Shane a postcard a few days after the draft. It read:

Congratulations on a one-of-a-kind high school career. It will be some time before someone like you comes along again. Also, I want to say congratulations on the draft and I still can't believe that we let you slip through our hands, but K.C.'s loss is L.A.'s gain.

How Victorino's career might have turned out differently had he gone to the Royals is a question that will never be answered.

GREAT FALLS, MONTANA, POPULATION 50,000, calls itself the "Electric City," not because it promotes itself as a place of great excitement, but rather owing to the hydroelectric dams that lie on the nearby Missouri River. One of the area's claims to fame is that Meriwether Lewis and William Clark journeyed to Great Falls in the early 1800s to explore the newly purchased Louisiana Territory. Like Lewis and Clark, scores of young baseball players had ventured there since 1969 to explore big-league dreams. Before becoming the Great Falls Dodgers, the team had appropriately been named the Voyagers.

The 34 young men who saw action for the Great Falls Dodgers in the summer of 1999 arrived from a remarkably diverse array of places. The team's manager, Tony Harris, and two of its players were from Australia. Dave Detienne, Victorino's Nova Scotian roommate, was one of two Canadians on the roster. A tall Russian named Alexander Toropov was on the pitching staff. Another hurler came from Oxford, England. Add a smattering of Latin American players and it was as if the United Nations had relocated to rural Montana.

Before joining the team, Victorino shared what little he knew about the Treasure State with his hometown newspaper.

"I don't know much about Montana, other than it's boring, but that should give me the chance to concentrate on just baseball," he told *The Maui News.* "I look at this as a start of a journey."

Roommates Detienne and Victorino, one from a place of harsh winters, the other from a place of gorgeous beaches, were two of the players who came to Great Falls with great dreams.

Some of the young men who passed through town that summer left professional baseball after only a season or two. Others bounced around the minors for the better part of a decade before hanging it up. At least one member of the team wound up in prison. Of all the players the Dodgers organization thought enough of to send to rookie ball in 1999, only two made it to the majors within the next decade.

Their backgrounds as different as could be but their ambitions exactly the same, Victorino and Detienne quickly developed a kinship. They were roommates on the road, and in Great Falls they stayed in the home of a host couple named Bob and Elaine.

The two players from Maui and Halifax had worked hard to catch the eye of major league scouts not in the habit of making trips to far-flung locations like Hawaii and Nova Scotia. The lanky 6'3" Detienne, a 25th-round pick by the Dodgers in 1997, hoped to become one of only a handful of players from his province ever to make it to the bigs. As the first position player from Nova Scotia ever drafted by a major league team, he was off to a promising start.

This is how Detienne described the life of an aspiring baseball player in cold and foggy Halifax: "In Nova Scotia, we didn't have high school teams. By the time we got out on the field, it was already late June, and we played only 20 or 25 games. But baseball was something that I picked up at a young age and just loved. All of my development was done indoors at not-so-great facilities. Eventually, I got to go to national tournaments, and that's where I got my first exposure to any type of scouting."

Victorino's home was hardly a baseball hotbed, either. A frequent saying heard there, "*Maui no ka oi*," translates to "Maui is great." But the phrase never really applied to sports and especially not to baseball. At the time Victorino began his minor league career, only one player born on the island had ever made it to the highest level of baseball…and that was Tony Rego, who suited up for parts of two seasons with the St. Louis Browns way back in the 1920s.

Since Rego's days, a couple dozen Hawaiian players, the vast majority from Honolulu, had reached the major leagues. Formal ties between Major

League Baseball and the islands were largely severed in 1987, when the Hawaii Islanders, a Triple A team in the Pacific Coast League, ended a 27-year run. An MLB-affiliated winter league in Hawaii began play a few years after the Islanders departed.

In the spring of 1999, major league scouts discovered Maui had at least one outstanding baseball talent.

"It was exciting to go through the process of having scouts come to Maui to watch me play," Victorino said. "People hadn't really seen that before. I was like everybody else. I'd look around and wonder, *Who are all these people?*"

The Pioneer League's 76-game season had already started when Victorino joined his team in Medicine Hat. A couple days after his arrival, team manager Tony Harris called Victorino to his office before a game to ask about his availability.

"I had him leading off and playing center field," Harris recalled. "I was so excited to see this kid finally play and was sure he would accept my offer to get in there."

Harris had it all planned out. He figured Victorino would be raring to go, so the manager wanted to surprise him by opening his desk drawer and pulling out the lineup card with the name "Victorino" written across the top.

But to Victorino, the offer was more option than order. Because Harris had phrased it as a question, he chose to give an honest answer. He told Harris he was still adjusting to his new environment and did not yet have the type of glove he would need to play center field.

"Nah, not quite ready yet, Skip," he said. "Maybe in a few days I might be."

In his head, the manager was thinking, *You have to be kidding! Who the heck does this guy think he is?*

But he played it as cool as Victorino had.

"Okay," Harris replied, and he abruptly ended the talk.

Detienne came by Harris' office as the conversation was coming to an end. "I saw the look on Tony Harris' face, and I just laughed, because I still didn't know Shane that well and couldn't believe he had the guts to say he wasn't ready to play," Detienne recalled.

It may have surprised onlookers, but Victorino's response to his manager was in keeping with the somewhat controversial reputation he developed on his home island. Anybody in Maui who knew Shane Victorino, even in passing, knew he was *kolohe*, a Hawaiian word meaning rascally and mischievous. In high school, he not only led his teams in scoring but also in getting thrown out of games. Part of his difficulty controlling anger and impulsivity stemmed from having attention deficit hyperactivity disorder, or ADHD, which he would continue to battle in the minor leagues.

Uninitiated in the ways of Shane, Harris found his new charge's conduct anything but amusing. Later that week, the manager summoned Victorino again, this time with some news: "You were going to start last night. But since you wanted a couple days off, I decided to give you a week off. Never say you aren't prepared and ready to play. If [then-Dodgers manager] Davey Johnson had called today and asked if you were ready, would you have said you were?"

"Of course," Victorino admitted sheepishly.

It was the first of many lessons he would learn during his first weeks down on the farm.

"With all my involvement in Shane's career, I have never known him to be anything other than always ready to play from that point onward," Harris said. "It was important to let this rookie kid know that the tail doesn't wag the dog."

His initial dealings with his manager were less than ideal, but what happened the day Victorino finally ran out to center field for his first start with Great Falls redefined the meaning of a disastrous first day on the job.

Things began to go poorly even before the road game in Missoula, Montana, started, when Dodgers second-round draft pick Brennan King was hit in the mouth and lost a tooth during batting practice. With Victorino a couple weeks removed from a procedure to extract his wisdom teeth, dental problems were becoming a recurring theme for Great Falls players that summer. Maybe it was their proximity to all the nearby hockey rinks.

But King's injury paled in comparison to the one that occurred during the game to Jason Repko, the Dodgers' first-round pick. And it happened at the hands of Victorino.

In the third inning of the Missoula game, a softly hit line drive fell between shortstop Repko and center fielder Victorino. A Missoula player on third base, who had returned to the bag to tag up if the ball was caught, took off for home when he saw it drop. Victorino quickly picked up the ball and in one motion rifled it toward home plate.

More than a decade after the play, Victorino still recalled its details. "I hardly looked up, so I didn't see that Jason was probably no more than 10 or 15 feet directly in front of me," he said. "I winged the ball in as hard as I could, and it hit him in his temple. He went down and started convulsing. I'm thinking, *Oh my goodness, what just happened here?* The ball went all the way into right field, and we all ran over to see if Jason was okay. He was still convulsing, and I was just in disbelief."

Out cold for a few minutes, Repko was eventually able to walk off the field under his own power. But for weeks after the incident, he experienced symptoms of a serious concussion.

"It was scary, very scary, because we realized that might have killed him," Detienne said. "For a while, he was talking slower and not making much sense, like he was in a daze."

Repko made a full recovery and went on to play in the major leagues.

No one felt worse about the incident than Victorino. "That was one of my first memories of pro ball," he said. "It was incredible that something like that happened."

Lost in the horror of the mishap, deservedly so, was that Victorino earned his first professional hit in the game, a run-scoring triple that nearly cleared the outfield wall.

The run-in with his manager and the on-field accident made for a bad first few days in Great Falls. But Victorino would face many more challenges in that and future minor league seasons, the hardest of which was being away from the comforts and familiarity of his beloved Maui.

"I really missed home," Victorino said. "I remember calling my family every night and telling them I wasn't sure if I wanted to do this. I didn't know how tough it would be being away from my family for the first time."

WILD CHILD

THE LUSH RAIN FOREST, SPECTACULAR CLIFFS, AND WHITE-SAND beaches within a few miles of Wailuku give the town of about 13,000 in central Maui a strong aura of paradise. But at its core, Wailuku is not much different than thousands of other small communities that dot the American landscape. By day, men in neckties rush in and out of the local courthouse. In the late afternoon, the downtown workforce clogs Main Street with something closely resembling rush-hour traffic. And on summer evenings, Wells Park, situated in the heart of Wailuku's business district, teems with people of all ages, including Little Leaguers getting their first taste of baseball on the park's dirt field.

Down the left-field line of the diamond, beyond a chain-link fence, is a house with a dilapidated exterior and a forgotten garden. Back in the days when the home was occupied and flowers were in bloom, Shane Victorino and his older brother spent endless summer hours there in the company of their grandparents. Shane, whose head of dark, bushy hair earned him the nickname "Spongehead," grew up listening to the ping of metal bats hitting baseballs, as well as the thud of stray foul balls hitting his grandparents' roof.

"The sounds of baseball were embedded in me as a kid," Victorino said. "I spent a lot of time at that house playing catch with my older brother and grandpa while my parents were at work. Whatever my brother did, I would trail behind him. Anything he did, I wanted to do."

When his brother, Mike Jr., who was five years older than Shane, became old enough to go off and play in pick-up games with other children in Wailuku, Shane eagerly tagged along, even though he was a few years younger and much smaller than the kids who did battle on the local playgrounds.

"We'd play basketball or little home run derbies with a tennis ball, and Shane would always want to be a part of it," Mike Victorino Jr. said. "And he insisted on playing on the same team as his big brother. So we'd play games of two-on-two against guys who were usually five or six years older than Shane. That taught him to be a competitor from a young age. He wasn't as fast or as physically strong as us, but you could see he knew what he was doing. He could move and was real athletic. But he got his butt kicked from me sometimes, because we lost and I hated losing. He held his own, but we'd still lose. Sometimes I'd say, 'Enough already. I'm tired of losing. Get out of here.' I'd pick up a basketball and throw it at him as hard as I could, and he would run home crying. But you know what? He'd be back an hour later at the park saying, 'Can I play with you guys? Can I jump in?' Of course I said yes every time. He was my brother."

Shane wanted nothing more than to emulate his older brother. But the person with whom he had the closest bond growing up was his grandpa. Chester Nakahashi, his mother's father, was a retired tugboat captain who shared the house by Wells Park with his wife, Olive. Shane and Chester, separated in age by more than 50 years, were kindred spirits nonetheless. Both had a volatile personality that many found hard to control.

"When my grandpa got upset, the only one who could calm him down was me," Victorino said. "My grandpa would actually listen to me and not to any of his sons. We had that special bond. My grandpa was probably my best friend when I was a kid. We were like two peas in a pod."

When summer was over, an average childhood afternoon for Shane was school and then sports. On some days, while his grandparents rested, Shane went off to the local ballfields to play, always leaving behind a note like this one:

Dear Grandpa & Grandma,
Please come and watch my scrimmage. I play at Field 2 at 4:15 or 4:30. I walked down to the field.
Hope you come!!
Love,
Shane

Like clockwork, his grandmother, grandfather, and their white dog, Fluffy, would make their way to the field to cheer him on. "To my father,

Shane was everything," Joycelyn Victorino said of Chester's relationship with her son. "The minute he opened his mouth, it was all about Shane."

Olive Nakahashi also doted on her grandsons. "She was as close to an angel as I ever met on this earth," Mike Victorino Sr. said of his mother-in-law. "As bad as Shane would get sometimes, she'd always say, 'No, no, no, don't hit him. *Love* him. *Hug* him!'"

But something less positive was happening in the Nakahashi household that Shane did not fully grasp and act upon until he was in his late teenage years.

In his quest to make a quick buck, Chester was losing his life savings to gambling and con artists. In the early 1990s, when Shane was about 10 years old, Chester got suckered by two telephone scams that led him to send tens of thousands of dollars to Spain in exchange for what he thought would be millions of dollars in lottery winnings.

"My father-in-law was gullible," Mike Victorino Sr. said. "He thought the golden ring was always right around the corner. He loved gambling and going to Las Vegas. I used to have people come up to me and say he owed them money. I would just pay them off and not say anything about it."

Later, when Chester's behavior continued to spiral out of control, an intervention by Shane helped him get his life back together.

Chester and Olive Nakahashi's second-youngest daughter, Joycelyn, was prom queen, high school class president, and a member of the National Honor Society at St. Anthony High School. After graduation, she worked as a counter agent for the now-defunct Mid-Pacific Airlines at Kahului Airport. In 1988, she became secretary for the International Longshore and Warehouse Union.

Mike Victorino, who grew up on the Big Island of Hawaii and moved to Maui in 1973, always juggled multiple jobs, including selling insurance door to door, managing a McDonald's, and driving tourists to scenic island locales. He also found time to get an associate's degree in business from Maui Community College.

He met his future wife while both were working at McDonald's. Joycelyn was a teenager earning pocket money and Mike was in a management training program.

"I was 22, and she was still in high school," Mike Victorino Sr. recalled. "I wanted to take her to the prom, but she already had a date. I wanted to take her to the Chrysanthemum Ball and somehow found a way to win that battle. I ended up marrying her, so I guess I ended up winning the war."

Mike Victorino's and Joycelyn Nakahashi's family backgrounds were emblematic of the forces that helped shape the culture of the Hawaiian islands in the 1800s, a century in which the native population was ravaged by disease and in which the island became a territory of the United States. Mike, a third-generation Hawaiian, had great-grandparents who emigrated from Portugal to work on sugar plantations. Joycelyn was of Japanese, Chinese, and native Hawaiian heritage.

Shane Patrick Victorino was born on November 30, 1980, in Wailuku. His first name pays homage to the titular character in the 1953 film starring Alan Ladd, one of his father's favorite movies. His middle name is reflective of his family's strong Catholic faith.

Until the age of seven, he lived with his parents and older brother "upcountry" in Maui, in the village of Makawao, where Mike and Joycelyn Victorino moved after getting married in 1976.

The Victorinos moved in 1987 from Makawao to a four-bedroom house in Wailuku Heights, a middle-class subdivision nestled in the West Maui Mountains. The home offered a majestic view of the island's coastline and was just five minutes from Joycelyn's childhood home near Wells Park.

After their busy work days, Mike and Joycelyn Victorino carved out time for their sons. "The rule in this house was we all come home every night and eat together and pray together," Joycelyn said. "When we had dinner, there were to be no phone calls, no radio, no TV. Everything was shut off. Dinnertime was family time. That was the rule in my house."

Even rambunctious Shane managed to stay tranquil during these evening hours when his mom cooked roast beef, lomi lomi salmon, kalua pig, or chicken katsu. Shane cleaned his plate so that he would earn some guri guri, a beloved Hawaiian frozen dessert.

The older Shane got, the more his parents recognized his hyperactivity. Mike Sr. saw that his son was showing some of the same behavioral traits he had as a child. "His mom was very good in school. I was a very poor student. I was like Shane. I couldn't stand structure and was always in trouble. My parents got to know all the principals very well," he said.

To help compensate for some of the lessons Shane was not grasping at school, his parents got him involved in the Boy Scouts. There he learned valuable social and life skills. When Victorino returned home after his first season of minor league baseball, he was awarded the rank of Eagle Scout, the organization's highest distinction.

Sports were a godsend for young Shane, because away from the athletic fields, he had an uncanny knack for hurting himself.

By the age of five, he had visited the emergency room *eight* times. His mishaps included a bicycle accident that occurred while he was frantically waving to his mother and not paying attention to the road in front of him. The gruesome result of the crash was a bike spoke through his ear.

"He was very accident prone," Mike Victorino Sr. said. "Once I was having a meeting at our house. All of a sudden I heard a thud from the bedroom and my older son shouted, 'Daddy, daddy, come quick, Shane's bleeding!' What happened was Shane dove off the bunk bed and hit his head on a toy truck. He cut his head open. That put an end to my meeting."

Shane got the stitches, but Mike Jr. suffered the spankings each time his little brother got hurt.

"I got dirty lickings for every one of those events, because I was supposed to be watching him," Mike Victorino Jr. said. "But that wasn't an easy thing to do. One time we were at my friend's house watching television. One minute, Shane was there, and the next minute he was gone. I went outside to look for him but couldn't find him. Then we heard a lady screaming down the street. We ran down and saw Shane there standing next to a bike. The bike was all busted up, and it looked like Shane was about to run away. It was pretty obvious that he got hit by her car. The lady was traumatized, and Shane was ready to just go off and find something else to do. That was my brother in a nutshell. He was a crazy kid."

Shane's unfettered energy even led to the expulsion of the Victorino family dog, an Akita that one day made the mistake of getting too rough with him. "The dog jumped on Shane, and Shane got so mad that he jumped on the dog and bit it," his father recalled. "I was afraid for the dog, so we got rid of it."

This type of unrestrained behavior did not translate well to a classroom setting. "I had hyperactivity problems," Shane said. "I was always on the teachers' last nerve. Looking back on it, I don't know how they put up with me. I think some of them recognized I just had a lot of energy, but a lot of them just wanted to wring my neck every day."

When Shane attended Emmanuel Lutheran Preschool in nearby Kahului, his parents got almost daily phone calls about their son's disruptive behavior. His father wondered what all the fuss was about and decided to get a closer look at the classroom dynamics. With the permission of the school principal, he observed Shane and his class from a closet. Even he was surprised at how difficult it was for his son to sit still. Eventually, Joycelyn Victorino met with school officials to discuss the situation.

"We came to a mutual agreement to take Shane out of the school, because there were teachers threatening to quit if we didn't," she said. "I was surprised that trained professionals couldn't manage a four-year-old, but in the best interests of everyone, I told them we'd just go ahead and take him to a different school."

While Shane was in grade school at the Maui Individualized Learning Center, his parents sought evaluations by a pediatrician and by school doctors. Based on these tests, Shane was diagnosed with attention deficit hyperactivity disorder, or ADHD, a medical condition that leads to inattentiveness, hyperactivity, and impulsivity. The American Academy of Pediatrics estimates that between 4 and 12 percent of school-age children, the vast majority of them boys, have the disorder.

Though kids with ADHD have a hard time focusing attention on many everyday tasks, they often have the ability to "hyperfocus" on a specific subject or hobby. Shane, who took medication for his disorder, poured all his energy and concentration into sports. "My parents saw sports as an avenue to use some of my energy," Victorino said. "I think it was a challenge for them because I was so energetic and so hyper and so all over the place all the time."

Shane felt driven to play as many sports as possible.

"A lot of kids want to focus on just one sport," he said. "I think it helped me a lot as a kid to play multiple sports. One, it helped me stay in shape and keep busy, and two, it kept me from getting too wrapped up in any kind of frustrations with one sport. Once one season was over, I'd move on to another and then another after that."

Athletics were indeed a year-round obsession for Shane and his brother. Mike Jr. became a three-sport star at St. Anthony High School while Shane was still in junior high. "We never took a break from sports," Mike Jr. said. "That's why we never got into surfing or body boarding or any ocean activity. During the summer, we'd travel all over, to the mainland, to Oahu, to the Big Island. We never had any downtime."

His parents viewed sports as a year-by-year commitment, which meant there was no quitting in the middle of a season. "We encouraged them to play, and we demanded they played and practiced hard," Mike Victorino Sr. said. "And I said, 'If you start the year with this team, I don't care if they're 0 and 25, you're going to finish. If you start something, you finish it before you jump to the next team.'"

On weekends, sports were a family affair. At the 1996 Hawaii Cup, a soccer tournament held each summer on Maui, Shane scored several goals, Mike Jr. coached a team, and Mike Sr. was the tournament director. Mike Sr. also was the public address announcer for Shane's Pony League baseball games.

ALWAYS ON THE GO AND SIX TIME ZONES behind the eastern United States, Shane spent relatively little time in front of the television. But during his preteen years, he caught quite a few Atlanta Braves games on WTBS, the superstation that broadcast all over the country. His affinity for Deion Sanders, a two-sport athlete and then a member of the Braves, turned him into a fan of the team.

"My brother was my role model, but the guy on TV that I wanted to mimic was Deion Sanders," Victorino said. "He was a quick, explosive athlete who could change a game in the snap of a finger. In football, he was either returning a punt for a touchdown or making an interception. In baseball, he was either beating out a bunt and stealing a base or running a ball down in center field. That's the kind of player I wanted to be."

And that was the kind of player he was becoming.

By the time Shane reached junior high, his older brother was noticing changes. The scrawny kid who nipped at the heels of the older boys on the playground, begging them to let him join their games, had developed into a superb athlete. "Shane was in seventh or eighth grade, and we went to Oahu to watch a University of Hawaii football game," Mike Jr. recalled. "I was already a high school all-star at defensive back on Maui. We were in a parking lot, and I told Shane to come at me. I started backpedaling, and before I could even turn and run, he was already behind me. I was thinking, *Wow, this kid is pretty fast.*"

The next time Mike Jr. had a chance to show off his brother's speed was while attending the University of Hawaii–Hilo on a baseball scholarship. This time, he decided to have some fun with it. "Shane came to visit me at college," his brother said. "We were at a friend's house having a good time when I decided to make a little wager. I said that Shane could beat the fastest guy on our baseball team in a sprint down the highway. Everybody put a little money in, and almost all of it was on the other guy. But Shane just smoked the guy. He went by him like he was standing still."

Having come of age playing sports against much older kids on Maui, Shane was more than prepared to compete against his peers by the time he got to St. Anthony High School, the alma mater of his mother and brother, in the summer of 1995. He hoped to play five sports at the school that had a student body of fewer than 400. Unfortunately, he could not fit basketball into his already jammed athletic schedule. So he settled for participation in four—football in the fall, soccer in the winter, and baseball and track in the spring.

Despite his modest size, he experienced immediate success for the Trojans, which made him an enormous fish in a small pond. The location of his hometown only elevated his status level. Not only was the pond he played in small, but it was thousands of miles away from almost every other pond in the United States.

Upon entering high school, Shane got a piece of advice from his brother, who had played baseball, football, and soccer at St. Anthony. "I told him to never judge himself on what he did on this island," Mike Victorino Jr. said. "I told him to look past that and to judge himself on what he could do at the state level, and after that, to rate himself on what he could do on the national level. I knew he could go places if he worked hard enough."

Shane listened to his brother, whose hand-me-down equipment he wore with pride. "I idolized him and wanted to be like him," he said. "Whatever he did, I did. I wore No. 2 in football like him, wore No. 8 in baseball like he did, and wore No. 10 in soccer like he did. The path that I took was through him."

As a freshman, Shane outran seniors at track meets. As a sophomore, he made all-league at wide receiver and defensive back. In baseball, he traveled to California between his freshman and sophomore years to play in a youth all-star tournament. Most impressively perhaps, he was named the Maui Interscholastic League's player of the year in soccer as a sophomore.

"I still say to this day that his best sport was soccer," his father said. "He'd have two or three guys on him and they still couldn't cover him. He had that ability to stop on a dime, turn, and go all the way to the opposite side of the field and score a goal."

The sport Shane most enjoyed playing was football.

"I loved the adrenaline of it," he said.

His athletic ability and enthusiasm did not endear him to everybody, however. "Shane had a bull's-eye on his back," his brother said.

In some cases, he might as well have drawn that target on himself.

In his teenage years, it became evident that the biggest impediment to Shane's development as an athlete was Shane himself. The same impulsivity issues that plagued him as a child threatened to overshadow some of his exploits on the field. He was on the verge of becoming known as much for his outbursts directed at teammates and opponents as for his game-changing plays.

Mike Victorino Jr. recalled one such incident that took place at the Hawaii Cup soccer tournament when Shane was 14 years old. "Shane's team was playing a team from the mainland," Mike Jr. said. "He scored a goal and then he ran over to the opposing sideline and gave the parents and coaches the finger. It got so bad that police officers had to come in to settle everything down. Shane just didn't care. He did what he wanted to do. Nobody could figure him out."

Shane's parents sensed that his antisocial tendencies were attributable to his attention deficit hyperactivity disorder. Though Shane had been diagnosed at a young age, he had never received thorough treatment for the condition, just prescription drugs to help him control the symptoms. His parents took him to see Dr. Alfred Arensdorf, a well-respected child psychologist in Maui whose own son had ADHD. Arensdorf concluded Shane was not a bad kid, just an excitable one.

"It was getting to the point where he risked being disqualified from sports," Arensdorf said. "He wasn't making it academically, and he wasn't behaving well enough for some coaches to want to coach him. I felt there were things that could be done to help him."

The treatment was not going to take effect overnight, however. In the meantime, Shane continued to struggle with his emotions.

Around the time he started meeting with Arensdorf, Victorino's football coach at St. Anthony suspended him for the last game of his freshman season for insubordination. "I got into it with one of my coaches, and I told him I was going to transfer to public school and come back the next season and beat the crap out of [St. Anthony High School]," Victorino recalled.

The coaching staff felt Victorino's threat was disrespectful to his teammates and school.

"The public school people were constantly after him to transfer, and he knew that," said Kevin O'Brien, who was offensive coordinator of the varsity squad at St. Anthony during Victorino's playing days. "[Head varsity coach] Charley Ane gave his full backing to the decision to bench him. He wanted to teach him a lesson."

Ane, a Honolulu native who played several seasons for the Detroit Lions in the 1950s, had a way of getting through to Shane.

"Charley was very critical in Shane's development," O'Brien said of his coaching mentor, who passed away in 2007. "Shane saw in Charley someone who had attained the highest level in professional sports. He had credibility with Shane because he had played in the NFL. Charley was a big man who had the loudest voice of anybody I've known in my life. He wouldn't let Shane get away with anything. And Shane saw how he carried himself and what he expected on the field and in life."

For example, whenever a funeral was held at the church on St. Anthony's campus, Ane would command his players to stop playing, remove their helmets, and pay respects until the procession passed.

The benching of Victorino at the end of his freshman season triggered another public spectacle, this time involving Shane's grandfather, Chester.

"My grandpa came out onto the field during the game and wanted to fight the head coach, because I wasn't playing," Victorino said. "I had to restrain him, and my uncles had to restrain him. It caused a big scene."

O'Brien was on the sideline during the incident.

"That was one of the worst things I've ever dealt with," he said. "The grandfather came down from the stands and started yelling at us, 'Let the boy play! Put him in the game!' Shane started yelling at his grandfather to go away. I stood with my arms wrapped around Shane for about five minutes. He was bawling."

During his sophomore year, Victorino broke his ankle, causing him to miss half the football season.

"He was in a cast and on crutches for four weeks," O'Brien recalled. "While he was out, we went to Kauai for a game and slept in a school cafeteria the night before we played. The next morning all his teammates were complaining that Shane woke them up by walking around on his crutches all night. It became a running joke between us. I told him that I bet he sleeps no more than two hours a night."

Shane's restlessness carried over to the classroom, where O'Brien was his world history teacher.

"Sitting in a classroom for even 50 minutes was a lot of work for him," O'Brien said.

On the football field, however, Victorino's aptitude was undeniable. The season opener of his junior year was a typical game for the quarterback-tailback-kicker. He scored two touchdowns: one on a 60-yard run and another on a 30-yard fumble return. He also threw a touchdown pass, booted a field goal, and added two extra points.

In another game that season against Lahainaluna High School, he set a Hawaii state high school record, which has since been broken, by splitting the uprights with a 48-yard field goal. Later in that same game, however, he was ejected for committing a personal foul against an opposing player. The referee thought he saw Victorino punch the player, but witnesses to the incident later cast doubt on whether he actually had.

High school fans could read all about Victorino in the local newspaper. The game stories proclaimed him a "one-man wrecking crew," while the letters to the editor featured writers both defending and criticizing his conduct.

Thanks in part to Victorino and starting quarterback Mika Pico, the Trojans won eight league football games during Victorino's junior year in 1997, more victories than they had in the seven previous seasons combined. The 1997 season included a 44–0 drubbing of rival Baldwin High School, the large public school that had once courted Victorino.

As the two best athletes at St. Anthony, Pico and Victorino developed a friendly rivalry.

"Shane needed someone to push him," O'Brien said. "Here was this guy Mika who was frankly a better football player than he was. Mika was the one who pushed Shane athletically. No one else could, and that was exactly what Shane needed."

Pico played football at a small California college before returning home to Maui where he became an electrician.

Stacey Yamamoto, a star on St. Anthony's girls soccer team, joined the school's junior varsity football team because the team was one player shy of being able to field a team. She did so well kicking extra points and field goals for the JV that she moved up to the varsity as a backup to Victorino. Playing alongside him, she observed his ability to take over a game.

"Let's just say he was cocky on whatever field he played, but he could afford to be," Yamamoto said. "He was part of the reason I got to kick. He ran so much and did so much during a game that when it came time to kick an extra point, he would be in need of a rest."

Victorino was one of Yamamoto's biggest supporters.

"We had a preseason game against Hilo High School where we were winning big, and we let Stacey kick off," O'Brien said. "The kick-off team is designed so that the kicker is the last one back. Sure enough, the Hilo High kid breaks it right up the middle, and Stacey has to make the tackle. She takes two steps toward him, turns sideways, and the guy runs into her and goes down. Shane was the first one on our team to run on the field after the play. He was more excited about it than anyone."

Baseball was less popular than football at St. Anthony. Only about a dozen players came out for the team, and it took Victorino a while longer to distinguish himself from other talented players in Maui and the rest of the state. Neither his play nor his conduct made him the center of attention in his early high school days, though he did become a four-time All-Maui Interscholastic League player on the diamond.

"When he played baseball, you didn't see the behavioral issues you saw when he was playing other sports," Dr. Arensdorf said. "He was such a disciplined baseball player. Part of that might have been that he grew up with his dad announcing games from behind home plate. He knew his dad had always been right there."

Through medication and counseling, Victorino succeeded in bringing the symptoms of ADHD under control. "As he got older, we got him on long-acting stimulants that crept up to the right level and trailed off gently and didn't carry the potential for dependence," Arensdorf said. "I wanted him to have a medicine that would take him through his sports training and homework."

In addition to drugs, Arensdorf also talked with Shane about behavioral modification strategies.

"The major thing we worked on was strategies for dealing with his anger and with people who rubbed him the wrong way. It was a big challenge for him to learn how to get along with people he didn't have a natural click with. There were coaches on that list, but it was mostly teachers. With coaches, if he got benched for something he did, he'd blame the coach if he didn't play and the team lost. He knew that things would've gone better for the team if he had been out there. He'd get really angry about it. I finally got him to do problem solving. We looked at a sequence of events that got him into trouble and traced it back to a point where he could have done something to avoid a problem. He was good at that. And I think it helped him."

His work with Dr. Arensdorf also contributed to improved performance in the classroom and better relationships with classmates.

"I told him that if he put the same kind of energy into academics that he put into sports, that he could be a 4.0 student," Arensdorf said. "I don't think he got it up that high, but he started doing very well. There were certain classes and teachers an athletic kid just wasn't going to be tuned in on. Some teachers didn't relate to athletes. A couple of them wanted St. Anthony to just be a college prep school. They thought of athletics as kind of a concession to the dark side. But Shane worked to do well in those classes, too.

"The odds are not in favor of kids with ADHD performing anywhere close to their potential. But Shane started making real progress. He became a real gentleman around the women in his class. And he helped tutor kids in the grade school as a community service project. These were kids that were just like him when he was young."

In addition to the personal satisfaction he got from graduating from St. Anthony with a better than 3.0 grade-point average, Shane's accomplishments in the classroom pleased his mother. "It was always high on her wish list for me to do well in school," he said. "And I proved that I could do it, which made her very happy. Dr. Arensdorf was very inspirational in my life. He helped me understand how to control my emotions and channel my energy in the right way. He was definitely a big part of helping me grow. What I'd tell somebody who has a child they think has ADHD is that it's nothing to be ashamed of. It's an imbalance, and it's something that needs to be treated. Don't be ashamed or afraid to go get help."

Shane's challenges as a child and teenager helped motivate his father to get involved in public service.

Mike Victorino Sr. had always been active in civic life on the island, serving as a member of the local PTA and director of the Maui County Fair Association. In 1998, he took his involvement a step further by winning election to the Hawaii State Board of Education. Even though his sons had attended private school, the elder Victorino believed strongly in the state's public education system. "I had graduated from public school and wanted to make sure we kept the system on track in dealing with special needs and other issues," he said.

SHANE'S SENIOR YEAR WAS MARKED by emotional growth and continued excellence in athletics.

After being named the male athlete of the year by *The Maui News* in 1999, Victorino said, "I'm a gamer. I hate to lose. Going to a small school taught me a lot, like how to overcome a loss. It shaped me into the athlete I am. I know I'm ready to take that last-second shot, kick the game-winning field goal, whatever."

He had racked up so many honors that some started referring to St. Anthony High School as "Shane Anthony" during his final year. A nerve pinch injury, or stinger, prompted Victorino's football coaches to avoid calling plays where he might aggravate his injury. He was used mostly as a decoy during his senior season.

His participation in baseball and track in the spring required multitasking.

"There were baseball games and qualifying track meets at the same time," Mike Victorino Sr. said. "Shane would drop his baseball pants, change his shoes, and run over to the track to qualify. He'd run the qualifying heat and be back before the inning started."

This led to some creative managing by his baseball coach, Llewelyn Awai, or "Coach Lew" as he was known. "It took a lot of commitment for him to do baseball and track, so I didn't want to deny him that opportunity," Awai said. "Sometimes I'd have to go out and give the umpire a bad time about something to give Shane a little more time to get back to the baseball field."

Awai, who had planned to retire when his son graduated from St. Anthony in 1997, stayed on at the urging of the Victorino family to guide Shane through to graduation. His steadying hand helped Shane confront his bouts of immaturity. Sometimes that meant sacrificing wins in favor of teaching lessons. The coach did whatever he could to let Victorino multitask during games, but practice was sacrosanct. He also adhered to a strict code of fairness.

"There was a really important game we needed to win to qualify for the state tournament during his senior year," Awai said. "Shane was at a weeklong soccer camp trying out for a team that was going to travel to Europe. Even though he missed baseball practice, he expected to play when he came back. I really was in a situation where I had to decide if I wanted to wrap up the championship or not. I decided not to do it. I had to bench him. It wouldn't have been fair to the rest of the boys who came to practice if I didn't. I think he learned a lesson from that. He learned that practice is important, that discipline is important. He mostly was a very coachable player. He didn't like to lose, and he gave you 100 percent. He also picked up the younger players. But practicing wasn't something he liked very much."

As he neared graduation, Shane cut back significantly on the type of incidents that drove his coaches crazy, including a habit of leaving practice early with female friends. "Everybody was his girlfriend," Awai said. "He was that type of guy."

Many on the island embraced his personality, warts and all.

"A lot of people thought he was too proud, but he was just a confident young man," said Lilyana Koa, a social studies teacher at St. Anthony and a "team mom" for the football team. "Children are gifted in different ways, and Shane put his energy into what he did on the field."

In his last year of high school, the right-handed hitting Victorino batted .458 and reached base an astounding 65 percent of the time while playing shortstop, manning center field, and pitching on a field whose name paid tribute to Ichiro "Iron" Maehara, a founding father of Maui baseball.

The Maui-born Maehara played in the 1930s on one of several teams on the island operated by sugar companies. During World War II, he competed on the diamond against U.S. military teams, helping to foster relations between the mainland and the island's Japanese American population. Though Maehara never made it off Maui as a player, his knowledge of the game prompted the Dodgers to offer him a scouting job in the 1960s. In that capacity, he steered a Honolulu high school pitcher named Sid Fernandez to the Dodgers. Later, as a member of the New York Mets, Fernandez played a key role in the team's 1986 World Series victory against the Boston Red Sox.

Some were beginning to think Victorino had a chance to follow in Fernandez's footsteps.

"We saw how good he could be," said Craig Okita, another of Shane's coaches and a former college baseball player. "He was a really good hitter. I saw he had the tools. It was just a matter of him concentrating on what he did."

Speed was his greatest asset. At the 1999 state track meet, he won the 100-meter dash, the 200, and the 400, setting a record of 10.80 seconds in the 100 that still stood in 2014.

Though he could outrun just about anybody, Victorino was not pushed to learn to switch hit, a skill considered advantageous for small and quick players.

"We tried it, but he was slapping the ball and grounding out to third base a lot," Awai said. "I allowed him to switch hit, but it came to the point where I realized I wasn't going to be able to teach him the right way to do it."

Lyle Cummings, a friend of Victorino, saw him mature during his senior year. "He knew he had something special, and he changed into a different person that year," Cummings said. "He took on leadership and pushed the other boys on his team to be at his level."

Despite his maturation, Shane Victorino remained a polarizing figure on the island of Maui. His awesome talent was still overshadowed in some circles by his history of emotional outbursts. Some people either did not know he had ADHD or thought the disorder was not a real medical condition.

At the end of the school year, St. Anthony athletics director Pat McCall tried to put Victorino's high school years in perspective.

"Not only has he brought recognition to our school, but everyone who has coached him or played with him has seen a superior athlete," McCall told *The Maui News*. "But he has also grown a lot, which has been very crucial. Shane has been in a fishbowl ever since he got here, so every one of his faults has been publicized and duly noted. A lot of good things he's done and a lot of the growing he's done has always been followed by, 'Yeah, but do you remember when…' I think to his credit he has been able to survive that. He has matured immensely."

IN THE DAYS FOLLOWING THE 1999 AMATEUR BASEBALL DRAFT, Victorino had to weigh his options and make up his mind quickly. Should he try his luck at professional baseball on the mainland or stay at home and be a two-sport college athlete? Or was there a way to do a little of both? Victorino asked the Dodgers if they would allow him to play college football during the baseball off-season. The answer from Dodgers scout Hank Jones came quickly: no chance.

After a few days of introspection, Victorino decided to play baseball.

His grandfather, Chester, helped him organize his thoughts in the lead-up to his decision.

"His grandpa had a talk with him and advised him to go where his heart was telling him to go," Arensdorf recalled. "It was his grandpa who helped him think through a lot of his decisions."

But ultimately the choice was his.

"Before he made the decision, he went into his room and closed the door," Mike Victorino Sr. said. "He was there for a while. We didn't hear any noise, so we thought he was asleep. His mom opened the door and there he was kneeling at his bed praying. When he came out, he said, 'Mom, Dad, I want to forego college and take my chances in baseball.' His mom was devastated because she wanted him to get a college education. But he said he could always go to school later."

Joycelyn Victorino felt a lot better when the Dodgers included $60,000 in Shane's signing bonus to help pay for college if his baseball career ever hit a plateau.

In his senior yearbook, a tuxedoed Victorino is pictured above a quote from two-sport athlete Bo Jackson: "Set your goals high and don't stop until you get there."

Shane had high goals. Now he just had to reach them.

3
ON THE FARM

VICTORINO MADE A FEW MISSTEPS DURING HIS ROOKIE SEASON in Great Falls, Montana, but he performed well enough in 1999 to earn a call up the following year to Yakima, Washington, the Dodgers' Class A team in the Northwest League. In Montana, Victorino hit .280, good for only 52nd in the Pioneer League. But his season included a 14-game hitting streak and a team-leading 20 stolen bases and 53 runs scored. His on-base percentage of .335—about half what it was his senior year of high school—was merely a reminder that he would never again be as big a fish in as small a pond.

With a short season of professional baseball behind him, Victorino settled into the decidedly unsettled life of a minor league player. His first season in Montana yielded respectable statistics on the field and good friendships off. Though he still fought homesickness, he embraced his new and radically different lifestyle. In Montana, the process of cultural assimilation meant swimming in muddy rivers instead of the clear ocean. But he knew the Pacific would still be there for him in the off-seasons, and knock on wood, if he ever got called up by the Dodgers. Los Angeles had some pretty good Polynesian restaurants, too, which was yet another reason for him to aim for the big leagues. For now, he would get by on the notion that any food tasted pretty good after a long bus ride to Medicine Hat, Billings, or wherever his team was going.

After the season in Great Falls, Victorino showed some Aloha spirit by inviting his Great Falls roommate Dave Detienne to train with him in Maui. Every day started early for the two young ballplayers and included hitting, throwing, running, sprinting, and lifting weights. That regimen was followed by an afternoon nap and a big meal prepared by Victorino's mother.

"As an east coast Nova Scotia boy, Maui was a huge cultural contrast for me," Detienne said. "I loved it. It was great hanging out with Shane's family, going to family luaus, and doing a lot of stuff you can't do as a tourist. It was a great way to spend time in the off-season."

Before Victorino headed to Yakima for the 2000 season, he had some important family business to tend to in Maui. He realized the time had come to confront his grandfather about a pattern of behavior that was destroying his life. It was bad enough that Chester Nakahashi had squandered his money on get-rich-quick schemes and gambling trips to Las Vegas, but in the process, he had been neglecting his wife, Olive, who was slowly succumbing to Alzheimer's disease.

Over the years, no one had stressed the importance of family to Shane more than his grandfather. But the man who helped him develop his core values in life had strayed from what he knew to be right. An intervention was necessary, and everyone in the Victorino family knew Shane had the best chance of making it work. Shane and Chester were both extremely emotional people, and when one was in need of a firm hand, the other could be counted on to provide it.

"The turning point where I knew I needed to do something was when he asked me for some money that he wanted to send overseas to somebody he trusted," Victorino said. "He said it would benefit the whole family. This had happened before, and people always ended up fooling him and taking everything he had. I went to his house and told him I wasn't going to give him the money because I had no idea who these people were that he was talking to on the phone. He could tell I was upset with him."

Shane, who was 19 years old at the time, knew a lot hinged on the conversation. He drew in a deep breath and told Chester what he expected of him. "Grandpa, please think about Grandma and what she's going through," Shane said. "That is what should be most important to you right now, not these other things that you go off and do."

Chester had never once lost his cool with Shane. But if it was ever going to happen, this was the time. Shane looked his grandfather squarely in the eye. There was no turning back now.

"Grandpa, I ask that you stop going to Vegas and be home for her," he said.

The old man stood stunned, almost knocked off balance. Shane braced himself for an angry outburst, but one never came. Instead, Chester tenderly hugged his grandson.

Shane had a lot of time to think about the exchange on his way back to the mainland. As badly as he wanted to make a name for himself on the diamond, that was not what mattered most. And life did not stop for baseball.

AN EXTENDED CHANCE TO PLAY A GAME THEY LOVED is what sustained Victorino and his minor league compatriots. While most of their high school teammates were sitting in dorm rooms or working "real jobs," these guys were getting paid, at least a little bit, to play baseball. The journeys through the night to play three days here and four days there were part of building a baseball résumé.

In Great Falls, Victorino stretched a dollar about as far is it could go. He was so frugal with his spending that he saved enough of his $650 monthly paycheck to avoid having to work in the off-season. He barely used the credit card his mother furnished him with before he left for the mainland.

"You're not doing it for the money or the lifestyle," Victorino said. "You're doing it because it's something you love. That's what keeps you going. Sure, it could be grueling sometimes, but you accept that and just keep trying to get better. Long bus rides, staying in hotels, and having roommates are what make the experience unlike any other. You just stick it out and hope one day you'll make it to the top. As a lot of people say, you go from the doghouse to the penthouse when you get to the big leagues."

How about the extraordinary pressure to succeed, to survive and advance to the next level? Perhaps because the experience was so new, the atmosphere—at least for a little while longer—was somewhat relaxed.

"At the lowest levels of the minors, playing baseball is still a dream for everyone, and nobody's really knocking on the door yet," said Derek Michaelis, a teammate of Victorino's at several minor league stops. "Sure, there were guys the organization put a larger investment in and gave more opportunities to, but there was a lot of equality. Everybody had a chance to show what he could do. We were a bunch of very talented baseball players who didn't know how to play the game yet."

In the spring of 2000, Victorino reported to the Yakima Bears, another of the Dodgers' Low A teams. Coming into the season, Victorino was rated the 13th-best prospect in the Dodgers' system by *Baseball America*, a respected trade magazine.

Some of the guys sent to central Washington with him were teammates from the year before in Great Falls. Others were freshly drafted, including his new roommate, Nick Alvarez. Victorino, who signed a professional contract out of high school, was still a teenager. Alvarez, a recent graduate of Saint Thomas University in Miami picked by the Dodgers in the 26th round of the 2000 draft, had recently turned 23.

"When I first met Vic, I thought, *Whoa, I can't deal with this kid!*" Alvarez said. "It was like I was back in high school with him running around like crazy all the time. But then I realized, *Wait a second, he* was *in high school two years ago.* At first his energy was kind of overwhelming, but he's an extremely colorful character, so I just embraced the situation. He really grew on me. I tried to be like an older brother to him."

Victorino needed good friendships and a strong support network that season, because the promotion to Yakima came with a couple of unexpected twists. The Dodgers, an organization that had originally heard about Victorino through word of mouth, had spent the past year evaluating his skills, and based on their observations, player development officials decided to order up some big changes. In Yakima, Victorino would move from center field to second base. And he would no longer hit exclusively from the right side of the plate. At 19 years of age, he was going to learn to switch hit.

The Dodgers felt Victorino's strong arm made him a good fit for second base. His move to the infield also suggested the Dodgers had surveyed their farm system and noted an abundance of good outfielders.

Position switches were part of playing in the minors. Many young players drafted out of high school do not take the field at the same spots they played at the prep level. If that were the case, every minor league team would have mostly shortstops and pitchers, the positions normally reserved for the most athletic players on a high school team. As long as a player landed at a spot that maximized his chances of playing in the major leagues, he was not going to gripe.

Detienne said his friend resolved to make the best of the situation. "He wasn't really happy about moving to second base, but he was going to give it a try," Detienne said. "My thought on it was that he was such a good center fielder that it was ridiculous to put him anywhere else."

The affinity Victorino developed in Great Falls for center field made the move to second base difficult to swallow at first. "I really liked playing center," he said. "You see it all in center field. It's the closest thing to a bird's-eye view. To me, the picture of what's going on in the game doesn't get any better than through the eyes of a center fielder."

Though he would have preferred staying in the outfield, Victorino felt he could adapt to a new defensive position without too much anguish.

The assignment to pick up switch hitting was a far different story, however.

"I remember thinking, *How am I going to learn to hit left-handed?*" he said. "But they were adamant that I could do it if I worked at it."

Most players who learn to switch hit do so as kids, taught and trained either by parents, private instructors, coaches, or another interested party who thinks a young player might have a future in the game. As a child on the baseball fields of Maui, Victorino did not have anybody coaxing him in that direction. Except for a few left-handed at-bats in high school, where his coach had noted that he tended to haphazardly slap at the ball, he had never seriously considered trying to switch hit.

"We never thought about it," Mike Victorino Sr. said. "It just wasn't one of those things that ever crossed our minds."

The obvious advantage of developing the ability to switch hit at a young age is that a player has ample time to develop and become familiar with movements that, at first, can feel awkward.

Victorino's teammates in Yakima watched him take swings with hitting coach Damon Farmar without an ounce of envy.

"I couldn't imagine trying to do it at the age he was, particularly when you're going up against professional pitchers," Michaelis said. "It's hard enough to hit them with your natural hand."

The potential payoff for Victorino and the Dodgers organization made it a gamble worth taking, however. By standing in the left-handed batter's box, the speedy Victorino would be two crucial steps closer to first base and more apt to beat out infield hits.

His four months in Yakima were neither a resounding success nor an epic failure. Victorino hit only .246 in his second season in the minors, an average brought down by his left-handed at-bats. On the bright side, he finished strong, hitting over .300 in August, the final full month of the minor league calendar.

On defense, every ball that came his way turned into an adventure, both of the good and bad variety. He averaged an error every six games but also made a good number of jaw-dropping plays.

A typical Victorino play at second base, according to his roommate Alvarez: "There'd be a ball hit up the middle, and you'd think for sure it was going to be a hit. But he'd somehow reach out and grab it. The problem was he might end up throwing it into the third row of seats."

Victorino's own assessment of the season was equally blunt. "I had trouble with the balls hit right at me, but any ball to my right or left, I made it look pretty easy," he said. "I battled through that year, and at times it wasn't very fun. Learning two new things in a short season was extremely difficult."

Despite his struggles in 2000, hitting coach Damon Farmar had high praise for him at the end of the season, in which Yakima was crowned Northwest League champions.

"This is his first full year switch hitting, and he's made tremendous strides," Farmar told the *Yakima Herald-Republic* in September 2000. "He's more aggressive, his pitch selection is greatly improved. Things that often come later for guys, he's grasped really quickly. I've seen him walk more, seen him lay off pitches out of the strike zone more, he's bunting more. He's always been aggressive, but before it was aggressive out of the strike zone."

Farmar, the father of future NBA player Jordan Farmar, also liked what he saw from Victorino at his new infield position. "He's a tremendous athlete, the best second baseman in the league by far," he said. "I've seen him make major league plays in the field, plays you don't see by a lot of guys a lot further down the line than he is."

An added bonus that season was that his family made a trip to Yakima to see him play professional baseball for the first time. Up until that point, in-season communication between Shane and his family had been limited to phone calls and handwritten letters.

An example:

Mom & Dad,
Well hello to the two of you. I hope that all is going well. I appreciate that you went out of your way to send the goodies. Like I said it means the world to me when you do things like that. Keep this check for yourself. Everything is going good. I'm having a blast!!
Love:
Shane

Victorino's teammates, though they had not met his parents before, had warm feelings toward them. Throughout the season, Mike and Joycelyn Victorino sent Shane care packages with pineapple, macadamia nuts, and other Hawaiian treats, and Shane always shared the bounty with the rest of the team.

When Joycelyn saw her son in action in Yakima, she officially made peace with his choice to put off college to pursue a professional baseball career.

"My heart was pounding and pounding," she said. "After the game, he talked to some high schoolers. There were at least 50 or 60 kids there, and he spoke from the heart about his experiences. I was so proud of him."

Victorino did what he was asked to do in Yakima. He had been a good soldier and embraced new challenges.

But then the Dodgers came to him with another bit of news. At his next minor league stop in Wilmington, North Carolina, he would go back to playing center field and resume hitting right-handed only.

The Great Yakima Experiment was over—at least for the moment.

AFTER THE 2000 MINOR LEAGUE SEASON, Victorino went home to Maui for a few weeks to play softball with his buddies, fish and dive with his uncles, and enjoy his mother's cooking.

He enjoyed his time at home so much that when the day came for him to fly to Arizona to take part in the Dodgers' instructional league, he lost track of time and almost missed his flight. As he rushed to pack his bags and get to Kahului Airport, Victorino phoned his grandfather, Chester, to let him know he would not have time to stop by and say good-bye in person. Chester told his grandson not to worry, that he would go over and meet him at his departure gate. These were the days before the 9/11 terrorist attacks, when people without tickets could go through security. At the airport, Victorino checked in for his flight, passed through security, and headed for the gate with his father. He waited for Chester as long as he possibly could, but seeing no sign of him, eventually he had to board the plane. Only later did he find out that his grandfather had gone to the wrong set of gates.

About a half hour into the flight, one of the co-pilots came down the aisle asking if there was anybody named Shane on the plane.

"Yeah, that's me," Victorino said, removing his headphones.

"I ran into your grandfather before I got on the plane, and he said he loves you and wishes you good luck in the instructional league," the co-pilot told him. "He said he'll see you when you get back to Maui."

Unfortunately, that never happened. Chester Nakahashi, his grandson's best friend and biggest fan, passed away two weeks later at the age of 73.

"I got a call while I was in instructional league from my dad telling me that Grandpa had passed away," Victorino said. "I remember sitting back in my bed in my hotel room basically in shock. It hurt a lot, because we were so close. But I'll never forget how he somehow got that message to the pilot to tell me he loved me."

Nakahashi died in his sleep beside his ailing wife, Olive, who was in the last stages of Alzheimer's. At his grandson's insistence, he had been by her side throughout his final months of life. A year to the day Chester was buried, Olive Nakahashi passed away peacefully at her Wailuku home. Several years later, Victorino sponsored a golf tournament in Maui, attended by several of his teammates on the Philadelphia Phillies. The event raised more than $100,000 for the Aloha Chapter of the Alzheimer's Association.

In the months before his death, Chester stopped making trips to Las Vegas and mailing large sums of money to strangers halfway around the world. Following a heartfelt conversation with his grandson, Nakahashi publicly shared the story of his financial mistakes at an event held by the American Association of Retired Persons in Honolulu. By doing so, he hoped to raise awareness of scams that target seniors.

Victorino himself would later move to Las Vegas, a popular travel destination for Hawaiians that is sometimes referred to as the "ninth island." Surrounded by temptation in Sin City, he would benefit from the knowledge of what gambling did to his grandfather.

His education as a professional baseball player in full bloom, Victorino and several of his Yakima teammates prepared to leave the rainy Northwest and travel 3,000 miles east to live and play in a place of vibrant youth.

In April 2000, Victorino arrived on the campus of the University of North Carolina Wilmington for the first and only season of the Class A Wilmington Waves. The three-month, 60-game seasons of Great Falls and Yakima were a thing of the past. From here on, his seasons on the farm would consist of twice as many games, a major milestone for a minor leaguer. The Wilmington roster was stocked with prospects, prompting manager Dino Ebel to call the squad a "dream team." The team included three of the Dodgers' top four picks in the 2000 amateur draft as well as several of Victorino's teammates from Great Falls and Yakima. He was also reunited with his rookie ball manager, Tony Harris, who served as the Waves' hitting coach.

Harris was happy to have the chance to continue building a personal and professional relationship with Shane. "Shane's personality would be best described as infectious," he said. "His funny, caring, friendly personality is one to always remember.

"I had always written him up in our internal reports as a major league prospect. I could see as a talent evaluator that he had the tools to play at the highest level. It was a matter of whether he would work hard enough, and he proved that he would do that."

Victorino, batting leadoff for Wilmington of the South Atlantic League, felt back in his comfort zone.

"Coming into the year, I had a really good feeling," he said. "I was back in center field and hitting right-handed only, but I felt like what I had learned the year before, even though it was difficult sometimes, made me a better player."

Jerry Weinstein, the Dodgers' director of player development, focused on Victorino's defense in a preseason assessment of the team he gave to a Wilmington newspaper.

"We feel like with his running ability and instincts for the ball, he will be a real exciting outfielder," Weinstein said.

A few weeks into the season, it became clear that some on the team might be enjoying themselves a little too much while virtually living on the college campus. Several players, including Victorino, were knocking the cover off of the ball...but only while playing on the road. Victorino's home-road splits defied logic. In 40 at-bats at Brooks Field in Wilmington, he had a paltry four hits. On the road, he was hitting well over .300.

After two seasons in sleepy Great Falls and Yakima, many of the Waves were breaking out the party hats.

"It was a large temptation," Michaelis said. "I was married the entire time, so I didn't participate in a lot of the revelries of some of the other guys. But undoubtedly they were occurring."

As Victorino struggled to find consistency at the plate, another aspect of his game was blossoming, thanks in part to the help of former Dodger Maury Wills, who gave Victorino and other members of the team a private lesson in the art of the stolen base.

Victorino absorbed the information and went wild on the base paths in Wilmington, swiping 47 bases in 60 attempts.

And before long, he found his swing, both at home and on the road. The Dodgers chose Victorino as their minor league player of the month for July 2001, a month in which he hit .316, swiped 14 bases, and knocked in 14 runs. In August, however, Victorino landed on the disabled list for the first time in his professional career with a sprained ankle suffered while crashing into an outfield wall.

For the season, he hit .283, the highest batting average in his three years of pro ball.

His strong year in Wilmington came at an opportune time. The organization's process of winnowing out lightly regarded players became more intense at this level. Fifteen of his 33 teammates from rookie ball in 1999 were already out of professional baseball by 2001.

Though he dropped down on the list of the Dodgers' top prospects, he did well enough to survive and advance to the next level. At the end of the season in Wilmington, the Dodgers called him up to high Class A ball in Vero Beach, Florida, for the playoffs. His career trajectory got another major boost when he learned his 2002 assignment would be at Double A Jacksonville. It now seemed realistic that he might one day get a chance to take a dip in the Pacific as a member of the Los Angeles Dodgers.

WITH EVERY MULTIHIT GAME, a minor leaguer felt a step closer to his big-league dreams. But with every 0-for-12 slump, a player's entire universe could be temporarily thrown into disarray as he asked himself the question, "Why am I doing this again?"

By 2002, Victorino was in his fourth year of professional baseball. Though he had steadily progressed through the Dodgers' system, he was hardly immune from the peaks and valleys of the minor league existence.

When he joined the Double A Jacksonville Suns in 2002, the book on Victorino was still filled with a lot of question marks. In Single A, he had established himself as a base stealer and a defensive stalwart, but his failure to succeed at switch hitting raised concerns about whether he possessed enough offensive tools.

It took the eye of a baseball man with polished instincts to identify that Victorino needed to resume working on his switch hitting if he hoped to keep advancing through the farm system. That man was former major leaguer Gene Richards, Victorino's hitting coach in Jacksonville.

"You ever switch hit before?" Richards asked him during spring training, knowing full well the answer.

"I tried it in my second year of pro ball."

"How about you give it another shot?"

"I'm not sure I want to try it again."

"I think you can do it. You can run, and you're athletic enough. Let's work on it."

Though he chose not to come right out and say it, Richards was communicating his opinion that Victorino's chances of succeeding in— or even making—the major leagues likely depended on conquering both sides of the plate.

"By taking another run at being a switch hitter, he had a chance to bring something extra to the table, to gain an edge that would help separate him from the competition," said Richards, a left-handed hitter who batted .290 with the San Diego Padres and San Francisco Giants from 1977 to

1984. "But I treated it with care. If we had tried it and he had failed, I might have lost him."

A knock on Victorino's offensive game at the time was that he hit too many fly balls. It did not matter if Victorino was fast enough to be rounding second base when a ball was caught; it was still an out. Richards felt Victorino could better use his blazing speed by hitting balls on the ground and legging out hits, especially as a left-handed hitter.

So Victorino went back to work, spending extra time with Richards in the batting cage every day for the first half of Jacksonville's season. There, they went through a battery of drills. In some, Victorino practiced swinging a bat with one arm to improve the overall mechanics of his stroke. In others, he swung a sledgehammer to build arm strength.

Victorino had worked that spring training with Dodgers legend Tommy Lasorda, who managed the team for 20 seasons and continued to serve the organization in an advisory role.

"I felt if he could swing down on the ball and hit more line drives that it would be a big addition to his game," Lasorda said. "The talent was there, but nobody could seem to get it out of him. He was a willing worker, but sometimes he would give you the impression that he wasn't too concerned about the game. I used to holler at him a little bit, but he knew it was constructive and that I thought the world of him."

During that 2002 season in Jacksonville, Llewelyn Awai, Victorino's coach at St. Anthony High School, came to Florida on business and stopped by to see Jacksonville play a road game at Orlando. The Victorino family was also in town for the game. When Awai arrived at the ballpark and saw Shane's mom, she frowned and told him that Shane would not be playing that night. He had acted up during the previous night's game and was paying for it with a seat on the bench.

Awai stormed down the bleachers to confront Victorino, who was on the field warming up with the rest of the team.

"I came 5,000 miles to watch you sit out?" Awai yelled.

After the game, Awai caught up with Victorino.

"What happened?" his former coach asked.

"It was some stupid thing," Victorino told him. "The big boss from the Dodgers was here, and he didn't like something I did."

Victorino told Awai that he had thrown his helmet and bat in frustration.

"I thought I broke that habit," Awai said. "These people mean business. Somebody high up with the Dodgers is here and you're doing those things. You have to conduct yourself like a man."

Unsure of his timetable for taking cuts from the left side in an actual game, Victorino returned to Jacksonville after the Southern League all-star break in 2002 to find Richards waiting for him.

"You ready to hit left-handed in a game?" Richards asked.

Sensing his pupil's uncertainty, Richards did not wait for an answer. Victorino was barely hitting over .200 as a right-handed hitter midway through the season, so Richards felt it was an ideal time to shake things up.

"You're doing it. You're going out there tonight, and this is going to be a new start to your switch-hitting career," the coach said.

It was settled, and the outcome showed Richards' instincts were right.

During a 20-game stretch in July and August 2002, Victorino went 25-for-69, a run that included a 13-game hitting streak. Victorino also stole 45 bases that season, tied for second most in the Southern League.

Most important to his coaches, his late-season offensive success came from both sides of the plate. His switch-hitting skills were still a work in progress, but in contrast with his first go-around, he made enough progress to eliminate any thoughts of abandoning the experiment.

The biggest endorsement of his development in Jacksonville came near the end of the 2002 season when Victorino was one of three position players selected by the Dodgers to play in the Arizona Fall League, a month-long showcase for baseball's top minor league talent. Every major league team is permitted to send only six prospects to the fall league, and the 180 players are divided onto six teams. A whopping 36 alumni of past fall leagues participated in the 2013 MLB All-Star Game.

In Arizona, playing for the Peoria Javelinas and alongside future major leaguers including Mark Teixeira, Justin Morneau, and Brandon Webb, Victorino elevated his game to a new level. In 109 at-bats—including many from the left side—he hit .330 with 36 hits in 34 games.

"Getting invited to the fall league was an honor, and I felt like I played well enough there to catch some eyes," Victorino said.

The Dodgers had to be impressed with his progress, Victorino assumed. But despite his recent successes, his career path was about to change abruptly and in a way he did not see coming.

4

A Shot at the Big Time

AT THE CONCLUSION OF THE 2002 SEASON, THE DODGERS AND every other big-league team evaluated the talent in their minor league systems to determine which farm players should be made off-limits to other teams and which should be left vulnerable to potential suitors.

It was the annual rite of December known as the Rule 5 Draft, in which organizations create a select list of protected players and risk losing prospects who fail to make the cut.

As the draft rules of the time dictated, any player who signed a professional contract at 18 years of age or younger and had been with the same organization for at least four years was available in the Rule 5 Draft, unless the player's existing team placed him on the protected list, otherwise known as the 40-man roster.

Victorino met two of the eligibility criteria for the draft: he signed with the Dodgers when he was 18 and had spent four years in the organization's farm system. If the Dodgers chose to leave him off the 40-man roster, a group composed of both major and minor leaguers, he would be dangled out to other teams.

The purpose of the Rule 5 Draft is to prevent organizations from hoarding prospects in the minor leagues. Any team that takes a player in the draft has obligations of its own. The drafting team must pay the original club $50,000, and the draftee must remain on his new team's 25-man major league roster the entire season. If that does not happen, a return policy kicks in and the player is offered back to his original team for $25,000.

Were the Dodgers impressed enough with Victorino's skills to keep him from the clutches of other organizations that might have an interest in him?

From his quick promotion to Double A Jacksonville to his selection to play in the prestigious Arizona Fall League, he appeared to have a future with the organization. But with other players in a farm system showing equal or greater promise, it does not take much to go from prized prospect to odd man out. The Dodgers had acquired a center fielder named Wilkin Ruan from the Expos in the spring of 2002, and the farm system directors thought enough of Ruan to indicate he would have a chance to play at Triple A Las Vegas in 2003.

Ruan likely took the last spot on the 40-man roster, meaning Victorino was up for grabs going into baseball's 2002 winter meetings. But it was hardly a guarantee that he would be leaving the Dodgers. For that to happen, another organization would have to step forward in the Rule 5 Draft and take a risk that he was ready to play in the major leagues immediately.

That team turned out to be the San Diego Padres, who selected the 22-year-old Victorino with the 19th pick in the 2002 Rule 5 Draft. He was one of 28 players who went in the draft that year. One of those players had the perfect Rule 5 name: Jerome Gamble, who went from the Reds to the Red Sox.

Bill Bavasi, the Dodgers' director of player development at the time, said the organization made a tough call in leaving Victorino unprotected.

"We had to take a long, hard look at him," Bavasi told the *Wilmington Morning Star* after the release of the organization's 40-man roster. "He will be a good player off the bench or an extra outfielder in the big leagues. I look for him to have a long career in the majors. I also, though, wouldn't put it past him to become an everyday player in the majors."

The whole Rule 5 process is an inexact science. Wilkin Ruan went on to have a good year in Triple A and was promoted to Los Angeles later in 2003. But he had only the proverbial cup of coffee in the majors, finishing his brief big-league career with just 52 at-bats. He was out of baseball by 2009.

Victorino felt scorned by the Dodgers, but he tried not to lose focus.

"Each year, I was hoping to be put on the roster in Los Angeles," he said. "Was I frustrated that they let me go? Yeah, I was, because I thought I had earned a place on the 40-man roster. I guess there were just other guys who fit their model a little bit better. I saw it as an honor that another team thought enough of me to give me a chance."

The decision not to protect Victorino disappointed some of the coaches in the organization who helped mentor him.

"I expressed the opinion that I thought they were giving up on him a little too quickly, but they didn't see him as I saw him," said Gene Richards, Victorino's hitting coach in Jacksonville in 2002. "As things turned out, it might have worked to his advantage, though. The Dodgers, by letting him go, may have increased his desire to prove to people he could succeed."

Tommy Lasorda, who worked with Victorino to help him improve his game, was surprised the Dodgers left him unprotected.

"I worked with a lot of guys over the years, but I didn't see many guys who improved as much as he did," Lasorda said. "I didn't have anything to do with those [Rule 5] decisions, and the next thing I knew, he was gone."

The meaning of what transpired was open to interpretation. On one hand, the Dodgers had not thought highly enough of him to protect him. On the other hand, the Padres snapped him up in the belief that he could not only play at the highest level of baseball but that he could do so right away.

Victorino turned his attention to doing what he could to thrive with the Padres.

"I thought I had a good chance of making it in San Diego," he said. "The funny thing was that I played in the fall league with guys from the Padres, and [general manager] Kevin Towers and all their people were there to watch them. I guess they watched me, too. It was nice to know they thought a lot of me. So I wanted to go out and try to make it with them and make it a great experience."

Indeed, Towers had been impressed with Victorino. "We had very favorable scouting reports on him going into that winter, so when we were looking to the Rule 5 Draft, he was a guy who certainly stood out," Towers said. "We knew we were getting close to moving into Petco Park, which was going to have a real expansive outfield, and we were looking for a table-setter, somebody with a lot of speed who could ignite an offense and play solid 'D.' Even though he was young, we thought he fit that profile.

"I remember going to see our players in the Arizona Fall League and seeing him play. At that point, we didn't know if he would be protected by the Dodgers or not. Once the protection list came out and we saw he was exposed, he was really kind of a no-brainer selection for us. A center fielder with speed and the potential to be an offensive player was something we didn't have in our system.

"The Rule 5 Draft is a very cheap way to extract talent from another organization that doesn't have room to protect a player. It's probably not that the Dodgers didn't value Shane. I'm sure it was that they had a lot of depth and they couldn't protect everybody."

Victorino's friends in Maui were not sure what to expect when he came back home in the off-season as a prospective major leaguer. *The Maui News* had documented his every move during minor league stops in Great Falls, Yakima, Wilmington, and Jacksonville. But now he was on the brink of making the San Diego Padres. Would he let that go to his head, or would he be the same old Shane?

Only time would tell.

But one thing was for sure: no one expected him to play that winter in the competitive softball league he had joined in high school and continued to play in during his minor league off-seasons. Nobody wanted him to get hurt at such a critical point in his career.

His friend and softball teammate, Lyle Cummings, took him aside and made it clear that he would not be suiting up for the games in Kona on the Big Island of Hawaii. Cummings was a big and intimidating man who usually had the final word in matters.

Victorino had other ideas.

"We were out practicing, and Shane was ragging me about letting him play in the softball tournament," Cummings said. "I kept telling him no, but he kept asking me. He asked me every day. Finally I said, 'Okay, I'll let you play, but you can't tell your mom about it. If anything happens to you, your mom and your brother would kill me.'"

Victorino played well in the tournament. He made some acrobatic catches in right field and had several extra-base hits. He was playing his heart out and had avoided doing anything to risk injury—until a game late in the tournament when he tagged up from first base on a fly out and slid hard into second base to beat the throw.

Cummings called timeout and came hurtling out of his team's dugout.

"Shane, what the hell are you doing?" he barked at his friend.

"What?" Victorino said brushing dirt from his pant leg.

"You're going to get hurt! I don't need you breaking your leg here. I told you what would happen to me if you got hurt."

"Yeah, I know, but we're going to win," Victorino told him. "I'm here to win."

And sure enough, with Victorino leading the way, the team won the 16-team statewide tournament.

IN SPRING OF 2003, VICTORINO VALIDATED his new general manager's belief in him and made the Padres' roster. To do so, he beat out veteran outfielders Brady Anderson and Roberto Kelly for a roster spot. When the Padres left their spring training camp in Peoria, Arizona, to head north in late March, Victorino was one of five outfielders that joined them. With the team battling injury problems, Padres manager Bruce Bochy indicated Victorino might even have a chance to see regular playing time.

He was still a Rule 5 guy, however. Winning a spot on the Opening Day roster was only the first step. Now there were two paths on which he could be taken: if he stayed with the Padres all season, they could keep him in the majors or return him to their minor league system the following season. But if they cut him from the 25-man major league roster that season, he would be offered back to the Dodgers.

About 135,000 people saw Victorino and the 2001 Wilmington Waves play 69 home games. Two years later, nearly half that many came to just one game in San Diego, the last Opening Day at Qualcomm Stadium.

Victorino had crossed that magical threshold into the major leagues, something he described as a trip "from the doghouse to the penthouse." The express elevator had taken this 22-year-old from a lone season in Double A all the way to the big leagues. Now all Victorino had to do was show he belonged there.

The huge crowd in San Diego was just one of several things the Rule 5 acquisition found hard to fathom. Where to start? How about with the fact he was on a major league roster with baseball's all-time career leader in games pitched, Jesse Orosco. Victorino remembered Orosco as the pitcher who recorded the last out in the New York Mets' 1986 World Series triumph, the one aided by Victornio's fellow Hawaiian Sid Fernandez. Orosco's major league debut in 1979 came seven months before Victorino was born.

On Opening Day 2003, the Padres faced Barry Bonds and the defending National League champion San Francisco Giants. Less than a year earlier, Victorino was one of many guys struggling to make it to the majors. Now he was there and playing on the same field as one of the game's most prolific sluggers.

"I was in shock more than anything," Victorino recalled. "I remember walking out there to a full house at Qualcomm Stadium, looking around, and thinking, *Oh my goodness!*"

If Victorino felt overwhelmed by his new surroundings, he did a good job of not openly showing it.

"What impressed me about Shane was his maturity level," Towers said. "He was a highly confident young man. He felt like he belonged. Sometimes you get kids who are in awe when they get to the big leagues and kind of are just in survival mode. But I never saw that in him, and that's something I really liked about him. Even when he struggled, he felt like he belonged."

Like Cinderella at the ball, Victorino wanted to make the experience last. He knew that if his clock struck midnight and the Padres offered him back to the Dodgers, the chartered planes would transform into buses, the five-star hotels into cheap motels, and the sizeable per diems into puny daily allowances. He was the only member of the Padres making the major league minimum salary of $300,000 at the start of the 2003 season, but that was still about 10 times more than his highest wage in the minors.

It appeared likely that Victorino's acclimation to the major leagues would come mostly through pinch-running appearances and as a late-inning defensive replacement.

On April 2, 2003, in the Padres' third game of the season, Victorino made his debut as a pinch runner for Xavier Nady in the bottom of the ninth inning with the Padres trailing the Giants 5–3. With Victorino on first and Ryan Klesko on third, Sean Burroughs struck out to end the game. It was a mundane beginning but one Victorino will never forget. "It was absolutely amazing to see all those guys out there who I admired so much," he said. "But when I ran out there for the first time, I felt comfortable. This is the game I had played my whole life, and I was just going to keep playing it the same way I always had."

The next afternoon, he grounded out in his first big-league at-bat, a pinch-hit appearance against the Dodgers, of all teams. Next in his line of firsts came his first major league start, in left field later in that series against L.A. In four plate appearances, he walked, grounded out twice, and laid down a sacrifice bunt that led to a key Padres run.

Before that game, Dodgers general manager Dan Evans told *The San Diego Union-Tribune* he hoped Victorino harbored no ill will toward the organization that had left him vulnerable in the Rule 5 Draft.

"If [the Padres] eventually don't have enough roster spots, we'd be interested in having him back," Evans told the newspaper. "I like his energy. I like him as a person. We didn't have enough spots to keep him. If you don't have enough spots, you can't fret about it. If you lose guys [in the Rule 5 Draft], it just means you've got talent coming. We all thought he could play here."

Evans said he even discussed the possibility of reacquiring Victorino by trade before the start of the 2003 season.

The Dodgers may have still wanted to be friends, but Victorino had moved on. "I wasn't holding a grudge or anything. But there was no reason for me to look back," he said.

Victorino flaunted his defense in the series against his former club. On one play, he made a good running catch in left field. On another, he got a ball in from the outfield quickly that led to a runner being thrown out at the plate.

Victorino was also picking up some valuable pointers from Padres coach Davey Lopes on how to steal bases at the major league level. Lopes, who stole 38 consecutive bases without being thrown out as a member of the 1975 Dodgers, worked on building Victorino's confidence on the base paths. His protégé responded by swiping seven bases in nine attempts while with San Diego.

Victorino's first major league hit came on April 20 against the Colorado Rockies, a third-inning single to right field against pitcher Shawn Chacon.

An injury to Padres outfielder Mark Kotsay in May gave Victorino more chances to start. Brand new to the majors, Victorino suddenly found himself in the role of regular center fielder and leadoff hitter...and he struggled mightily. During a stretch of 10 starts in May, he got mired in a 4-for-33 slump. Later that month, he was still hitting just .151.

With Victorino scuffling and the team stuck in last place, Padres manager Bruce Bochy began looking for other options. When Kotsay went on the disabled list, the team called up outfielder Jason Bay from Triple A Portland. They also claimed outfielder Gary Matthews Jr. off waivers.

Around this time, Victorino got called into Bochy's office.

"He told me he had some bad news," Victorino said. "It had become a numbers game, and I had become the odd man out."

The odd man out. That had an unpleasant and familiar ring.

On May 23, the Padres designated Victorino for assignment, a nice way of saying he was cut.

The next day, newspaper readers in San Diego awoke to a *Union-Tribune* headline proclaiming Victorino the Padres' "latest Rule 5 flameout." San Diego had taken a spin on the roulette wheel, and the house had taken the team's money, the accompanying story proclaimed.

In retrospect, Towers believes the Padres mishandled Victorino. It was a case of too much, too soon for the young Hawaiian.

"We weren't very good that year and probably played him a little bit more than we should have," Towers said. "He got a little overexposed, which I think was really tough on his development at that time."

Dismissed by the Padres, the only way Victorino was going to stay in the majors was if another big-league team claimed him off waivers and put him on its 25-man roster for the remainder of the season. That was extremely unlikely based on his performance in San Diego.

So the Dodgers got another crack at signing their former sixth-round draft pick to a minor league deal. And that is what they did, assigning him back to Double A Jacksonville, where he spent the 2002 season.

The potentially bad case of déjà vu prompted a phone call from Eric Tokunaga, the Hawaiian scout who first took an interest in Victorino prior to the 1999 amateur draft.

"Hey look, the Dodgers sent you down to Double A, but you know you don't belong there," Tokunaga told him. "So just go out there and prove to them that they're wrong. Keep playing, because you know you're good enough to play in the major leagues."

The words comforted Victorino, but for the first time, he started to wonder if he would always be the odd man out, the victim of a numbers game, a player with good all-around skills but one not quite impressive enough to make the majors and stay there.

From the crowd of 62,000 on Opening Day at Qualcomm Stadium, Victorino flew east to Jacksonville to rejoin his old team that played in a stadium that held 11,000.

So much for his time in the major league penthouse. He was back in the doghouse.

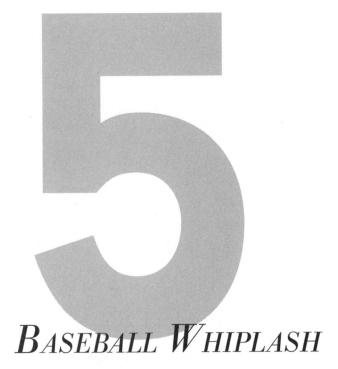

5
BASEBALL WHIPLASH

THANKS TO SHANE VICTORINO'S SLIGHTLY HEAVIER POCKETS, the Jacksonville Suns ate well on the night he returned to the minor leagues. He dipped into his nearly two months of big-league pay to order a spread from the Olive Garden after a game in Orlando. His teammates welcomed the respite from their usual postgame meal of fried chicken or pizza, and most were happy to have Shane around again. As they devoured breadsticks and pasta, he regaled them with tales of his brief life in the majors.

Victorino had not planned for this demotion, and when the team returned to Jacksonville, he belatedly realized he had no place to stay. Nick Alvarez, his roommate at Single A Yakima in 2000, offered to take him in. Alvarez found Victorino to be the same fun-loving guy who bounced off walls, gabbed constantly, and played video games until the wee hours of the morning. On a brutally hot Sunday in Jacksonville, Alvarez got hurt trying to make a catch against the outfield wall. Victorino ran over to check on him and to plead with him to stay in the game so they could suffer in the heat together. "Shane looked at me and said, 'Don't worry about it. I'm out here. I'll cover all this ground. You just stand there and look pretty,'" Alvarez said.

But behind the smile and good humor, Alvarez noticed his friend seemed to have a greater sense of purpose.

"Nobody who gets a taste of the big leagues wants to come back down," Alvarez said. "But he came back hungry, real hungry. And he was a bit more mature. He knew where he wanted to be, and he knew what he needed to do to get there. He had no doubt that he was going to make it back."

Determination aside, Victorino could not help but think that the Dodgers, by leaving him unprotected in the Rule 5 Draft, and the Padres, by not keeping him on their major league roster the entire 2003 season, had rejected him as a ballplayer and a person. Was the game he had loved his entire life just an unforgiving business? One day he was regarded as a top prospect, but by the next, he was reduced to a few lines of agate type announcing his release.

He lacked perspective at those moments. In his mind, he had failed and was now moving backward athletically for the first time in his life. In reality, he had simply been unable to achieve immediate success at a level of baseball far higher than any he had played before. He tried to repress these irrational thoughts, but he was alone and lonely and still just 23 years old. He also still grappled with ADHD. After he turned 18, he stopped taking medication for the disorder in the hope it would go away on its own. In some ways, his condition had improved, partly through therapy he got from Dr. Alfred Arensdorf, the child psychologist in Maui. He demonstrated less impulsivity than before, but he was still prone to lapses in concentration and focus.

Shortly after he returned to the minors, Jacksonville was on the road near the town of Sevierville playing the Tennessee Smokies. Victorino hit a home run in the game but afterward could not shut off his brain. As his teammates packed up their gear and loaded the team bus, he walked out of the ballpark into the warm Tennessee night. He went down the long ramp leading to the road and kept walking out onto Route 66, a road whose name alone is synonymous with America's wandering spirit.

He heard the roar of the bus as it drove past him, but he did not look up. He had some serious thinking to do. His mind buzzed with thoughts as he asked himself variations of the same questions: Did I make the right decision by signing a professional baseball contract? Has my career peaked? Will I ever again get a shot in the major leagues? If I walk away from baseball, what other options do I have?

Over the next 15 minutes, he hastily made a decision to return home and enroll at the University of Hawaii. Maybe he could convince head coach June Jones, who had recruited Victorino out of high school, to still offer him a football scholarship. Either way, he was going to walk away from baseball.

"I was at one of those crossroads," Victorino said. "I definitely loved baseball, but I was so frustrated and upset at the game. I thought I was over it and wanted to move on. I was still young and thought that if I went back to school, I might be able to pursue another profession."

Back at the motel, Victorino sat and stared up at the ceiling. At about 2:00 AM, his cell phone rang. It was his brother, Mike, calling to congratulate him on the home run he hit earlier that night.

"Hey, bro, good game. I saw on the Internet that you hit a home run," Mike Victorino Jr. said.

"What's so good about that?" Shane shot back. "What's so good about me coming to Double A and hitting a home run? Big effing deal!"

Then he dropped his big news on his brother.

"Mike, I don't belong here. I'm over this. I'm coming home," he said.

His brother realized he had a serious situation on his hands and called for backup. Shane's father got on the phone and listened to his son's litany of reasons for wanting to come back home. Mike Victorino Sr. took it all in, and when his son was done talking, he laid out the situation for him.

"If you decide to come home, we'll support your decision 100 percent," the elder Victorino told his son. "But if you quit and give it all up, that's it. You won't go back. Listen to me, this is what I want you to do: give yourself three weeks. If you're still unhappy and still feel like you want to come back, then you should. But give yourself three weeks and see what happens."

Shane's brother was less charitable, but his reaction came from the heart. Mike Victorino Jr. had been a standout baseball player in high school and was good enough to play Division I college baseball at the University of Hawaii–Hilo. But by his early twenties, he had already started a family. He dropped out of college after two years and went back to Maui to be with his future wife and two children. Since 1997, he had worked as a longshoreman.

"I told him, 'Bro, you're not coming home. You were the one who decided to go professional. We told you to go to college and get an education, so you wouldn't have to work as hard as Mom and Dad. You made that decision, so you're not coming home. You have a chance that a lot of guys never get. Home will always be here.' My dad gave him a few weeks. I didn't give him any timetable. I just told him he wasn't coming home."

Shane agreed to wait and see if his moment of crisis passed.

"I went to bed that night and really thought about it," he said. "I showed up at the field the next day and had a great game. I took it a day at a time and started to feel better. What it came down to is that I had a moment of doubt, but I decided I couldn't give up on something I always dreamed of doing."

ON THE FIELD, VICTORINO QUICKLY FOUND his hitting stroke again with Jacksonville. In nearly 300 plate appearances, he batted .282, and in mid-August 2003, he was called up for the final two weeks of the season at Triple A Las Vegas. There he was reunited with Gene Richards, the coach who oversaw his successful transition to switch hitting in Jacksonville two years earlier. Victorino hit .390 in his first 11 games at the Triple A level, a run that included a 5-for-5 game.

Roaming the outfield, Victorino turned heads with his throwing arm. His pinpoint accuracy was in stark contrast to the wildness he displayed while playing second base earlier in his minor league career.

"In the outfield, the quicker you get the ball from the glove to your hand, the longer you have to wind up, and you can make a full arc with your arm," explained former Phillies center fielder Garry Maddox, a defensive standout during his playing days. "That way, you can put everything into your throw. In the infield, it's different because you never get the opportunity to really wind up and let it fly. You're always short-arming it or something like that."

Mike Victorino Sr. checked back in with his son at the end of the Triple A season.

"Things were looking up by then," his father recalled. "I called him up and said, 'When you coming home? You said you were coming home.' He just laughed, but I think he learned something from that whole experience. He was ready to give it all up. I didn't convince him to stay. I just thought it was a better idea to take some time and see what happens."

The sting of not having caught on with the Padres had largely worn off, but Victorino still had lingering concerns about his future with the Dodgers.

"I did well in Vegas, and I thought I'd have a chance to get called up to L.A.," Victorino said. "Unfortunately, that didn't happen. I thought that winter I'd at least get put on the [40-man] roster, but that didn't happen either. It was okay, though. I knew if I went back to Vegas the next season and did well that I'd eventually get my shot."

WHEN CAMP BROKE in the spring of 2004, Victorino indeed found himself headed back to Vegas.

Las Vegas is known as Sin City because of the various forms of debauchery it offers. The town is also called Lost Wages for its habit of separating people from their cash. But for the young men sent to Las Vegas to play baseball in summer temperatures that often exceed 100 degrees, a more accurate nickname for the sweltering city is Low Wages, where most players tried to get by on about $2,000 a month.

"There was so much going on and so much to do there, but we were playing baseball, and it's not like we could afford much," Victorino said.

Pitcher Edwin Jackson, a teammate in Las Vegas, said the stands at Cashman Field were often eerily quiet on game nights.

"We didn't have much of a fan base," Jackson said. "You could sit there and count the number of people who came to most games."

When Victorino and his teammates did hit the town, it was usually for dinner at a neighborhood restaurant away from the Las Vegas Strip. They tried to create their own fun. On one outing to a sushi restaurant, Victorino was the ringleader of a group that dared Jackson to eat a large clump of wasabi, a fiery Japanese horseradish, with no beverage to wash it down.

"He actually did it," said Joe Thurston, a Las Vegas teammate and friend of Victorino. "We were kind of nervous about what the aftereffects would be and what we'd tell our manager had happened. Shane loved it. He had had a lot of sushi encounters in Hawaii and thought this was pretty funny."

And just as he was known to take an extra base by stretching a double into a triple, Victorino was also known to stretch out jokes, which occasionally got him in trouble with teammates.

"If somebody did something wrong in a game, we'd laugh and joke about it afterward, give the guy a little bit of a hard time," Thurston said. "Victorino might take it to the extreme, and that was the kind of thing that could get some people frustrated with him. He would maybe tell that extra joke that took things over the edge. There'd be times when he'd get into shouting matches with people over that."

Victorino needed all the laughs he could get in the first months of the 2004 season, because he and his manager, former major league catcher Terry Kennedy, had some problems with each other. The relationship hit a low point during a June series at Tacoma when Kennedy instructed Victorino and his fellow outfielders to play a "no doubles" defense to make sure nothing got behind them.

"Someone hit an absolute laser over Victorino's head in center field, and it short-hopped the fence," said Thurston, the second baseman in that game. "When we came back to the dugout, Kennedy began yelling and screaming at him. I thought it was really inappropriate. It wasn't Victorino's fault. But Kennedy's going on and on saying, 'When I say no doubles, I mean no doubles!' That incident seemed to me like a sign that Shane didn't have the support of the Dodgers organization anymore. It seemed like Kennedy was just out to get Victorino."

A pick by the Dodgers in the 2003 amateur draft also affected Victorino's standing with the organization. The Dodgers used a sixth-round selection on a 6'4" slugger named Matt Kemp, a center fielder from Oklahoma who made an almost immediate splash in the minors. Kemp's performance knocked every other outfield prospect a peg lower on the organization's depth chart.

The highlight by far of Victorino's 2004 season in Las Vegas came on the diamond but not during a game.

It happened over Memorial Day weekend when a group of local Little Leaguers were invited to run onto Cashman Field alongside members of the Las Vegas 51s.

Several of the young players' mothers sat in the first rows of the stands, cheering loudly and snapping pictures. One of the women caught Victorino's eye, and he later found a way (not through her son) to pass along his phone number.

A couple days later, Victorino and Melissa Smith went out for the first time. Melissa worked for the Las Vegas–based Ultimate Fighting Championship organization. She was into kickboxing and showed off some of her workout gear to her date. Intrigued by what he saw and already a big UFC fan, Shane grabbed some equipment of his own and started trying out some moves.

"Do you want to fight?" Smith asked jokingly.

Her date eagerly took her up on the offer.

The bout lasted a matter of seconds. Victorino, a bit overeager to impress, lifted his foot and landed a kick that hit Melissa squarely in the face.

"I took off my gloves and threw them on the floor and said, 'I'm not playing with you anymore,'" Smith recalled with a smile.

"What can I say, my competitive nature definitely came out that night," Victorino said.

Shane and Melissa literally hit it off on that occasion, and they arranged a second date for when Shane returned from a road trip to the Pacific Northwest in a few days. Unfortunately for them, that ended up being the series when Kennedy laced into him for letting a ball go over his head.

While in Tacoma, Victorino found out he was being sent back to Double A Jacksonville. The Dodgers' farm directors told him they felt he had lost some of his confidence hitting left-handed. At Triple A, he was hitting over .300 from the right side of the plate but below .200 from the left side. That perhaps justified a demotion, but his stormy relationship with Kennedy certainly did not help.

In the seemingly never-ending game of musical roster spots, former rookie ball teammate Jason Repko was called up from Jacksonville to take Victorino's place on the Triple A roster.

His instructions to leave Las Vegas made little sense to Melissa, who was not a particularly big baseball fan.

"Can't you just come back to Vegas?" she asked when he told her the news over the phone. "Can't you just say you don't want to leave?"

"No, they tell me where to go. I don't tell them where I should be," he said.

So for the 10th time in five years, Victorino packed his gear and prepared for another change of scenery. Like every other player fighting for a shot at the big time, he had signed up for this nomadic lifestyle. His moment of crisis the season before had affirmed his desire to keep plugging along. Back and forth, up and down. Have bat, have glove, must travel. Run into a manager who dislikes you, and prepare to slide down the ladder.

Even in Victorino's absence, he was still a target of Kennedy's scorn. In the series following his departure, the 51s were playing in Edmonton when the manager heard a familiar tune playing in the visitors' clubhouse.

It was "Yeah" by the artist Usher, the hit song Victorino used as his walk-up music on his way to the batter's box.

"Isn't this Shane Victorino's song?" Kennedy asked.

Some players, including Thurston, confirmed that it was.

"Well, you see where this song got him, don't you? It got him back to Double A," the manager said.

BACK IN JACKSONVILLE YET AGAIN, Victorino put together the best three-month stretch of his minor league career to that point. In a complete turnabout from Las Vegas, he hit far better and with more power left-handed.

In 294 at-bats with Jacksonville in 2004, Victorino hit .327, which was 92 points higher than he hit in Las Vegas the first part of the season. And in slugging 16 home runs, he displayed a level of power he had never shown before. Before that torrid 75-game stretch in Jacksonville, he had a total of 18 homers in five and a half seasons of minor league ball. Perhaps as a result of his focus on proving himself at the plate, he stole only nine bases. But by that time, his ability to swipe a bag or two in a game was well established.

Alvarez said he learned a lot about his friend in the second half of the 2004 season.

"For whatever reason, things weren't working out in Triple A for him," Alvarez said. "I don't think [the Las Vegas 51s] read him the right way. I know there were some things going on between him and the manager and the group of players they had there at the time. But he took that experience and learned from it. When he came back to Double A, he played at a level I had never seen him play at before. He became an all-around player. And he was the first one on the field, and the first one in the cages. He just took it to another level."

It seemed only a matter of time before Victorino, who was still not on the Dodgers' 40-man roster, returned to Las Vegas or maybe even got his first shot in Los Angeles.

"Absolutely, Shane is on the verge of heading back up to Triple A," Dodgers minor league field coordinator Terry Collins told the *Florida Times-Union* during the 2004 season. "He's regained that confidence in his hitting from the left side, which is why we brought him here. It's not just his batting, though, it's his overall play. Like the other day when he was rounding second base when his routine fly out to center field was caught. That's the type of hustle and play that got Shane to the major leagues a couple of years ago with San Diego."

Though they were separated by thousands of miles, Shane and Melissa's relationship blossomed in the summer of 2004. Melissa traveled to Jacksonville several times so the couple could spend time together. Melissa had grown up on Alaska's Kenai Peninsula, three hours south of Anchorage. Though the climates of Alaska and Hawaii were quite different, the two states had strong cultural similarities because of their geographic isolation. Both were slow-paced and very family-oriented. Smith, a single mother who received a degree in business and finance from the University of Alaska–Anchorage, had a warm but no-nonsense personality that appealed to Shane.

Victorino stayed with Jacksonville for the remainder of the Double A season, but there was talk of a possible September 2004 call-up to Los Angeles for the major league stretch run. That did not materialize, either, but the positive chatter strongly indicated that the Dodgers had designs on protecting him on the 40-man roster. That would help convince him the Dodgers believed he fit into their plans for the future.

Then again, there were no guarantees in the life of a minor leaguer, especially one who had experienced as many detours as Shane Victorino.

TIME TO SHINE

AFTER BOUNCING AROUND THE UNITED STATES FOR THE MAJORITY of his professional career, the idea of picking up and leaving the country was probably the furthest thing from Shane Victorino's mind in 2004.

The notion was borne out of a casual conversation before a game between the Jacksonville Suns and Birmingham Barons, the Double A affiliate of the Chicago White Sox. Birmingham hitting coach Manny Trillo, a Venezuela native, took Victorino aside and asked about his plans for the coming off-season. Shane was noncommittal. He assumed he would go to Las Vegas to see his girlfriend, then spend a few weeks in Maui.

"Have you considered playing winter ball in Venezuela?" the former major leaguer asked him.

Trillo, who in 1969 was selected in the minor league portion of the Rule 5 Draft by the Oakland Athletics, knew a thing or two about fighting to get noticed by big-league clubs.

The thought of going to Latin America had never occurred to Victorino.

"Would you like to play winter ball?" Trillo pressed harder.

Victorino bounced the idea off his agent. They decided to pursue it further.

Near the end of his 2004 season in Jacksonville, Victorino got a call from Ruben Amaro Sr., a scout for the Philadelphia Phillies who also worked with Águilas del Zulia of the Venezuelan Professional Baseball League. Trillo, a coach on the team, had put Amaro in contact with him.

Victorino realized he could stew for a couple months wondering if he would get a spot on the Dodgers' 40-man roster or he could go to Latin America to play baseball and, if the Dodgers left him unprotected, impress scouts from other organizations. He made up his mind to go to Maracaibo, Venezuela, for the 63-game season. Before leaving the country, he gathered up his meager belongings and moved in with Melissa and her son, Keenan, in Las Vegas. After years living on his own all over the country, Shane had found love and companionship with Melissa, who supported his decision to try and give his fledgling career a boost.

"He was still considering going back to school, but he decided to tough it out one more time," she recalled. "He saw it as a chance to have fun and play baseball on his own terms. It had started to feel like the Dodgers were treating him like a business transaction."

During Victorino's second month in Maracaibo, the Dodgers released the newest version of their 40-man roster. Again, Victorino was left off it, meaning any team that wanted to take a chance on him could once more do so in the Rule 5 Draft. For the duration of his stay in Venezuela, he tried not to dwell on the off-season drama of staying with an organization that did not seem to value him or breaking in with another one that thought he might be major league ready.

"I thought I was going to get protected by the Dodgers, but I didn't," he said. "I didn't know if somebody was going to take me in the Rule 5 Draft again or not, so I just focused on playing baseball. And I had a great time just doing that."

Pete Mackanin, the manager of Águilas del Zulia and later a bench coach for the Phillies, got a good taste of Victorino.

"Players go down there to hone their skills, to get at-bats, and to improve their style of play and abilities," Mackanin said. "That's what he was there to do, and it paid off for him. He was close to a five-tool player. He was well-liked by the people in Maracaibo and highly respected throughout the league because he played so well that winter. I was surprised he was left unprotected because of the skills he showed. He definitely made a good impression on me. I was a coach with the Pirates at the time, and I tried to get the Pirates interested in him."

The change of scenery had done him good. In Maracaibo, Victorino hit .280 with nine home runs and 38 RBIs in 214 at-bats.

"Those months in Venezuela were everything to me," Victorino said. "It was an experience I'll always remember. It was great to go to a different country to play baseball, to see the passion and understanding those fans have for the game. When other players ask me about winter ball, I tell them they should absolutely go if they have the chance. I was there at a time when there were a lot of things going on in the country. You had security guys holding M16 machine guns sitting on the field in foul territory with dogs. It made you really understand how lucky we have it in the United States."

The winter ball season was starting to wind down when Victorino got the news that for the second time in his young career a team had selected him in the Rule 5 Draft, held that year at baseball's winter meetings in Anaheim. This time he went to the Philadelphia Phillies as the seventh overall pick. Major league teams selected nine players from the Dodgers' farm system in the draft, by far the most of any organization.

It was no coincidence that Phillies scout Ruben Amaro Sr. wanted Victorino to play winter ball. The Phillies had liked him for a while, and his solid play in Venezuela had only made him more intriguing to the organization and Amaro's son, Ruben Jr., who was an assistant general manager for Philadelphia.

"He was a guy who was already Rule 5'd, so he was on our radar screen," Amaro Jr. said. "We had him on one of our lists of prospects that may or may not be available that winter. We thought his left-handed swing was kind of a work in progress, but clearly his defensive attributes and speed were big assets. And he had a good arm for a guy who was not very big.

"We put together a list for the Rule 5 Draft, and our scouts really liked how he played in Venezuela. I talked to my dad quite a bit about him. One of the players there at the time was Tomás Pérez, who I knew for many years and who played for our organization. I checked in with him on Victorino, and he had some really positive things to say, too. My dad said he could run, he was hitting extremely well, he was stealing bases, and he was playing an outstanding defensive outfield. You set your [40-man] roster around November 18. From there, you have almost three weeks before you decide if you want to claim somebody. We figured let's give it a shot, and we ended up Rule 5'ing him."

For Victorino, it was the same situation he had found himself in two years earlier when he had gone to the Padres. He would try to win a roster spot at Phillies spring training and hope to stay on the team's major league roster for the entire 2004 season. If the Phillies dropped him, they would be required to offer him back to the Dodgers, an organization that was starting to feel more and more like purgatory for him.

AFTER HIS ADVENTURE IN VENEZUELA, Victorino made his annual off-season trip to Maui. Back home, his softball buddies were gearing up for another statewide tournament.

In previous off-seasons, he had talked his way on to the team, rejecting the concerns of teammates who feared he might get hurt and derail his chances at making the major leagues. This time, however, his friends refused to budge.

"I let him play before, but when he got picked by the Phillies, that was it, no more," said friend Lyle Cummings. "This was his big chance. I didn't care how much he ragged me. I wasn't going to let him play."

Lilyana Koa, a teacher at St. Anthony High School, observed him around the athletic fields in Wailuku. "When he was home, he was running and going to the batting cages," she said. "He had such great skills in so many sports when he was in high school, but you could see that he knew he had to keep working if he wanted to achieve his dream."

In February 2005, Victorino reported to Phillies spring training in Clearwater, Florida. Coming into camp, the Phillies had an abundance of quality outfielders. Newly acquired Kenny Lofton was expected to take over the starting duties in center field from Marlon Byrd, who was coming off a disappointing 2004 season. Veteran Bobby Abreu had the right field job locked up, and Pat Burrell was a mainstay in left. The Phillies had another solid option in utility outfielder Jason Michaels, who contributed good numbers off the bench the season before. The best-case scenario for Victorino was to make the team as a fifth outfielder. His edge was that the Phillies had picked him in the Rule 5 Draft, which meant they not only thought he could make it in the majors, but they also had good reason to want him to.

It appeared as spring training opened that four players would vie for the final spot on the team's 25-man roster: Victorino, Byrd, journeyman infielder Jose Offerman, and a highly regarded first baseman named Ryan

Howard, who clubbed 46 home runs in the minors in 2004. Incumbent first baseman Jim Thome, who had hit 89 homers in his two seasons with the Phillies, was not going anywhere, but some speculated that Howard could get a shot in the Phillies' already crowded outfield.

These were tough roster decisions for the front office and new skipper Charlie Manuel, whose last managerial job had been with the Indians in 2002. If Victorino was the front-runner for the last outfield spot, Byrd made a very compelling case for himself by hitting nearly .400 in his first 14 games in the Grapefruit League.

The biggest question mark about Victorino remained his hitting. During the spring, he did little to inspire confidence that he could handle big-league pitching. He hit just .157 with one home run and two RBIs. The best that could be said for him that spring was that he reinforced his reputation as a great defensive outfielder and a threat on the base paths.

Manuel's evaluation of Victorino in *The Philadelphia Inquirer* told the story: "He's shown me his tools, the fact that he can run and play center field. He has a good arm. Like I said before, he needs to be a little more disciplined at the plate and work the count. Have a better approach. I think those are things that he needs to work on. He has the potential to be a very good player. He's not a polished product yet."

On March 31, 2005, four days before the start of the regular season, Victorino got demoted to Triple A Scranton/Wilkes-Barre. Byrd, despite his outstanding spring, followed him down a few days later after the Phillies decided to carry only four outfielders on the Opening Day roster. Ryan Howard, who hit .315 with three home runs during spring training, was also sent back to the minors to further develop his skills. That left Jose Offerman as the winner of the final-man-on-the-roster sweepstakes.

Victorino had simply not made the grade.

"We wanted to see what he could do offensively, and what he basically did was show you one of his tools every single day," Ruben Amaro Jr. said. "But he never put them all together for an extended period of time during the course of the spring. He was given chances to play. We just felt like he wasn't going to make our club."

There was no comparison between Howard's and Victorino's respective situations. Howard was assured to be back in Philadelphia at some point in the coming months. Victorino, on the other hand, was back in limbo. The demotion to Triple A meant he had no chance of making the Phillies' Opening Day roster, and it also signaled the start of a three-day process that would determine his baseball fate. One of three things would happen after that 72-hour period: he would be claimed off waivers by another team; taken back by the Dodgers; or, if neither of the first two happened, become a free agent.

It was a very quiet few days. No team claimed Victorino off waivers, and the Dodgers said "no thanks" to welcoming him back to their organization. That is when Amaro Jr. went to work, trying to convince Victorino to sign a minor league deal with the Phillies.

"We started the process, for lack of a better word, of schmoozing Shane to let him know he was a guy we liked and who could benefit from being in our organization not just that year but long-term," Amaro said. "I think he liked the situation, and I think it ended up being a great move for him and for us."

If there had been more time for him to test the free-agent market, Victorino might have looked in other directions. With the season about to start, however, he felt his best bet was to stay with the Phillies. Still only 25, he was already with his third organization. He hoped Amaro truly believed in him and that he could eventually find a home in Philadelphia.

"The Phillies gave me a good opportunity to make the team in spring training, so I knew they liked me," Victorino said. "I wanted the opportunity to play at Triple A without worrying about going up and down. I thought it was a good chance to really prove myself."

Scranton/Wilkes-Barre manager Gene Lamont recalled looking forward to seeing Victorino on his team in 2005.

"I knew he had to be a talented kid, but I was kind of surprised that the Phillies drafted him, because their outfield positions were pretty set," he said. "But I thought he was good enough to be a big-league player. We were lucky that we were able to hold onto him."

Victorino had experienced a number of defining moments during his six-year professional career. There was his initial breakthrough as a switch hitter in Jacksonville, his opportunity to play in the Arizona Fall League, and his weeks with the Padres as a Rule 5 draftee. But it seemed likely that his upcoming season with the Red Barons would go a long way toward determining his baseball future.

HIS ABYSMAL SPRING TRAINING BEHIND HIM, Victorino prepared for his next battle. This time it was not against another player gunning for the same roster spot but rather with himself, to prove beyond question that he could hit from both sides of the plate. His love-hate relationship with switch hitting seemed destined to end either in marriage or breakup with Scranton/Wilkes-Barre. His coaches believed he could make it as an everyday major league player if he developed consistency with his left-handed hitting skills.

"He had such athletic ability, but he just couldn't put it together left-handed," said Sal Rende, the batting coach for the Red Barons in 2005. "For him, hitting right-handed came so naturally that he could go five or more games without an at-bat from that side and still hit a home run when a left-handed pitcher came in. That wasn't the case from the left side."

The pressure was on, and Victorino's response to it would show if he was ready to make it back to the penthouse.

"I knew how important it was for me to have a good year," Victorino said. "I wanted to do whatever I could to make that happen."

Like he had at Double A Jacksonville in 2002, he spent time with his hitting coach to try to gain confidence as a left-handed hitter.

Rende's work with Victorino was a "last-ditch effort" to get the young player to master switch hitting. "He was one of those kids who had passion and fire, and he was so much fun to be around, because he could joke," Rende said. "He would take a bad swing and say something stupid, and then we'd go on to the next swing. We did something we called an off-center drill where we'd throw the ball from in line with where the second baseman would play. So it'd be cutting across the outside part of the plate. He'd have to hit it into left-center field, which created a swing path for him. That was a key thing for him, creating a consistent swing path. He was getting a feel for where everything needed to be at a given point in an at-bat. Once he found that rhythm and that swing path, he could apply it in a game without worrying about it, because his muscle memory was kicking in."

With Rende on medical leave for a month at the start of the season, Victorino struggled at the plate. By mid-June, he was hitting only around .250. But upon Rende's return to Scranton/Wilkes-Barre, Victorino absolutely took off, hitting for average and power from both sides of the plate as the team's leadoff man.

"The power kind of surprised me because of how small he was," Lamont said. "As the season went on, you could see he had a nice, short, compact stroke. I knew he should be playing in the big leagues from the middle of the season on. I kept mentioning that to the Phillies, but they just didn't have room for him right then."

His Red Barons teammate Ryan Howard got the call to Philadelphia in July 2005, but Victorino stayed put and continued to terrorize International League pitchers.

"Scranton was a tough place to hit homers, and Shane hit most of his home runs at our ballpark," Rende said. "That was a big accomplishment. It was just a phenomenal year, and it was so much fun to watch him, especially in the second half of the season."

The Phillies front office trusted Lamont, a longtime baseball man who had helped groom players for decades.

"Gene Lamont had been around a lot of center fielders in the game for a long time," Amaro Jr. said. "I remember him saying Andy Van Slyke was one of the best center fielders he'd ever been around when he was in Pittsburgh. And he felt Shane was every bit as good as Van Slyke. That was pretty high praise. When you have a coach or manager of that stature making those kinds of comments about a player, it makes you stand up and listen."

Victorino finished the year on a 22-game hitting streak. Despite his struggles early in the season, he lifted his average to .310. His power surge that began the year before in Jacksonville carried over to the 2005 season, in which he hit 18 home runs. He stole only 17 bases, but he legged out 16 triples, the most of any player at any level of professional baseball in America that year.

Some of the pitchers he faced wondered where in the world this dynamo had come from.

"I had never heard of the guy before, but the way he burst onto the scene that year, you saw somebody who was really talented, had a lot of power, and really enjoyed playing," said Justin Miller, who faced Victorino in 2005 while pitching for Syracuse of the International

League. "At the Triple A level, it could be a long season, but he was going out there in the last week of August and having as much fun as the first week of the season. You saw his competitiveness and his desire to be a major leaguer."

At season's end, Victorino was named the International League's Most Valuable Player. The only blemish to the season was that the Red Barons finished last in the league's North Division.

Despite the huge numbers he put up that year, Victorino still somehow missed being ranked as one of *Baseball America*'s top 20 prospects in the minor leagues.

A.J. Hinch, a Scranton/Wilkes-Barre teammate who later became manager of the Arizona Diamondbacks, enjoyed observing Victorino during the 2005 season.

"When I first met Shane, we were at very different ends of our careers," Hinch said. "He was at the beginning, bouncing around after being a Rule 5 pick, and I was at the tail end of my career, looking to get into the front office or managing. I took some time because I wanted to get to know him. He was a high-strung guy, physically talented but still learning how to play the game and to use his skill set. He was such a young guy, but he was already on his third organization. But he had maintained his energy and enthusiasm. I didn't want to be a Crash Davis–type, but I was the oldest player there. And with Shane, I was always trying to find out how his mind works."

At one point during the season, Victorino's coaches also started wondering about the inner workings of his mind.

"I got kicked out of a game, and I went in the clubhouse and watched him play center field on TV," Lamont said. "There were a couple balls hit in that game that he didn't catch. I knew how good he was in center field and thought he should have gotten to them. The next game I watched him very closely again, and the same thing happened. After the game, I told him that I thought he should be able to get to some of those balls. I told him it looked like his concentration wasn't very good. That's when he told me he used to take medication for attention [hyperactivity] deficit disorder, but he had stopped taking it. So I mentioned that to the trainer, and he did some tests."

Victorino had been diagnosed as a child with ADHD, but now he learned he had the adult form of the disorder. It had not gone away on its own as he hoped it would. So after a six-year break, he started taking medication again. To be permitted to do so, he got a "therapeutic use exemption" from Major League Baseball, because ADHD drugs are on baseball's banned substances list. Ritalin and other ADHD drugs are stimulants that calm sufferers of the disorder but have the opposite effect on people consuming the pills recreationally. In 2012, more than 100 major leaguers held such exemptions.

"I think the medication helped his concentration," Lamont said. "It didn't help his ability, it just helped him focus. He was very, very good to begin with. It probably made him a little bit better."

Victorino credits Rende with making him a complete hitter and Lamont with keeping a watchful eye on him. "Gene was one of my favorites in the minor leagues. He had my back," he said. "That talk he had with me turned out to be really important. I don't know if getting on medication was the extra thing I needed to be able to focus and channel my energy. But ever since that day, I've been back on it. And when I take it, I'm calm and focused on what's going on around me."

The medication helped him off the field, as well. When on medication, he could do routine things other people take for granted, like watch entire movies.

"I was very supportive of him getting back on it," said the future Melissa Victorino, whom he continued dating while playing in Pennsylvania. "It balanced him out and helped with his attention span. It's a night-and-day difference when he takes the medication."

Hinch, who was a psychology major at Stanford University, saw the evolution of a player occur right before his eyes. "He was so talented, and people were waiting for him to put it together," he said. "I think for him it was a matter of slowing it down. Most guys on their way up attack the game with such vigor and aggressiveness that they don't use their heads when they play. He was a small guy with a lot of power. A lot of young immature players try to show that off. They don't realize there are other ways they can impact the game. It finally came together for him that summer. He was maximizing all his skills as opposed to showing off all his skills. I'm a big fan of his, maybe because I saw him go from a raw, unpolished player to one of the most electric players in the game. And it happened quickly. The physical ability was there. It was the mental side that clicked."

Victorino attributed his watershed season in Scranton/Wilkes-Barre to the development of his body and mind.

"I realized it's the guy who has mental toughness to keep grinding every day who can separate himself," Victorino said. "And you have to realize you're not going to succeed all the time. You just have to find a way to readjust yourself and do the little things that make you better."

Phillies manager Charlie Manuel, who nearly kept Victorino on the 25-man roster after spring training, was pleased to read the glowing reports coming out of Triple A. The "little man with the big swing," as Manuel described him to reporters, was doing exactly what he had failed to do during a disappointing spring training.

"The year at Scranton showed his passion and determination and his confidence in himself and the push and drive he has," Manuel said. "He earned a chance with us."

On September 1, 2005, the day after he won the International League's MVP award, Victorino was one of six players called up from the minors to join the Phillies' 40-man roster.

With the Padres, Victorino had gotten a brief taste of April and May baseball in the major leagues. Now he would have a chance to see how the big boys did it in September, in the middle of a pennant race, no less. At the time of his call-up, the Phillies led the National League wild-card race, with the Astros, Marlins, Mets, and the surprising Washington Nationals (in their first season since moving from Montreal) nipping at their heels. Meanwhile, the Phillies trailed the Braves by four games in the National League East.

Victorino's role that month, according to Manuel, was to occasionally fill in for outfielders Kenny Lofton and Jason Michaels and also to make pinch-running appearances.

A few days after joining the Phillies, Manuel showed his confidence in Victorino by letting him hit against Astros closer Brad Lidge in the ninth inning of a tight game at Citizens Bank Park. The move prompted questions from the local media about whether it was wise to rely on an untested player in such a big situation. Victorino battled Lidge for 10 pitches before grounding out. The at-bat served as an initiation to the pressures and scrutiny of September baseball.

Houston went on to sweep the Phillies, who by that time had fallen behind both the Astros and the Marlins in the wild-card race. In the final game of the Astros series, Victorino collected an RBI single that briefly put his team ahead. It was his first major league hit in two and a half years.

Later that month, with the Phillies still in the thick of the playoff hunt, Victorino experienced the biggest thrill of his young career. In the top of the ninth inning of a game at Atlanta, the Phillies and Braves were deadlocked in a scoreless pitchers' duel between Jon Lieber of the Phillies and Tim Hudson of the Braves. Michael Tucker got the Phillies on the board with a two-out RBI single. Braves manager Bobby Cox left Hudson in the game to face pinch hitter Victorino with two runners on base.

"It was crunch time," Victorino said. "We were trying to make a playoff push, and this was a crucial game. I got a 1-2 slider from Hudson and put a good swing on it. I saw the outfielder stop running and knew it was gone. Then I remember thinking, *Did this really just happen?* As I ran around the bases, I saw how ecstatic the bench was."

The game meant so much to the Phillies that the veterans on the team chose to skip the ritual of giving a rookie who had just hit his first career homer the cold shoulder when he returned to the dugout. The Phillies went on to win the game 4–0, keeping their playoff hopes very much alive.

After the clutch home run, the ball he hit out was nowhere to be found, so Victorino settled for the lineup card from the game as a memento.

Owing to his year at Triple A and clutch performance with the Phillies, a new set of questions surrounding Victorino started swirling: With two players on the 60-day disabled list, if the Phillies made the postseason, would Victorino win a spot on the playoff roster? And looking ahead to 2006, had he positioned himself to contend for a starting job in the outfield?

The first question became moot when the Phillies, despite winning more games than they had in any season since going to the World Series in 1993, finished the year two games behind the division-winning Braves and one game behind the Astros for a wild-card berth.

Debate over the second question started the moment the Phillies' 2005 playoff hopes got dashed.

Victorino made the most of his 17 major league at-bats that September. His five hits included two home runs. He knocked in eight runs and scored five.

Perhaps his incredible year at Triple A had been more than a fluke. It was now up to the Phillies to decide if he truly fit into their long-term plans.

MAKING IT

MOST KIDS WHO GROW UP PLAYING BASEBALL REACH THE END of their "careers" after Little League, or if they are lucky, high school or college. Anybody good enough to draw the interest of major league scouts is a truly exceptional talent. That said, few if any players spend time in the minor leagues just to soak up the experience and walk away. After toiling down on the farm, each yearns for a taste of the big leagues, even if only for a few games. Whether or not a player makes the leap from minor leaguer to major leaguer can brand him in his own mind as a success or failure.

In contrast to the major leagues, where team success is more highly valued than individual performances, the minor leagues are an every-man-for-himself kind of place.

"As much as we all want to win, wins and losses are not the most important thing," Los Angeles Dodgers minor league field coordinator Terry Collins told the *Florida Times-Union* during Shane Victorino's 2004 season in Jacksonville. "My job today is to make sure these guys get better. That's all I care about."

Player development directors, whose livelihoods depend on grooming talent, have to see it that way.

But a minor league player has a different and somewhat paradoxical take on the importance of team. A player's closest friends and confidantes are his teammates; they are really the only ones who can even remotely understand the joys and frustrations of life on the farm. By the same token, his teammates are the same guys he is trying to outperform in order to get noticed and promoted to the next level.

For a player to prove, for example, that he is an organization's second baseman of the future, he has to show he is the best player at that position in the farm system. Fearing he might be overtaken in the organization's depth chart, a Triple A shortstop might wonder how his counterpart at Double A is doing. Or a catcher at Double A might keep close tabs on the backstop his organization just drafted in the first round. Minor leaguers have to be a little bit paranoid, always looking ahead and behind to see if someone might be standing between them and their hoped-for destiny.

So what happens when a player who has spent years on the same diamond as a bunch of other talented athletes is one of the few to make it to the big time? The ancient Greek playwright Aeschylus said, "Few men have the natural strength to honor a friend's success without envy." If Aeschylus had met Shane Victorino's buddies, he might have reevaluated that sentiment.

An overwhelming majority of the guys Victorino was with in the Dodgers organization never reached the major leagues. As one of his former teammates, Derek Michaelis, put it, "I played at every level except for the one that matters." Though they did not quite make it, Michaelis and others who played with Victorino viewed his success with nothing but delight. "Whether he made it to the big leagues or not, Shane would have been one of the first guys I would have remembered playing with," Michaelis said. "You can't *not* remember Shane Victorino. I just always liked the guy."

Among the players who suited up with Victorino in the minors, each had his own reason for giving up the dream.

Michaelis, who played parts of six seasons in the Dodgers' system, was released by the organization in 2005. Rather than looking for an opportunity to play in an independent league, he opted to go back to Rice University to complete his degree in economics.

"I'm 6'7", left-handed, and could hit the ball a mile," Michaelis said. "I just didn't do it often enough, and I struck out too much. I was a physical specimen, intriguing to scouts, but I never put together a full season."

One of the people Victorino turned to for support while struggling as a Rule 5 draftee with the Padres in 2003 was Dave Detienne, who first met Victorino in Medicine Hat, Alberta, Canada, when the two were roommates in rookie ball.

"When you're going through tough times, you just need to get someone you can trust on the phone," Detienne said. "I hope I was able to help bring Shane back to reality and get him back on track."

Detienne's professional baseball career was sidetracked by government bureaucracy, of all things. He was traded from the Dodgers to the Mets and offered a Triple A contract in 2005, the same year Victorino had his watershed season for Scranton/Wilkes-Barre. Detienne, a Canadian citizen, had impressed the Mets with his ability to play multiple positions, and assignment to their affiliate in Norfolk was a major step forward for him. He had never played above Double A in the Dodgers' system.

"I saw an opportunity to make it to the big leagues," Detienne said. "It might have been as a utility player, but that was fine. I just wanted to play in the big leagues. I was ready to go to Triple A when the Mets called and said they needed a little more time to get me a work visa. They said not to worry, that it wouldn't be an issue. But two weeks turned into a couple months, and finally they said there was nothing they could do."

Detienne could not resolve his immigration issues and had to sit out the entire 2005 season. "It was devastating," he said. "I finally had momentum. All that grinding away in Great Falls [Montana] and the other places I played, and someone had finally noticed. I had an opportunity, and there was nothing that was going to stop me. I kept in touch with the Mets during that season, but after the season, they revamped their player development system, and all the connections I had were gone. When I went looking for a team, the first question out of everyone's mouth was, 'Where did you play last year?' Then I had to explain everything that happened."

Detienne turned to the independent leagues for the 2006 season. Still unable to latch on with a major league organization, he spent the 2007 season playing independent ball in Gary, Indiana. In 2008, he spent a few games with another independent club in Edmonton before deciding his heart was not in it and he retired at the age of 28. He took the $72,000 signing bonus he had saved for eight years and made a down payment on a house in the Vancouver area for him and his wife.

"To this day I have a very hard time accepting how things turned out," Detienne said. "But I'm glad I'm able to turn on the TV and see Shane play."

When Victorino returned to Double A Jacksonville following his brief stint with the Padres in 2003, teammate Nick Alvarez invited him to share his apartment. It was a particularly rough time for Victorino, whose first go at the majors had been a flop.

Alvarez, a Miami native who spent two seasons in the minors with Victorino, invited Shane and a couple other teammates to his family home during the Southern League all-star break.

"We spent a few days relaxing, not thinking about baseball at all," Alvarez said. "It did us a lot of good."

Alvarez retired in 2006 after learning he was being demoted by the Dodgers from Triple A to Double A. He is now a successful businessman who owns three gyms in Miami. Although he sometimes regrets his decision to walk away from the game, he is thrilled that Victorino's persistence paid off for him.

"Shane's very confident, and a lot of times, you can confuse that with arrogance," Alvarez said. "But anybody who got to know him recognized exactly what kind of person he is. He's somebody you wanted to do well. And when he made it to the majors, I and a lot of other guys who played with him were really happy."

Victorino did not blaze through the minor leagues to get to where he was. He faced adversity and challenges, which made him a stronger player and person. And the guys he got to know on the way there helped him immensely.

"These guys are the closest thing to your family," he said. "Sure, everyone has their own interests in mind, and it can be a cutthroat game in regards to that, but off the field, there's friendship and a sense of loyalty. Nobody's going to stab each other in the back. I'm friends with many of the guys I played in the minor leagues with. Unfortunately, a lot of them didn't get to the big leagues. But they still look at me as the same guy they played with in the minors."

In the time off between the 2005 and 2006 seasons, Victorino avoided most of the angst and uncertainty he carried with him until that point. After plugging away for years, he had achieved a breakthrough. The door was now open.

In April 2006, for the second time in his career, Victorino opened a season in the major leagues, this time as the fourth outfielder for a Phillies team that the year before had finished in second place in the National League East, two games behind the Braves. Despite a solid 88–74 record, the team came up a game short of the Astros in the wild-card race. That meant the Phillies had missed the postseason for the 12th straight year.

The team Victorino joined in 2006 appeared well-positioned to compete again for a division title. Three of his teammates—Pat Burrell, Chase Utley, and Bobby Abreu—were coming off 100-RBI seasons. And that group did not include Ryan Howard, a midseason call-up in 2005 who had 22 homers and knocked in 63 runs in just over 300 at-bats, a performance that won him the National League Rookie of the Year Award. A slew of big bats helped the 2005 Phillies finish second in the National League in runs scored.

Joining the Phillies roster to help fill a void left when veteran center fielder Kenny Lofton signed with the Dodgers was center fielder Aaron Rowand, who was fresh off helping the Chicago White Sox win the most recent World Series.

It was going to be a tough lineup for Victorino to crack, but he hoped to have enough opportunities to build upon his solid performance from the previous September. Before the new season started, team management gave him a vote of confidence by unloading one of the players most likely to compete with him for playing time in the stacked outfield. The team dealt Jason Michaels, who shared center-field duties with Lofton in 2005, to the Cleveland Indians for relief pitcher Arthur Rhodes. A high opinion of Victorino's ability had something to do with the trade; the criminal charges filed against Michaels for scuffling with a Philadelphia police officer the previous summer might have had something to do with it, too.

During spring training, the 25-year-old Victorino got a few extra chances to show off his skills while All-Star right fielder Bobby Abreu was away playing for Venezuela in the inaugural World Baseball Classic. Victorino had hit only .253 in the Grapefruit League, but behind the stat lines, his manager observed talents and personality traits he felt could be nurtured.

"I observed the confidence he has in himself and the push and drive he has," Charlie Manuel said. "He earned his way to the major leagues, but he had to go through a growing-up process before it happened. He had such good talent, but you gotta really study the game and learn who you are. Shane loved playing baseball, and some people might have misread him as being nonchalant when he first signed to play. But I thought it was just important for him to start working with the right people, the right coaches who could push his buttons and get to him. But that wouldn't have worked if he didn't take the most important step of growing up."

With a starting outfield, from left to right, of Burrell, Rowand, and Abreu, Victorino set realistic goals for the 2006 season.

"I didn't know to what extent I was going to play, so I prepared myself for whatever opportunity I might get," said Victorino, who was slated to make $330,000 in 2006. "The idea was to work hard, knowing I had the opportunity one day to be an everyday major league player."

John Kruk, an ESPN broadcaster and member of the Phillies' broadcast team in 2006, was struck by Victorino's swagger.

"When he made the team, I thought he'd probably be a good fourth or fifth outfielder, a guy who could steal a base and play good defense," said Kruk, who played on the 1993 Phillies team that lost in the World Series. "When he started coming off the bench, I was struck by how cocky he was. For a guy who didn't play very much, he was really cocky."

Other baseball people believed Victorino was a budding star who could help shore up their outfields. Tampa Bay manager Joe Maddon said his team looked into trading for him, and Gene Lamont, Victorino's manager at Triple A Scranton/Wilkes-Barre in 2005, was quick to tell his new bosses in Detroit how much he thought of his former player.

"When I got to the Tigers in 2006, I mentioned him," Lamont said. "I said he's not just a hard player, he's a heck of a good player. But I think by then the Phillies realized what kind of player he was, and they weren't interested in trading him."

Seeing limited at-bats, Victorino started slow in his rookie season in Philadelphia. In April 2006, he hit below .200 as the team got off to a sluggish 10–14 start.

As it turned out, his big chance to get his foot through the door came when teammate Aaron Rowand almost put his face through an outfield fence.

In mid-May 2006, in the first inning of a game at Citizens Bank Park against the Mets, Rowand, his back to home plate, took off in a dead sprint after a Xavier Nady fly ball. Unable and unwilling to stop himself, Rowand made a spectacular catch before violently crashing into the chain-link fence. He crumpled to the ground in pain but immediately lifted his glove hand to show he had secured the ball. In pursuit of a catch that quelled the Mets' two-out, bases-loaded rally, Rowand broke his nose and suffered fractures to bones in his face, which more closely resembled a battered prizefighter than a baseball player as he walked off the field.

It was a stunning play and one that gave Rowand immediate cult status to Phillies fans always searching for worthy successors to beloved center fielders of years past, like Richie Ashburn, Garry Maddox, and Lenny Dykstra.

Victorino came off the bench that day and contributed two hits in a rain-shortened 2–0 win for the home team.

The circumstances were far from ideal, but Victorino was going to get his shot as a starter, at least for a while.

"You never wish that kind of thing on anybody," Victorino said. "But you have to be prepared to go out there when you get your opportunity, and I definitely was ready. I knew I was going back to the bench when Rowand got healthy, but I hoped that what I did while I was out there would open their eyes."

The day after Rowand's injury, Victorino rapped out four hits against the Reds in the major league debut of 22-year-old lefthander Cole Hamels, who tossed five shutout innings in a Phillies win. With Victorino in center and Hamels on the mound, the future of the team was revealing itself.

While filling in for Rowand, Victorino played like someone who never wanted to go back to the bench. He started 11-for-19 with four doubles, two triples, and a home run. Later that season, as if he were reaching out to fans one by one to introduce himself, he belted a home run at Fenway Park that awarded a Philadelphia man $1,000, the prize in a local contest where players "hit for" fans. Over the course of the season, Manuel experimented with his exciting young player by batting him in different places in the lineup, including fifth, sixth, and leadoff.

Victorino learned quickly the challenges of hitting in the major leagues. In another game that season at Boston, he took swings against knuckleballer Tim Wakefield, whose pitches often came in at around 60 miles per hour, and against Manny Delcarmen, whose fastball has been clocked in the high 90s.

"That wasn't something I had seen before," Victorino said. "It was so different facing Wakefield and then having a guy come in and throw flame balls."

Around this time, Victorino picked what would become his long-standing "walk-up music," the song played over the public-address system as players make their way to the plate. His choice was "Buffalo Soldier" by Bob Marley. The lyrics of the song about the first regiments of African American soldiers in the U.S. Army could be applied on a lesser scale to his own struggles to make it to the big leagues: "Fighting for arrival, fighting for survival."

Victorino's journey to the majors had been circuitous, but a Phillies teammate who made his major league debut in May 2006 was perhaps the poster child for the power of perseverance. Catcher Chris Coste had spent 11 years in the minors before getting his first shot in the big leagues at the age of 33. Coste went on to hit .328 for the Phillies in 2006.

Manuel could relate to the experiences of players like Coste who toiled for years on the farm.

"I was in the minors for six years before I made the majors," said Manuel, a former left fielder who went on to star in Japan. "It gets tough from a financial standpoint and from the standpoint of being frustrating. You see other guys go up, and you think you're just as good or better than them. But there are such a thing as late bloomers, players who get better in their late twenties or early thirties. Coste was a survivor."

And so was Victorino.

In a game at Shea Stadium against the Mets in late May, Victorino did his best Rowand impersonation by doing a belly flop on the warning track to make a catch. His hitting, speed, and defense prompted Phil Sheridan of *The Philadelphia Inquirer* to muse, "It's almost as if Shane Victorino emerged from the collective wishful thinking of Phillies fans the way Joe Jackson walked out of that cornfield in *Field of Dreams*. That's fitting because just like Shoeless Joe, Victorino is about to turn around and disappear into the corn. Metaphorically speaking, of course."

To no one's surprise, Victorino returned to his reserve role when Rowand got back. But he had made the most of his chance to play, emerging as one of the bright spots in what was a disappointing first half of the season for a team that had expected to compete for a division title. The Phillies won a dismal nine of 27 games in June, and at the All-Star break they trailed the Mets by 12 games. Victorino was hitting a respectable .277.

"I think doing what I did during those weeks kind of helped the Phillies realize that maybe they should give this kid a shot," Victorino said.

The attention of restless fans and media at that point in the season was squarely on Manuel.

It was a time of transition for the team. Abreu, Burrell, and shortstop Jimmy Rollins were the mainstays of the Larry Bowa era, a stormy four-year period in Phillies history remembered as much for the team's losing seasons as for its manager's temper tantrums. Bowa, in addition to being ejected from 22 games during his tenure, clashed publicly with several players.

The stories of the days under Bowa lived on long after Larry left the building.

"I know [Bowa] was someone who used to like to get on guys," Victorino said. "I wasn't here for that whole spiel. Every person is different with regards to stuff like that. It's hard for me to say if I would have been uncomfortable playing for him. Maybe I would have loved it, maybe not."

The firing of Bowa near the end of the 2004 season and the hiring of Manuel later that year represented a seismic shift in the direction and personality of the team. Those fans and players who liked Bowa, the shortstop on the Phillies team that won the World Series in 1980, saw him as a perfect fit for a city that lived and died with its sports teams. The frequent images of Bowa in the dugout, pacing back and forth, veins protruding from his neck, embodied the soul of the Philadelphia fan. But it was clear that Bowa was not getting the most out of his players. In the mind of then–general manager Ed Wade, that necessitated a change at the top. Wade could not have conjured up a personality more different from Bowa than Manuel.

Manuel, the son of a Pentecostal preacher, was rural-Virginia folksy and far less apt than Bowa to fly off the handle and berate his players.

"Was it a contrast? No, not at all," Jimmy Rollins joked. "Bowa was a tense guy. When he played, he was tense, and he was tense as a manager. You felt like you were walking on eggshells with him at times. It was worse for pitchers than position players. He just didn't like pitchers."

Victorino liked playing for Manuel, and it bothered him that the fans and media were not as quick to warm to him.

"It was awful showing up at the ballpark and seeing some of the signs telling Manuel to get out of town," he said. "It wasn't him, it was us. We knew we were a better team, but unfortunately in this game, the manager is always the one who gets scrutinized, who gets fired. He's not the one on the field. The players on the field are ultimately responsible for what happens. The manager can only run out the best team he has every night. I'm sure Charlie felt the pressure, but he stayed positive. When you have a manager like that, you want to show up to play, and you want to win."

WHEN THE TEAM RETURNED TO ACTION following the All-Star Game, change was in the air. Recently hired general manager Pat Gillick decided to stick with Manuel but opted to shake up the team in other ways. Two weeks after the All-Star break, with the Phillies at 49–54 and 13½ games behind the Mets in the NL East, the team traded Bobby Abreu and pitcher Cory Lidle to the Yankees for four minor league prospects.

As bad as the season had been, the Phillies were only five games behind the Reds in the National League wild-card race at the time of the Abreu deal.

The "kid" was going to get a shot.

"Once we made the move with Abreu, that was Shane's chance," Manuel said. "I think the way he played for us earlier in the season dictated to us he could be an everyday player."

Not everyone, however, was convinced that Victorino could fill Abreu's shoes.

Before the trade was consummated, Sam Donnellon of the *Philadelphia Daily News* noted that it would be difficult to replace a guy who consistently scored and knocked in 100 runs a season. "Unless you truly believe that Shane Victorino would give you a better stick and a better glove out in right field night in and night out—and, clearly, you are nuts if you do—then Abreu's your man," Donnellon wrote.

Ruben Amaro Jr., who was an assistant general manager of the team under Gillick, said the Abreu deal symbolized a change in direction for the team. "Pat felt like it gave us more payroll flexibility and a chance to look at some kids with a different type of energy," Amaro said. "The rest was just Shane overachieving. If we hadn't had somebody waiting in the wings, we would have been more reluctant to move Bobby. To his credit, [Victorino] created his own situation."

Over the span of a few days, third baseman David Bell, catcher Sal Fasano, and relief pitchers Rheal Cormier and Ryan Franklin—who had a combined 40 years of major league experience—also left the team. The Phillies brass wanted to give some younger players a chance to play, even if that came at the expense of getting back in the playoff hunt.

But aided by Ryan Howard's power explosion, second baseman Chase Utley's 34-game hitting streak, and Victorino's steady play in right field, the team became a strong playoff contender, playing torrid baseball in August to climb within one game of the Padres in the wild-card chase at month's end.

In late August, the Phillies decided to add a piece to the puzzle, making a move to bring in a veteran pitcher they hoped would provide leadership for the stretch run. Jamie Moyer, a Philadelphia-area native, was more than just a veteran. He was a 43-year-old with 20 years of major league service when the Phillies acquired him from the Mariners, Gillick's former team, for two pitching prospects whose combined ages totaled just one year less than Moyer's. But Moyer, a soft-tosser who got by on guile, certainly did not intend for 2006 to be his last season. In fact, he had vetoed a trade a year earlier to the Astros because Houston refused to discuss a longer-term deal. In Philadelphia, Moyer proved he had a lot left in his arm. In eight outings with the team in 2006, he posted a 5–2 record and was later rewarded with a two-year contract extension.

"We were excited when he came over from Seattle," Victorino said. "He brought us that veteran experience. He had played in the playoffs in Seattle before. It was great just watching him go about his business. Whenever there was a pop-up, he'd yell, 'Two hands! Two hands!' He's saying to do it that way, because it's the right way to do it. He reminded guys about the little things you need to do to play the game the right way."

In early September against the Marlins, Victorino again showed he was willing to risk bodily harm to help the team win. During a close play at the plate late in the game, he rammed into burly Florida catcher Miguel Olivo, who outweighed him by 40 pounds. He sprained his left wrist in the process of scoring the run. Before the incident, Victorino was hitting over .350 since taking over for Abreu in early August.

The play made a strong impression on his manager.

"We talked to him about running over catchers, because he's a little guy and we don't want him to get hurt," Manuel said. "But we also realized that when the day comes that he quits playing that way, then he won't be Shane Victorino. You gotta let him play."

Victorino had perhaps his best game of the year in a game toward the end of the season, a five-hit performance in a win against the Marlins. But by then, the Phillies had too much ground to make up, and they finished three games behind the Dodgers in the wild-card race.

Though the team fell short of the playoffs, the season had some high points. Howard followed up his outstanding rookie season by winning the National League Most Valuable Player Award. In 2006, Howard clubbed 58 home runs and had 149 RBIs. The Phillies led the National League in runs scored, but they also gave up a lot of runs. No Phillies pitcher won more than 12 games in 2006, and the pitching staff finished the year with a team earned-run average of 4.60.

The swapping of Abreu for Victorino was not about replacing one player with another similar one. It was about taking the outfield in a new and hopefully positive direction. The jury was out, but there was no denying that after Victorino joined the starting lineup for good, the team started winning.

Victorino finished the year hitting .287 with six home runs and 46 RBIs. Perhaps most significantly, he hit for a higher average from the left side of the plate after battling for years to effectively switch hit.

He also picked up a nickname—"the Flyin' Hawaiian."

"It came from a Mets announcer during a broadcast, and it just stuck," Victorino said. "I like it. I think it's an honor."

By the end of the 2006 season, John Kruk, who had earlier wondered about Victorino's potential as an everyday player, was completely won over. "Shane came in and gave them an attitude. He changed a lot of people's minds about what he could do out there," he said.

Victorino's first full season in the majors left him eager for more. "I got to observe great players on my team, guys like Ryan, Chase, Jimmy

Rollins, guys who were still early in their careers but so successful at what they did," he said. "To walk around the different ballparks and see guys on other teams who make the game look so simple, it was amazing to take it all in. We were so close that year, and it made us hungry to go to the next level."

THE START OF SOMETHING
SPECIAL

ERIC TOKUNAGA, THE MAJOR LEAGUE SCOUT IN HAWAII WHO had discovered Shane Victorino in high school and spread the word about his ability, viewed Shane's success not only as a remarkable personal achievement but also as a breakthrough for all Hawaiian players.

"The reason I started scouting was because I saw so many talented Hawaiian baseball players who ended up giving up the game," Tokunaga said. "There was nobody there to harness the talent and to talk to their families and encourage them to make their dreams a reality. Some of it has to do with stereotypes. Some people have this idea that Hawaiians are lazy, and all they want to do is eat plate lunches in the off-season. When I saw Shane, I knew he could really play the game. But he needed to beat a lot of odds to get where he wanted."

Entering the 2007 season, Victorino seemed assured of a starting job in the Philadelphia Phillies outfield. His solid 2006 proved he was capable of playing in the major leagues. The challenge of the coming campaign was to show he had the durability to be a regular player from Opening Day until October.

The previous season had taken a toll on his body. By October, he was experiencing more throbbing and soreness than he could ever recall.

"Mentally and physically, he really goes all-out in a game, and I think that's one of the biggest questions I asked myself, if he can play 162 games," manager Charlie Manuel told reporters before the 2007 season. "I think, right now, you'd probably look at him playing 135, 140 [games]."

Victorino's goal of convincing Manuel that he was a nine-inning, 162-game type of player almost got off to an inauspicious start—but for the best of all possible reasons.

He was in Philadelphia for the team's second-to-last exhibition game of the spring against the Red Sox when his fiancée, Melissa, called from Nevada to say she had gone into labor with their first child. Victorino immediately hopped a plane for Las Vegas, but unfortunately did not arrive in time to witness the birth of his daughter, Kali'a Makenna Victorino.

"I remember walking into the hospital room and seeing Melissa holding our child," he said. "It was definitely one of the most memorable days of my life."

The life of a major league player is such that life-changing moments that occur between late March and early October can only be savored for so long. So on the day after his daughter's birth, Victorino was back on a plane en route to the Phillies' season opener against the Braves at Citizens Bank Park.

Four outfielders were on the Phillies' Opening Day roster, with Victorino slated as the everyday right fielder. He was flanked by left fielder Pat Burrell and center fielder Aaron Rowand. For added support, the Phillies brought in free-agent Jayson Werth, a former teammate of Victorino's in the Dodgers organization.

"When I got [to the Phillies] in '07, the first thing I noticed was the energy and camaraderie in the clubhouse," Werth said. "It was different from any place I had seen. I thought it could blossom into something pretty special."

Former Phillie Garry Maddox, arguably the best major league defensive center fielder of the late 1970s and early 1980s, felt Victorino could excel playing a corner outfield position.

"There's less ground to cover in right field, and most balls hit to right are softer," Maddox said. "A lot of times you come up throwing, so putting him in right really gave him a chance to show off his arm."

A major project for Victorino in 2007 was to make better use of his speed. In 2006, Victorino stole only four bases, a far cry from the 45 or more bags he swiped twice in the minor leagues. New Phillies first-base coach Davey Lopes, who served on the Padres' staff during Victorino's stint with the team in 2003, vowed to help him reach his potential in this area. Going into the season, Victorino set a goal for himself of between 30 and 40 steals. Lopes thought that number could be closer to 50 if Victorino applied himself.

"The physical attributes were obviously there," Lopes said. "He had to develop the confidence factor and eliminate the fear of making a mistake or getting thrown out. It's about being ready to run, wanting to run, and being aggressive. You have to have those qualities to be a base stealer. The next level is choosing the right time to steal, so it's more than guesswork. For Shane, it was about looking at certain things on a pitcher's body that would tell him when he's going to throw over to first base versus going to home. Shane needed a little more push. I think sometimes players aren't as confident as they project themselves to be. You might get one pitch to steal on, and if you're not ready for it, then you've missed your chance. He had to establish that attitude where he could react instantaneously to the situation."

VICTORINO PLANNED TO STEAL BASES...and the team planned to win games. The latter intention was spelled out clearly and brashly at a media luncheon in January by shortstop Jimmy Rollins, who told the audience the Phillies were the "team to beat" in the National League East in 2007. "I know we are," he said confidently of a team that had not made the postseason since 1993. The prediction was based on his assessment that the team's young core of players, of which Victorino was now solidly a member, would continue to improve. The acquisition of starting pitcher Freddy Garcia, a 17-game winner with the White Sox the season before, further suggested the team had what it took to be a contender.

Rollins laid out his vision for the upcoming season, and in the process, provided bulletin-board material for every team in the division, especially the Mets, who were defending NL East champions. The New York media, always eager to seize on a story that pitted teams in the rival cities of New York and Philadelphia against one another, jumped all over Rollins' statement. During the first week of spring training, the *New York Daily News* splashed his face on its back cover, along with the words, "Silly Phillie." A story inside the paper quoted Mets third baseman David Wright shooting back at Rollins by saying, "Talk is very, very, cheap."

Victorino got a kick out of the attention paid to his teammate's comments.

"All he was trying to do was build confidence within the team, to get us pumped up," Victorino said. "He was trying to wake up the team, but some people put his words in the terms they wanted to."

In April, Rollins' words sounded hollow after the Phillies got off to a sluggish start to the season, losing six of their first seven games. The *New York Daily News* had some more fun at the shortstop's expense when Rollins made a key error against the Mets in the teams' first meeting of the year. "Rollins eats words and ball," the latest headline screamed.

Little was going right for the team—or for Victorino—out of the gates. Ironically, it was his attempt to show more aggressiveness on the base paths that got him in trouble with Manuel before the season was even a week old.

In a game against the Braves, with the Phillies leading 2–0 in the eighth inning and the heart of the Phillies order due up, Victorino was thrown out trying to steal third base for the second out of the inning. The Phillies ended up losing the game 3–2 in 11 innings. After the game, Manuel chastised Victorino for making a "terrible play." He was so upset that he benched him for the next day's game and gave Werth the start in right field. Another one-run loss in extra innings two weeks later to the Nationals dropped the Phillies to 3–10, the worst record in the majors. Afterward, Victorino vented his frustration.

"Everything is bitter around here," he told reporters after the game. "Sometimes you'd rather just walk out there and lose by 15 and walk off the field in the ninth. It's so frustrating. We're one hit away, we're one pitch away. It seems like we're one thing away from doing what we need to do, and it's just not falling into place."

It was still early, but the team was off to its worst start since 1982. Although division titles are not won and lost in April, a bad opening month would surely be to blame if they came up short in 2007 as they had in 2006. After the first month of the season, Victorino's average stood at .260. He had no home runs and eight runs batted in. And he was only hitting .219 from the right side of the plate. On the bright side, at least one thing was going according to plan: Victorino had swiped seven bases in nine attempts. In May, he would go on to steal nine bases without being caught.

But Victorino's struggles against left-handed pitching prompted Manuel in early May to again insert Werth into the lineup when the Phillies faced southpaws in Atlanta in back-to-back games. That decision did not sit well with Victorino, who voiced dissatisfaction to the media when he saw he was not in the starting lineup.

"I was shocked to see it," he told *The Philadelphia Inquirer.* "You just have to deal with it."

Long after the fact, however, Victorino said Manuel's decision was the right one. "I was struggling at the plate," he admitted. "Charlie has that special understanding of when you need that mental day off from baseball. People kept asking me if I was upset with him for doing that. I said some things at the time that made it seem like I was. But Charlie is a smart manager. He knew I maybe needed those two days off. It's such a mental game. When you're going well, you ask yourself what you're doing so that you can keep doing it. The reverse is true when you're not going well. But in some ways, you don't want to go too deep into it because you can easily overanalyze things and drive yourself nuts. Getting a day off is just what you need sometimes."

That was apparently the case with Victorino, who entered the final game of the Atlanta series as a defensive replacement and promptly unleashed a 300-foot dart on the fly from right field to throw out a Braves runner at home plate. Back in the starting lineup for the next series in San Francisco, he exploded for 10 hits and six stolen bases in four games.

The team's fortunes also turned around slightly. After posting a winning record in May, the Phillies stood at 26–27. But they trailed the red-hot Mets by eight and a half games, putting Rollins' preseason prediction in definite jeopardy.

More bad news for the team came in June when Freddy Garcia, whose record stood at 1–5, went on the disabled list with a shoulder injury. He would not pitch another game in a Phillies uniform.

Victorino had weathered some bumps in the first months of the 2007 season, but a Sunday afternoon in early June at Citizens Bank Park lifted his spirits as high as they had been since making the major leagues. On the occasion of Shane Victorino Figurine Day, the team gave away thousands of tiny dolls in the form of a hula-skirted Victorino playing a ukulele and flashing the "hang loose," or shaka, sign, which is made with a raised pinkie and thumb.

"That day was so special because everything in the ballpark was Hawaiian-themed and was a tribute to my culture and where I was born and raised," Victorino said. "It was amazing to see the bobblehead with the hula skirt and to hear the Hawaiian music playing between innings. It all just felt great."

The game turned out pretty well for the man of honor as well.

With the Phillies and Giants tied 8–8 in the bottom of the ninth inning, Victorino strode to the plate with one out to face San Francisco reliever Kevin Correia.

"It was starting to rain, and I said to myself, 'I'm going to swing for the fences here,'" Victorino said. True to his word, he swung and connected on a ball that carried over the fence in left field. "I didn't think I had hit it good enough for it to go out, but it did," he said.

The opposite-field shot was Victorino's first career walk-off home run. Amid his struggles and those of the team, it could not have come at a better time. The win brought the Phillies back to .500 and gave Victorino his most memorable baseball moment to date. As he rounded the bases, Phillies play-by-play announcer Harry Kalas, who started his broadcasting career in Hawaii, exclaimed, "Victorino *no ka oi*," or "Victorino is great," a variation on the phrase commonly heard on Maui to describe the island itself.

A few years later, Correia still vividly recalled Victorino's ninth-inning heroics in Philadelphia.

"It was a good pitch down and away, and he hit it out the other way," Correia said. "He's always been a tough out for me."

The Victorino family made sure that the celebration of Hawaiian culture in Philadelphia was shared with as many Mauians as possible. They ordered more than 50 boxes of figurines to distribute to children across the island. Appropriately, the shipment arrived at the harbor where Shane's older brother, Mike, worked as a longshoreman. In fact, shipments between the island and the East Coast had become commonplace; to provide himself a taste of home, Shane had boxes of *mochi*—ice cream wrapped with pounded sticky rice—sent to him regularly.

THROUGH THE SUMMER, THE FLYIN' HAWAIIAN continued to draw notice around the league. In early July in Houston, he leapt face-first into the right-field stands in an unsuccessful pursuit of a foul ball, a play that caught the eye of Astros closer and future teammate Brad Lidge. "It was probably four rows into the stands, and he did a flying superman into the seats," Lidge recalled. "Nobody in their right mind would have kept pursuing it all the way to the foul line, but he really believes in playing every play as hard as he possibly can."

A few nights later during a rain delay in Colorado, Victorino and some teammates dug in their heels and helped Colorado's grounds crew brave the blustery weather to gain control of a recalcitrant tarp.

Kevin O'Brien, a Colorado native and one of Victorino's high school football coaches, was sitting behind the visitors' dugout in Denver that night.

"The tarp got picked up like a wave, and there was someone [on the grounds crew] trapped under it," O'Brien said. "That incident was about more than just having fun in the rain. In my opinion, they might have saved somebody's life. And Shane was the first Phillie to run out there to help."After play resumed, Victorino capped the night with a two-run home run in a Phillies win.

The Phillies were generating excitement, but it was hard for the team to shake its reputation as losers. The countdown to a dubious distinction made that all too clear. On July 15, 2007, the statisticians proclaimed the Phillies the most unsuccessful team in sports history when the franchise became the first ever to lose 10,000 games.

In terms of the present, however, the Phillies had trimmed the lead of the first-place Mets to just five games, though neither team was playing like it wanted to take control of the division.

The Phillies finally got hot in the second half of July, and so did Victorino. He equaled a career high with five hits in Philadelphia's 26-hit onslaught against the Dodgers, the most by the team in a single game since 1985, according to the same statisticians who counted up all 10,000 of the team's losses.

Victorino was hitting nearly .350 in July and the team was a season-high seven games over .500 when he suffered the worst injury of his career while trying to break up a double play against the Chicago Cubs.

"I felt something rip in my calf," Victorino said. "It ended up being a strained right calf. It was definitely frustrating. I was having a great year and things were going in the right direction. And then that happened, and I had to go on the disabled list."

At the time, All-Star second baseman Chase Utley was also on the disabled list.

Before his injury, Victorino had fully rebounded from his slow start. He had 11 home runs and 32 stolen bases to go with a .284 batting average, and his 72 runs scored put him among the National League leaders in that category.

It was agonizing for him to sit while his team fought to get back in the playoff chase. He wanted to return to action as soon as possible, but others convinced him of the need to be patient.

"[In Double A Reading on rehab], I spoke to [teammate] Michael Garciaparra, who had had a similar injury," Victorino said. "He told me to make sure it was right, because he had come back too early and hurt it again. He said the last thing I wanted was to blow it out fully. He showed me his calf where that happened to him and there was a big indentation there. I knew I didn't want that to happen to me."

As Victorino healed, the Phillies continued to play well. By the time he returned to the lineup on August 22, the team was still eight games over .500, five games behind the Mets and squarely in the wild-card race. They were en route to their fourth consecutive winning month and led the National League in runs scored. But they had also yielded a bunch of runs to opponents. If the Phillies were going to make the playoffs, it appeared they would have to hit their way there.

In what continued to be a star-crossed year for the team, starting pitcher Cole Hamels went on the disabled list with a strained elbow just as Victorino and Utley, one of the league leaders in batting average, were returning. The 23-year-old Hamels had anchored a shaky rotation, leading the team with 14 wins at the time of his injury.

The goal of having every key player healthy at the same time had been elusive, but the team fought on with the pieces it had. And Rollins certainly would not have been to blame if they fell short of the playoffs. He was having a career year and would finish with 30 home runs, 94 RBIs, 139 runs scored, and 41 stolen bases.

DURING THAT SUMMER OF 2007, the baseball world watched while the San Francisco Giants' Barry Bonds closed in on Hank Aaron's all-time career home run mark of 755, long considered the most hallowed of sports records.

But something that should have been cause for celebration was instead met with disinterest or even anger by many fans. The cloud of suspicion hanging over Bonds for his alleged use of steroids was too much for them to ignore. There was widespread sentiment that Bonds' feats, a 73–home run season in 2001 among them, were not legitimate and exemplified a tainted generation in baseball. Some of the most prolific sluggers of the era, including Bonds, Sammy Sosa, and Mark McGwire, were linked to steroids, human growth hormone, or both. Star pitchers such as Roger Clemens had also been implicated in the use of performance-enhancing drugs.

Victorino, while reluctant to condemn any player who sought a chemical edge, never felt tempted to go down that road.

"It's unfortunate because our whole era will be looked upon as not being a clean era," Victorino said. "But I don't know how much these banned substances take your game to the next level. It still takes a special person and a special athlete to play this game. I still look at the guys who openly admitted it or are assumed to have taken banned substances as great athletes. They made a choice to do that, and they have to live with it. And because of that, there will always be a cloud over our era. I just never felt any need to do it. How much faster could they make me? How much more power could they give me? I can perform well enough without taking those substances."

He instead sought an edge in the gym.

In the early years of his career, Victorino's off-season fitness program consisted mostly of running and lifting weights. By the end of the 2007 season, he added exercises to help him gain and sustain strength during the season.

He enlisted the help of renowned trainer Keith Kleven, who had worked with athletes including golfer Tiger Woods and pitcher Greg Maddux. At first, Kleven feared Victorino would not respond to the new methods of getting his body in shape.

"When we first started, I questioned whether he could really hang in there and whether he was really dedicated," Kleven said. "He had to understand why we were doing some things different than he had before. We were getting into new techniques, things involving fast-twitch activity with the muscles and joints. He had to understand how important posture is, the mechanics of the body, specific movement patterns. As time went on, I could see everything starting to get better and better. He never rejected anything. Once he got going, he went until there was nothing left in the tank. He doesn't do anything halfway."

The techniques opened up a whole new world to Victorino. He went to Kleven's institute three times a week in the off-season for a 90-minute program consisting of 15 to 20 high-intensity exercises. He ran on an underwater treadmill, did a series of resistance training drills, and spent time in a Pilates studio, all the while working on improving the mechanics of his joints.

"It was a lot of high-repetition, low-weight training and a lot of emphasis on functional movements," Victorino said. "It helped me gain strength and keep it over a long period of time, instead of just getting it in short bursts."

The result of the program was a more nimble, lithe, and strong body. He added muscle to his 5'9", 175-pound frame, eventually bulking up to 190 pounds, which gave him a slightly stockier appearance. But on the baseball field, he remained as fast as ever. His workouts helped him add power and made him less prone to the type of injury he suffered during the 2007 season.

Kleven took precautions to avoid giving Victorino any substances that might land him in trouble with Major League Baseball. He stuck primarily to two dietary supplements—fish oil and a high-powered supplement called Nutriex Sport—that, among other things, helped protect connective tissue.

"These are ones that have been scientifically researched," Kleven said. "I wouldn't let him do anything other than these, because I didn't want to run into a problem of not knowing if it was cleared or not."

As the dog days of summer 2007 were coming to an end, the heat seemed to be getting to some of the Phillies. After surrendering two home runs in the ninth inning of a loss to the Padres, closer Brett Myers got into a fiery confrontation in the clubhouse with a newspaper reporter. Victorino was one of several players to get between the two men before they came to blows. The loss dropped the Phillies four games behind San Diego in the wild-card race.

The Phillies bounced back, however, to sweep the Mets in a four-game set in Philadelphia at the end of August, bringing them back to within two games of the division leaders. The rivalry between the two teams heated up a bit more during that series when the Mets accused the Phillies of stealing signs using cameras in center field.

The drama was intensifying, but Victorino could still play only a minor role. His calf continued to bother him, limiting his playing time.

The Mets reeled off eight wins in nine games to start the final full month of the season, and on September 12, the Phillies trailed New York by seven games with just 17 still to play. Barring a complete collapse, New York was going to make Rollins eat his words.

In the year of the 10,000th loss, people versed in baseball history had even more reason to view the Phillies' chances with extreme pessimism. This was a franchise that did not have a history of good fortune, the same organization that squandered a 6½-game lead in the waning days of the 1964 season, back when a National League pennant meant an automatic trip to the World Series. That collapse still haunted the city, and every player in a Phillies uniform had heard all about it.

But again, that was history.

Another sweep of the Mets, this time in a three-game series in mid-September at Shea Stadium, brought the Phillies within 3½ games of first place. But with only 13 games left to go, the Mets remained in control of their own fate while the Phillies still had ample work to do.

"We weren't worried about what they were doing," Victorino said. "We were worried about what we needed to do. We couldn't control what they did. We swept the Mets and kept crawling closer and closer. It wasn't something you think could happen. And when there was some kind of unbelievable finish, it usually happened against the Phillies, not to someone else. But everything just started falling into place for us."

The Phillies kept winning, and the Mets kept losing.

In the second-to-last series of the season against the Braves, who were complicating matters by also lurking in the playoff picture, Victorino hit a crucial home run to propel the Phillies to victory in one game, and he laid down a key bunt to help win another as the Braves dropped out of contention.

Entering the final weekend of the season, the Phillies and Mets had identical 87–72 records. The Phillies closed with a three-game series at home against the Washington Nationals. The Mets squared off at home against the Florida Marlins. As New York and Philadelphia duked it out for first, Washington and Florida battled to avoid the cellar in the NL East.

Several scenarios were in play. By the end of the weekend, the season could be over for either the Mets or Phillies. Or both might qualify for the playoffs, one as division champs and the other as the wild-card winner. Or, quite possibly, a 163rd game could be necessary if both teams wound up still tied in the standings.

A tiebreaking game between the Mets and the Phillies seemed a distinct possibility after both teams split the first two games of their final series and entered the last game of the season in a dead heat.

On that final Sunday, the early advantage swung to the Phillies when Mets starting pitcher Tom Glavine was roughed up for seven runs in the first inning against the Marlins. The scoreboard watchers 90 miles to the south in Philadelphia kept tabs as Florida maintained that big lead throughout the game, eventually prevailing 8–1.

Meanwhile, in Philadelphia, thanks to the combined efforts of 27-year-old slugger Ryan Howard, 44-year-old pitcher Jamie Moyer, and a boisterous home crowd that ensured a strong home-field edge, the Phillies clinched the division with a 6–1 win over the Nationals.

The Phillies had capped a historic comeback to win the NL East, ending a 14-year playoff drought in the process. It hardly mattered that the New York Giants beat the Philadelphia Eagles later that day at the Meadowlands. Baseball was king on this early fall afternoon. And though no one could have guessed that the Phillies would win the division title in the way that they did, they had won it nonetheless.

The respective records of the NL East rivals in the final 17 games of the season told the story: the Phillies won 13 and lost four. The Mets won five and lost 12.

Victorino, who started two games in the final regular season series and made a pinch-hitting appearance in the other, had willed himself onto the field for the miraculous stretch run. Seeing limited action because of his calf injury, he went only 7-for-34 in September. After his team clinched the division, he enjoyed every moment of the celebration. As the home fans went wild, he grabbed a fire hose from the field and treated the fans to a victory shower on a balmy 75-degree Sunday.

"I remember grabbing the hose and thinking, *Okay, it's time to have some fun*," he said. "Everyone was having such a blast. We were on such a high, and it was great to share it with the fans."

THE PHILLIES WERE PLAYING GOOD BASEBALL going into the October postseason, but they had the misfortune of running into a team that had simply refused to lose in the last month of the season.

Coming into the National League Division Series, the Colorado Rockies had won 14 of 15 games, including a one-game playoff against the Padres to break a tie for the wild-card.

As a division winner, the Phillies had home-field advantage in the best-of-five game series that opened at Citizens Bank Park on October 3, 2007.

Game 1 was a battle of aces, with 15-game winner Cole Hamels of the Phillies facing 17-game winner Jeff Francis of the Rockies. Colorado jumped out to a three-run lead in the second inning and never looked back, winning the game 4–2 to take home-field advantage away from the Phillies in the short series.

The Phillies dug an even deeper hole for themselves in Game 2 the next afternoon, losing 10–5.

After a day off for travel, the series moved to Colorado. For the Phillies, it was either win or go home for the off-season.

Philadelphia barely put up a fight in Game 3, managing only three hits and one run, which came on a solo homer by Victorino in the top of the seventh inning off Ubaldo Jimenez.

Just like that, the Phillies were out of the playoffs.

"We were all so gung-ho going into that series, and it came to such an abrupt end," Victorino said. "It hits you hard, because we had to do so much to get there. But it was a matter of running into the Rockies at a time that they were playing really well."

The Rockies continued rolling through the National League Championship Series before losing to the Red Sox in the World Series.

Despite its unhappy ending, the season had a lot of positive moments. The amazing comeback to catch the Mets topped the list.

Led by Jimmy Rollins, who won the 2007 National League MVP award, the team's young core showed it could win when it mattered most during the regular season. It was not a stretch to think that success in the playoffs would soon follow.

Rollins chose to focus on how quickly the team matured in the final month of the 2007 regular season and the playoffs. "The Mets were the first team to knock off the Braves after they won the division for so many years," he said. "And then we knocked off New York. When we won the division, it felt like the playoffs, because we hadn't won a division in so long. Everything else was gravy to us after that. But with that being said, we understood after the Rockies knocked us out that winning a division doesn't mean anything."

The team grew and so did its individual components, including Victorino, who responded to Davey Lopes' challenge to become a terror on the base paths. He stole 37 bases in 41 attempts. The nagging injury he suffered in July likely prevented him from swiping 50 or more.

"Trusting in [Lopes] and being aggressive allowed me to do what I did that season," Victorino said. "It was just a matter of going out there and doing what I was capable of doing."

His other goal, to play in as many of the Phillies' 162 games as possible, had not been achieved. Due to his calf injury, he appeared in only 131 games, 22 fewer than the season before.

Heading into the off-season, there was still a lot he and the Phillies wanted to accomplish.

9

UNFINISHED BUSINESS

CENTER FIELD IN PHILADELPHIA DOES NOT HAVE THE SAME mystique as, say, left field at Boston's Fenway Park, where the legendary Ted Williams ceded the job of patrolling the Green Monster to Carl Yastrzemski, who eventually gave way to Jim Rice. Together, the trio represented about 50 years of Red Sox baseball.

Yet from Shibe Park/Connie Mack Stadium to Veterans Stadium to Citizens Bank Park, the Phillies who have patrolled center field have created strong legacies of their own. Hall of Famer Richie Ashburn, who went on to broadcast Phillies games for decades; slick-fielding Garry Maddox, who jumped for joy after catching the last out of the 1980 National League Championship Series; and Lenny "Nails" Dykstra, whose nickname said everything, all won the hearts of many Philadelphia fans.

Since joining the Phillies as a September call-up in 2005, Victorino had seen action at every outfield spot. But in 2007, nearly all his starts came in right field because Phillies management felt Aaron Rowand was a better fit to play center. It was hard to argue with that. Rowand did after all win a Gold Glove in his second year with the team. Having the equally aggressive Rowand and Victorino on the same field made defense exciting. With each going full bore after balls hit in the gap, the outfield turned into a high-speed ballet of sorts. Neither was afraid to hurl his body into the wall or onto the warning-track dirt to make a play if it meant keeping the opposition from scoring a run.

"I thought [Victorino] was the best right fielder in the National League with his throwing and his speed," Phillies manager Charlie Manuel said. "He meant a lot to our pitching staff. He could throw guys out and catch up with balls."

Indeed, Victorino played a capable right field in 2007, picking up 10 assists in only 114 games. When Rowand signed as a free agent with the San Francisco Giants after the 2007 season, Victorino inherited the center-field position. As the de facto captain of the outfield, his level of responsibility was about to skyrocket.

"When you play center, you're in charge of the right fielder and left fielder and also of any infielder who might start coming out," explained Curtis Granderson, who by 2008 had established himself as one of the best defensive center fielders in the game. "The center fielder has his eyes on a lot of different things and has the best angle on the whole field to see where balls are being pitched. He has to stay focused on all 180 to 200 pitches in a ballgame because he sees them all, and that affects how a defense plays. When a ball's hit out there, the depth and the angles and the reads and the sun and the lights all come into play. These are things that a lot of fans don't see or appreciate. In Philadelphia, you have a crazy little wall out there in left-center field and a lower wall when you get to center field, so it's a must to be able to maneuver your body and still be athletic enough to make a catch."

Victorino looked forward to starting in center field, the position he had played most of his minor league career and one he considered "the centerpiece of the game."

During spring training, Maddox, an eight-time Gold Glove winner who was nicknamed "the Secretary of Defense," offered Victorino some advice.

"When the Phillies made the decision that Shane was going to be given the opportunity in center, the first thing I talked to him about was making sure he understood the importance of taking charge in the outfield, even though he didn't have as much experience as the other outfielders," Maddox said. "I told Jimmy Rollins that it was important that he support Shane, because that would make it easier for the other guys to follow Shane.

"Another thing I talked to him about was leaving his feet. In my career, I very rarely left my feet. I can't remember seeing Willie Mays ever leave his feet either. I've never seen anyone cover more ground by doing that. When you look at sprinters, they don't leave their feet to dive for the tape. They run through it. It's the same thing when you're playing center field.

I think just running that extra half step will get you to the ball a lot easier and more under control."

It was a lesson Victorino took to heart. Most of his best catches in the coming years ended with him on the dead run, not on the ground.

Victorino eagerly consumed everything Maddox had to say that spring training, but he also had some good-natured fun with the former Phillie.

"We were standing in the outfield and I was talking to him about playing the position and asking him some questions when a fly ball came out to us," Maddox recalled. "I reached out to catch it, but the ball went over my head. He started pointing and laughing. By the time he finished telling everybody what happened, he had the whole team laughing, too."

OTHER THAN LOSING ROWAND, the Phillies dealt with only minimal changes between the 2007 and 2008 seasons. One of the more significant moves from a stability standpoint was ownership's decision to give manager Charlie Manuel a two-year contract extension. The biggest on-the-field addition during the winter was closer Brad Lidge, who came over from Houston along with utility infielder Eric Bruntlett in exchange for outfielder Michael Bourn and reliever Geoff Geary. The addition of Lidge allowed Brett Myers to return to the starting rotation after a one-year stint as closer.

The off-season also featured some more sniping between Philadelphia and New York. In response to a claim by Mets outfielder Carlos Beltran that his team would win the National League East in 2008, Jimmy Rollins quickly reiterated his opinion from the year before that the Phillies were again the team to beat in the division.

The Braves, in the midst of an uncharacteristic three-year playoff drought, also hoped to compete in 2008. On paper, Atlanta appeared poised to score runs with Chipper Jones, Mark Teixeira, and Brian McCann leading the way. It would be up to John Smoltz, Tom Glavine, Tim Hudson, and the rest of the pitching staff to try to keep opposing offenses at bay.

As baseball writers and pundits weighed in with preseason predictions, most concluded the NL East was a race between the Mets and Braves. The defending division champs were getting little respect, perhaps because many believed their title came courtesy of an enormous collapse by the Mets rather than through their own exceptional play. The fact that the Phillies had been swept by the Rockies in the NLDS did not boost confidence in the team going into 2008.

Few questioned the talent of a lineup that featured the last two league MVPs, Ryan Howard and Rollins, and All-Star second baseman Chase Utley, who was coming off an injury-shortened 22-home run, 103-RBI season.

The knock on the Phillies was that their pitching staff, anchored by Cole Hamels, Jamie Moyer, and Brett Myers, lacked the depth necessary to compete over a 162-game season. The 24-year-old Hamels was coming off a 15-win season, and the ageless Moyer had chipped in with 14 wins the season before. But even if Myers regained his form as a starter, the Phillies still had big question marks in the fourth and fifth spots in the rotation. Kyle Kendrick, who won 10 games in 2007 and placed fifth in the National League Rookie of the Year voting, likely needed a strong sophomore season for the Phillies to keep pace. And then there was Adam Eaton, the team's fifth starter whose 10–10 record in 2007 looked terrific compared to the 6.29 ERA that came along with it.

As had been the case for the past several seasons, the offense was expected to carry the team. In 2007, the Phillies led the National League with 892 runs scored, an average of 5½ per game.

Two full seasons into his big-league career, Victorino had won over many skeptics. He had come a long way in a short time and had proven wrong the baseball people who pegged him as a borderline major leaguer.

"The Phillies took off when he solidified their outfield," said former Phillie John Kruk. "Once you get an established lineup, especially with guys who can switch hit like he can, you have something special. The knock on the Phillies [in the early to mid-2000s] was that there was no emotion. They were boring, they were dead. All of a sudden Shane came in and gave them an attitude."

But some in the Philadelphia media, at least implicitly, felt Victorino might have a hard time replacing Rowand.

Following an Opening Day 11–6 loss to the Nationals, Sam Donnellon of the *Philadelphia Daily News* wrote, "Along with the perennial concern about pitching, this winter's great Phillies anxiety was that something intangible was lost with the free-agent departure of Aaron Rowand. A hard-nosed, media-savvy face who met the throng that filed into the clubhouse every day, Rowand was a guy who not only added perspective to the day's proceedings but sent messages of his own via thoughtful answers to even the most inane questions."

Maybe the local media would miss Rowand, and maybe the team would, too, but not if Victorino had anything to say about it.

"When I first got to Philadelphia in 2005, I had pressure filling in for Bobby Abreu," he said. "Then when they traded Abreu, I had to say to myself, 'Okay, I'm not trying to fill anybody's shoes. I'm trying to create my own.' When Rowand left, he was a very popular player. So I had the same situation again. I just wanted to play the game the way I knew how. I knew I wasn't going to go out there and hit 30 home runs and drive in 100 runs. But maybe I could be a guy who can steal 40 bases and play great defense."

Victorino had passed most tests since joining the Phillies, but he still had some things to prove.

So did some of his teammates, most notably the newly acquired Lidge, who was looking for redemption in 2008. Lidge, a first-round pick by Houston in 1998, had once been a dominant closer for the Astros. In 2004, he broke Goose Gossage's National League record for strikeouts by a relief pitcher, fanning 157 batters in just 94⅔ innings. The following season Lidge set a career high in saves with 42 but struggled during the Astros' playoff run that ended with a World Series sweep by the White Sox. He eventually lost his closer's job at the start of the 2007 season, prompting his trade to the Phillies.

A resurgent 2008 would allow Lidge to live up to his nickname, "Lights Out," and at the same time keep the lights on for his career. Hanging in the balance was the ability of his new team to win crucial close games that could determine whether it made the playoffs or not. Lidge's quest for a professional rebirth was delayed when he hurt his knee in spring training and opened the season on the disabled list. But on April 7, Lidge pitched the ninth inning of a game against the Cincinnati Reds, surrendering a run on two walks, to earn his first save of the year. It was the start of a very special season for him.

Even the most talented teams are sometimes unable to overcome a rash of injured players. A week into the season Rollins went down for a month with an ankle injury that sent him to the disabled list for the first time since he broke into the majors in 2000. A few days after Rollins got hurt, Victorino left a game against the Cubs with a right calf strain. It was the same type of strain that kept him out of action for a large portion of the second half of the 2007 season. Not taking any chances, the Phillies put Victorino on the disabled list as well.

Despite injuries to the catalysts at the top of the lineup, the Phillies got off to a good start in 2008, finishing the opening month of the season with a 15–13 record. It was the team's first winning April since 2003.

Another player with a lot to prove in 2008 helped keep the team afloat while Rollins and Victorino were out. Left fielder Pat Burrell, in his ninth season with the Phillies, had the best April of his career. Playing in the final season of a six-year, $50 million contract, "Pat the Bat" hit .326 with eight home runs and 25 RBIs in the opening month.

Upon their return, Rollins and Victorino both played well. Victorino hit .322 and stole 11 bases in May, while Rollins hit .298 with six steals that month.

Victorino showed no ill effects of his injury in a game on June 7 against the Braves when he hustled to score from first base on an Utley hit. His mad dash home caused Charlie Manuel to joke that he would be tempted to put money on Victorino in a foot race against Big Brown, the horse favored to win the Belmont Stakes that weekend.

It was the kind of play his teammates liked to see.

"It's fun watching him hit the ball in the gap or down the line and watching his little legs scoot," Ryan Howard quipped.

Victorino atoned for a base-running mistake in a game at Atlanta by driving in the game's go-ahead run in the top of the 10th inning and then gunning down a runner at the plate in the bottom half of the inning to preserve a 4–3 win as well as Lidge's streak of 16 consecutive saves. In the final game of the Braves series, Victorino's three-hit performance helped the team cap a sweep on the road.

As the season progressed, the Phillies' starting pitching remained a concern, with Cole Hamels a bright spot in an inconsistent rotation.

Hamels' complete-game shutout of the Braves on May 15 lifted his record to 5–3 and lowered his ERA to 2.89. That game featured Victorino's first home run of the season and pulled the Phillies within a game of the first-place Florida Marlins, a team that got scant mention when the pundits were discussing preseason favorites to win the division.

The Phillies needed strong performances from Hamels in light of Brett Myers' struggles to regain his form as a starter. A loss to the Angels on June 21 dropped his record to 3–9. Following another poor start, Myers was demoted to the minor leagues for some tune-up work. At the back end of the rotation, Adam Eaton failed to win a game until his 11th start of the season. He too was sent packing for Lehigh Valley, the Phillies' new Triple A affiliate in Allentown, Pennsylvania.

Hamels was giving the team quality starts almost every five days, but the Phillies likely needed at least one more starter to bear some of the load. It helped that Jamie Moyer, as he had done since joining the Phillies in 2006, continued to put his team in a position to win almost every outing. In 2008, the Phillies went 22–9 in games started by the 45-year-old Moyer, who ended the season with 16 wins.

Moyer reflected on his late-career success at the start of the 2010 season. "To a certain extent, we're all still learning this game," he said. "If anybody ever says they have it mastered, they're lying. You see things happen, see situations come up, and you're always learning about yourself. When you stop learning or you become stagnant as a player, you start to go backward or the game ends up passing you by."

Lidge was making sure leads were not squandered in the late innings. At the All-Star break, he had 20 saves to go along with a 1.13 ERA. Lidge and Utley were selected to represent the Phillies in the All-Star Game at Yankee Stadium where Lidge turned out to be the losing pitcher in the 15-inning marathon. It was his only loss of the year and, though it might not have seemed important at the time to the Phillies, it guaranteed the American League representative home-field advantage in the World Series.

Victorino went into the break hitting .279 with 22 stolen bases. But he saved his best performance of the season for the final series of the first half. Against the Diamondbacks, he went 3-for-6 with a game-tying triple in the eighth inning of a contest the Phillies won in 12 innings. The next day, in a losing effort, he went deep twice against likely future Hall of Famer Randy Johnson.

Victorino's family was enjoying his accomplishments from afar.

From the time Shane was still in the minors, Mike Victorino Jr. had followed his younger brother's career very closely. Whenever possible, he sat in front of a computer and monitored his brother's games pitch by pitch. With the six-hour time difference between Philadelphia and Maui, that usually happened during breaks at work on the docks at Kahului Harbor. His mother, Joycelyn, who had a job up the road at the local headquarters of the International Longshore and Warehouse Union, soon got hooked on the practice, too.

"I'm his biggest fan," Mike Victorino Jr. said. "If Shane has a bad game, it's frustrating for me. I take it to heart, because I'm so proud of him. When he has a bad day, it's like the whole morale of the family goes down."

Mike Victorino Sr. could also rattle off his son's statistics, as well as those of the rest of the Phillies. His head for numbers—in his case, budget numbers—came in handy in 2008 when he successfully waged a campaign for a second term on the nine-member Maui County Council, the legislative and policymaking body for the islands of Maui, Kaho'olawe, Lanai, and Molokai. He would win a fourth term to the council in 2012.

Shane missed his family, but it helped that Philadelphia reminded him a lot of home.

"A lot of people don't realize it, but there are so many similarities between Hawaii and Philadelphia," he said. "Both are union and blue collar and have hardworking people. In Philadelphia, you have the old-school Italian families who have lived there for generations. In Hawaiian culture, everything's about the family."

THE PHILLIES LED THE METS BY HALF A GAME and the Marlins by a game and a half at the midsummer break, but Manuel sensed his team needed an addition to its family to repeat as division champs.

"I think we need a strong pitcher, a good starting pitcher," he told reporters shortly before the break. "I'm talking about a big pitcher. I'm not talking about a guy we've already got [in the system]. I think we need a force, somebody to go with Hamels. If that can be [Brett] Myers, that's fine. But we need a blue-chip pitcher, a proven big winner."

Several names emerged as possible candidates, and several Phillies were dangled as bait. Was Victorino, who by this time had clearly caught the eyes of other teams, one of them? General manager Pat Gillick would not say, but rumors that Shane could be traded for a pitcher were enough to create a minor panic for his fiancée, who lived in Las Vegas but spent a good part of the summer in Philadelphia.

"It would be a huge shock if we got traded," the future Melissa Victorino said. "There are fears of it every year. But that year it was really scary. I felt like he was going to have to pack his bags at any moment."

Melissa had formed strong bonds with the Phillies' wives, all of whom could relate to the unique challenges facing women whose spouses play professional sports. Some of the best tips she got were from Karen Moyer, who, like her husband, had been involved in the game for more than two decades.

"She was a really good person to go to for advice," Melissa said. "She was very honest and didn't sugarcoat anything. I think it's similar to veteran players taking younger players aside to tell them something. With the wives of players, it's the same way."

The rumors involving Victorino did not turn into reality. But the Phillies did make a trade, dealing three minor leaguers for Joe Blanton, a 27-year-old right-hander who had been having a dismal season with the Oakland Athletics. Blanton had posted a 5–12 record and a 4.96 ERA in 20 starts for the A's. In the previous three seasons, he had averaged 14 wins for the team.

The Phillies did not have the minor league prospects or the big bucks lying around to land the best available pitcher, Cleveland's CC Sabathia, who ended up going to Milwaukee before the All-Star break. Manny Ramirez, the top offensive player on the block, was dealt by the Red Sox at the trade deadline to the Dodgers. The Phillies had to settle for Blanton, a burly Kentuckian who they hoped would be enough to bolster their playoff chances.

Bill Conlin of the *Philadelphia Daily News* felt the price for Sabathia would have been too high for the Phillies. "The sellers giving up future

Hall of Famers on career down-ticks want major league–ready prospects who have survived the high-minors crucible," he wrote. "They want them gifted and they want to have those golden years before arbitration and free agency. That left the Phillies with one realistic, tradable option from the varsity—Shane Victorino. Fans, you didn't want to see a Phillies outfield next month without him in it."

On the night of the trade, Blanton flew to Florida to join his new team, which had beaten the Marlins 4–2 to remain in first place. The game featured many of the most positive things about the Phillies' season so far: Moyer notched his ninth win, Howard hit his MLB-leading 29th home run, and Lidge got his 21st save. Even Manuel showed some fire, getting ejected in the fifth inning for arguing that Victorino should have been awarded first base after being hit by a pitch.

The reception Blanton got from his new teammates in a Miami-area hotel told him a lot about the team. "I had been with the A's my whole career and didn't know anybody on the Phillies," he said. "I happened to be in the hotel lobby when the team bus got back to the hotel. Almost everybody came up and shook my hand and told me they were glad I was on board. I think that really summed up the quality of individuals on that team."

Those quality individuals needed to play quality baseball if they hoped to fend off the surging Mets.

New York beat the visiting Phillies 6–3 on July 23 to pull into a dead heat with first-place Philadelphia. The game helped inflame the simmering rivalry between the two teams. As Mets shortstop Jose Reyes rounded first base after hitting a tie-breaking three-run home run in the bottom of the sixth inning, he thrust his right arm in the air and extended his index finger, an act the Phillies considered excessive celebration.

"He's a very talented player and he can be one of the best players in baseball," Manuel said after the game. "But at the same time, he's got some growing up to do, and he's got some learning to do."

Later that season, Victorino would help the Phillies get a measure of revenge.

The day after Reyes' home run, the Phillies lost again to the Mets to drop out of first place. Since sweeping the Braves in early June, the Phillies were just 15–23. Manuel felt his team lacked leadership, and in late July, he called a clubhouse meeting to explain what he expected of them.

Victorino said the sit-down was good for both the manager and the team.

"I guess it seems like the right time in regard to what's going on," he told reporters after the meeting. "It's time for us to go. We've been in first place, and we're in second place now. It is time for us collectively to get going. It was really just Charlie sitting us down and giving us a pep talk."

The tactic worked. The Phillies finished July on a five-game winning streak, nudging themselves back into first place by a game.

An offhand comment in mid-August by Rollins temporarily overshadowed the neck-and-neck race between the Phillies and the Mets. Appearing on *The Best Damn Sports Show Period*, a nationally televised sports and comedy show, Rollins was asked whether it was difficult playing in a city known for its demanding fans.

"There are times," Rollins said. "I might catch some flak for saying this, but, you know, they're front-runners. When you're doing good, they're on your side. When you're doing bad, they're completely against you."

Over the following days, Rollins tried to clarify his provocative statement, which came in the midst of a four-game sweep by the Dodgers in Los Angeles, but some in the local media and blogosphere were not buying it. They pointed out that the Phillies had not fielded enough winning teams in recent years to ever give fans a chance of truly being front-runners. The storm surrounding Rollins passed rather quickly, but it certainly helped ratchet up pressure on the team to win.

In the clubhouse, Victorino tried to lighten the mood by leading cheers for a youth team from Waipahu, Hawaii, that was making a deep run in the Little League World Series.

"He's loud, but he helps keep things loose around here," Ryan Howard said. "I have to ask him all the time to use his inside voice."

Victorino, a neat freak who started many days by vacuuming his in-season apartment or off-season house, enjoyed commenting on the unkept state of Howard's locker as much as he did pranking teammates by "pantsing" them in the clubhouse or smashing a pie in the face of a guy doing a television interview.

In 2008, Waipahu went on to become the second team from Oahu in the past four years to win the annual tournament in Williamsport,

Pennsylvania. "I wanted them to come down to Philadelphia and watch a game, but they were having a luau that night," Victorino said. A later version of the team made it back to the tournament in 2010. When asked who their favorite player was, seven of the 13 players on the 2010 team said Victorino.

Victorino could not get enough of the young ballplayers from his home state, and if they caught the Phillies playing on TV while up the road in Williamsport, they would have seen Victorino make a play that bolstered his reputation as someone who did the little things to help his team win.

It happened in a game on August 19 against the Nationals. With Greg Dobbs at the plate, Victorino went from first to third base on an errant pickoff attempt by Washington catcher Jesus Flores. Victorino was sent back to first base, however, after it was ruled that the home-plate umpire interfered with Flores' throw to first base. Dobbs proceeded to hit a single to short left-center field and Victorino again legged his way to third base.

It was the kind of hustle Manuel had come to expect from the Flyin' Hawaiian.

"Without a doubt, those little things in the game are what count," Manuel said. "I don't take those things for granted, because I know how important they are. All those little intangibles are what he brings to the club."

The play also impressed Jesse Spector of the *New York Daily News*, a publication not usually in the business of praising Philadelphia players.

"When Chris Coste hit a sacrifice fly, Victorino scored the tying run," Spector wrote. "So Taguchi then grounded out to end the inning, highlighting the importance of a base-running play that could probably only have been made by Victorino, Jose Reyes, or [Olympic sprinter] Usain Bolt."

Also in late August, Manuel experimented with his lineup by putting the hot-hitting Victorino in the fifth spot in the order, right behind Howard. The Phillies won a few games in a row after the shake-up, including an 8–7 extra-inning victory against the Mets in which they battled back from a 7–0 deficit. That win helped key a 7–2 stretch at home during which Victorino hit .333 with two doubles, two triples, nine runs, and at least one hustle play that did not show up in any box score.

August's pitching star was none other than Brett Myers, who after getting called back from the minors delivered several solid starts, going 4–1 with a 1.65 ERA. He felt so good being back that he had a hard time leaving an early August game when Manuel came out to pull him. Myers' unwillingness to leave the mound led to a heated exchange with Manuel in the dugout.

Entering September, the Phillies trailed the Mets by a game. The 2008 season would again be a race to the finish in the NL East, with the team that came up short in the division in a good position to win a wild-card berth.

The Phillies headed into a key September series in New York with some advice from a man who had been in a few pennant races before. Former Phillies great Mike Schmidt began his e-mail to the team by imparting some generic words of wisdom and then got to the crux of the matter.

"The Mets know you're better than they are," Schmidt said in his note, a copy of which was posted on the clubhouse door. "They remember last year."

Myers went out and backed up Schmidt's bluster by throwing eight shutout innings in a 3–0 Phillies win. The Phillies took two out of three in that series but then lost two out of three at home to Florida.

The Mets won six out of eight at the start of September to open up a three-game lead. But the Phillies surged back with a seven-game winning streak, which included sweeps of the Brewers and Braves, to tighten things up again entering the last 10 days of the season.

The red-hot Phillies traveled to Florida for a critical series against the Marlins, who had won eight games in a row to pull within 5½ games of first place. The Phillies had won only six of 15 games against Florida coming into the three-game set at Dolphin Stadium. In the series opener, the Marlins outslugged the Phillies 14–8, roughing up Brett Myers for 10 runs in four-plus innings. In Atlanta, meanwhile, the Mets beat the Braves to go up by half a game in the NL East.

Two days later, the race had a much different complexion. Behind solid outings from Blanton and Moyer, the Phillies took the final two games of the Marlins series. Lidge chalked up his 39th and 40th saves in the wins. Atlanta took two out of three from the Mets to put the Phillies in control with six games remaining in the season.

The Phillies lost the next two against the Braves, including a 10–4 drubbing in the final game of the series. In the eighth inning of the finale, both benches cleared after Atlanta pitcher Julian Tavarez bolted toward third base to chase Victorino back to the bag. The unusual sight of a pitcher charging a base runner led to words between Tavarez and Victorino and to a parade of players coming onto the field to cool things down.

The Braves, a preseason favorite to compete for the division, may have been venting frustration at being 18 games out of first place.

The Phillies brushed off the incident and tried to get back to business, an important task considering the Mets had clawed back to within a game of first place entering the final weekend of play.

In a repeat of the matchups that closed the 2007 season, the Phillies played host to the wretched Nationals, while the Mets were at home against the Marlins. Milwaukee, which was tied with New York for the wild-card lead, had a home series against the Cubs.

The Phillies' 8–4 win against the Nationals in the series opener, coupled with a Mets loss to Florida, assured Philadelphia at least a tie for the NL East title.

Moyer took the mound the next day for a possible division-clinching game. He went six strong innings and the Phillies took a 4–2 lead into the top of the ninth. The Nationals scored a run against Lidge to make it 4–3. With only one out, the dangerous Ryan Zimmerman came to the plate with the bases loaded. Zimmerman lifted a ball toward center field that would have scored two runs if not for an amazing snare by Jimmy Rollins. The shortstop flipped the ball to Utley, who touched second and threw to first for a game-ending double play.

With that defensive gem, the Fightin' Phils had defended their division title and did not even have to wait until the last day of the season to do so.

The wild-card race, however, did come down to the 162nd game of the season. The Brewers beat the Cubs and the Mets lost to the Marlins, setting up a first-round playoff series between the Brewers and Phillies. For the Mets, it was the second straight year of self-induced heartbreak. The season provided a bitter sendoff to Shea Stadium, the team's stomping grounds since 1964.

Victorino saved some of his best performances for September. In a win late that month against Atlanta, a victory that put the Phillies 2½ games in front of the Mets, he extended a hitting streak to 11 games, a stretch during which the team won 10 times and Victorino went 21-for-43 with three home runs.

Victorino, who sat out the last game of the season, hit safely in 20 of the 24 games he suited up for in September, posting a .344 average. For the season, he hit a team-leading .293 with 36 stolen bases.

Several other Phillies also came up big when it mattered most.

Ryan Howard got hits in 21 games, hitting .352 with 11 home runs in September, a stretch that earned him high marks with NL MVP voters, who made him first runner-up to St. Louis' Albert Pujols. Utley also got a hit in all but three games he played in the final month. Moyer went 4–0 in the last weeks of the season to push his final record to 16–7.

And Brad "Lights Out" Lidge earned his nickname by saving eight crucial games in September, raising his season total to 41. Though there had been some close calls, such as game 161 against the Nationals, he did not blow a save all season.

Unlike the year before, Victorino did not douse the jubilant Citizens Bank Park crowd with a fire hose on the season's final Sunday. Instead he retreated to the trainer's room to get care for a right shin injury he suffered in a collision with Rollins during the eighth inning of the division-clinching game. A lot of players would have hit the showers after such an injury, but Victorino stayed in and scored what turned out to be an important insurance run.

He hoped another division title was just the beginning.

"We had a bitter taste in our mouth from getting swept the year before," Victorino said. "It made us hungry. We understood the situation a lot better in 2008. Either you better show up or you go home. That's what it's all about."

THE DAY AFTER THE LAST GAME OF THE REGULAR SEASON, Victorino took time to do something that for an hour or two made sports seem a little less significant. His trip to the pediatric intensive-care unit at Children's Hospital of Philadelphia had not been scheduled in advance by his handlers or the Phillies organization, nor was it intended as a prepackaged photo opportunity where an athlete visits with a sick kid. No, the visit to the hospital was made on the spur of the moment and was aimed at giving extra words of support to a young man from Maui whom he had befriended earlier in the season.

Shortly after his 14th birthday, Julian Rimm underwent surgery in Philadelphia to remove a cancerous bone tumor in his ankle. It was his second trip to Children's Hospital. The first was in June when his family, which has ties to Philly, came to get a second opinion on the cancer diagnosis Julian received in Hawaii. Before the June trip, Julian's mother, Gabi Galler-Rimm, reached out to Victorino's parents through mutual acquaintances in Maui to see if Julian, a sports fanatic, could say hello to Shane while in town. That led to an on-the-field meeting before a game at Citizens Bank Park.

The worst fears of Julian's family were realized when doctors at Children's Hospital confirmed that he in fact had cancer. They returned to Hawaii so Julian could begin nearly three months of chemotherapy treatment. Julian's surgery was scheduled for September back in Philadelphia. Before the procedure, he and his older brother got another chance to meet with Victorino at the ballpark.

When they parted ways that day, Shane gave Julian a hug and encouraged him to stay strong as he battled his disease.

That is where most stories of this kind end.

But Julian suffered complications from his surgery. In the process of having his tumor removed, he lost blood flow to his right foot. He was not only in great pain but risked losing the limb, which had become gangrenous.

When Victorino learned of the situation, he rushed to the hospital on an off-day before the playoffs to see his friend. For more than an hour, he sat with Julian and his family in the intensive-care unit. Victorino told Julian they were both suffering from leg injuries and showed him the gash on his shin that he got near the end of the season.

"Shane came by and really helped the situation," Galler-Rimm said. "It didn't get heavy. We didn't really talk about spirituality. He was just being uplifting. He was really trying to get Jules to focus on positive stuff, trying to get him to take his thoughts away from his pain.

"I'm being very sincere when I say that he had a huge impact on Julian's mental health. It was such hell, such darkness for us at that time, and here was this goofy Maui boy coming to cheer us up. Just being from Maui was our connection. We'll always connect to his sweetness and kindness. The Shane we got to know was a real sensitive, sweet, and kind person. This thing was so frightening to all of us, and Shane was such a great sport, such a great comfort."

ON THE BIG STAGE

WHAT GOT THE PHILLIES TO THE 2008 PLAYOFFS? THE MOST obvious answer was the sluggers (Ryan Howard, Chase Utley, and Pat Burrell hit a combined 114 home runs) and the speedsters (Jimmy Rollins and Shane Victorino stole a combined 83 bases), but just as important was the solid performance of an underrated pitching staff, which allowed the third-lowest number of runs in the National League.

That was a hopeful sign, because any team looking to advance in the playoffs needs good pitching.

The team that opposed the Phillies in the 2008 National League Division Series had perhaps the best arm in the majors at the top of its rotation. Since coming to Milwaukee from Cleveland in a July trade, 6'7", 290-pound hurler CC Sabathia had been dominant, winning 11 games against two losses with a 1.65 ERA. The Phillies would be hard-pressed to win the best-of-five series without taking at least one game started by Sabathia, whom the Phillies had not encountered that season. In a four-game home sweep of the Brewers the previous month, the Phillies had avoided facing the Brewers' ace.

"We knew we matched up well against Milwaukee," Victorino said. "And seeing them that close to playoff time gave us a good idea of who was swinging the bat well for them and who was throwing well."

With Sabathia looming as the Game 2 starter, it became imperative for the Phillies to jump out to a series lead at home in the opener. Milwaukee's Game 1 starter, Yovani Gallardo, was a wild-card pitcher on a wild-card team. He had missed most of 2008 with ligament damage in his right knee and had made only one appearance since May 1. Now the 22-year-old was being thrust into the limelight of playoff baseball.

Gallardo was up to the task, but so was Cole Hamels, whose strong Game 1 outing led to a 3–1 Phillies victory. A two-run second-inning double by Utley and a bases-loaded walk for Victorino held up as Hamels twirled eight shutout innings. A sold-out crowd of over 45,000 at Citizens Bank Park watched in the rain as Lidge came in to save the Phillies' first playoff win since 1993.

Brett Myers, a 10-game winner during an up-and-down 2008 season, took the mound in Game 2 against Sabathia, who was pitching on three days' rest for the fourth consecutive start.

The Brewers got out to a 1–0 lead in the first inning on a bases-loaded walk to J.J. Hardy, but Myers avoided further damage by getting Corey Hart to hit into an inning-ending double play. In the bottom of the first, Victorino, hitting second, stroked a one-out double, his first hit of the series. He also stole third base but was stranded there as Utley and Howard struck out.

Trailing by a run early, all the Phillies could have asked from Myers was to do what he could on the mound to keep them in the game. And he delivered with his arm as well as his bat.

With two outs in the bottom of the second inning of a 1–1 game, Myers stubbornly worked Sabathia for a nine-pitch walk that put runners on first and third for Rollins. Sabathia then walked him to load the bases, bringing Victorino to the plate.

Sabathia threw his sixth consecutive ball before finding the strike zone and then getting ahead of Victorino 1-2. Between the third and fourth pitches of the at-bat, Victorino, batting right-handed against the lefty Sabathia, assessed the situation.

"I was definitely looking for something in," he said. "I felt like he was going to come in with another fastball. The guy had just buried me with two fastballs, and I was late on them. I figured he'd think, *Why don't I just bury him again?* But he threw a slider and he left it up."

Victorino drove the ball deep down the left-field line. It did not stop carrying until it flew into the stands for a grand slam that gave the Phillies a 5–1 lead. Victorino took off around the bases, fist in the air. As he crossed home plate, he pointed at his father, Mike, who had come from Hawaii for the playoffs. The first grand slam of Victorino's career and in Phillies postseason history triggered a mass celebration at Citizens Bank Park that featured thousands of fans waving white rally towels given out before the game.

The next few hours were something for Victorino to savor. He had paid his dues with three organizations in the hopes of one day making it to this point. A pivotal playoff grand slam against one of the best pitchers in the game helped validate all his hard work.

"It gave me the confidence to say, 'Hey, I came up big in one situation. Why can't I keep doing it?'" he said. "I think that feeling carried over for the rest of the playoffs. It helped me build character."

Thanks to the grand slam, the Phillies had a comfortable four-run lead, but just as important, they had shattered Sabathia's air of invincibility. When Victorino faced Sabathia with two outs in the fourth inning, the hulking pitcher showed him the ultimate sign of respect by intentionally walking him with a base open and Chase Utley on deck. Two batters later, Sabathia was pulled from the game.

Victorino's blast gave the Phillies all the runs they needed. Myers allowed two hits and two runs in seven innings, and Brad Lidge came on in the ninth to lock up a 5–2 win. Lidge's second save of the series made him 43-for-43 in save opportunities during the 2008 season and postseason.

In the wake of Victorino's huge game, which included a grand slam, two doubles, and two stolen bases, Rollins decided to poke fun at Jose Reyes of the Mets, whose flamboyant home run celebrations had become a source of irritation in the Phillies clubhouse.

A day after his teammate's blast off Sabathia, Rollins took a newspaper photo of Victorino rounding the bases and touched it up so that his uniform number was changed from No. 8 to Reyes' No. 7. Rollins also taped a piece of paper with "Reyes" on it to the back of the picture of Victorino's jersey.

"They were teasing me, because they thought I looked like him rounding the bases," Victorino said. "In our clubhouse, we don't like when players do that kind of stuff, so they were giving me a hard time. It was a joke."

Victorino liked to engage in playful banter with opposing players, certainly enjoyed playing the occasional prank on teammates, and always stood out as a guy who played the game with enthusiasm. But how did his often flamboyant demeanor sit with guys who had been around the game for a long time?

"There are some guys who bug me, but he's not one of them," said Dusty Baker, who had spent nearly four decades as a major league player and manager through the 2013 season. "Cocky don't bother me. I heard that about myself when I played. He doesn't clown or showboat in what he does. That's what bugs me, guys who clown on you when they beat you. Victorino brings a lot of life and excitement to baseball. In a nutshell, he's a ballplayer."

The Phillies had a commanding 2–0 series lead with the next two games shifting to Milwaukee's Miller Park, but the Phillies could not finish off a sweep in Game 3. The Brewers scored two quick runs in the first inning off Jamie Moyer, the Phillies' regular season leader in victories, en route to a 4–1 win. The Phillies loaded the bases with nobody out in the top of the ninth inning, but a questionable interference call against Victorino on the base paths quashed a would-be rally.

With the win, the Brewers kept alive hopes of becoming only the eighth team in baseball history to rebound from an 0–2 hole in a best-of-five playoff series. As the Phillies and Brewers continued their battle, the Dodgers, who finished off a sweep of the Cubs later that night, waited to see whom they would face in the National League Championship Series.

The Phillies turned to Joe Blanton, pitching on eight days' rest, in Game 4. Since coming over from Oakland in mid-July, Blanton had shown himself to be a competent fourth starter. He did not lose a game with the Phillies, going 4–0 with nine no-decisions and a 4.20 ERA. Blanton's Game 4 opponent on the mound, Jeff Suppan, finished the 2008 regular season with 10 wins after averaging 14 the previous four seasons. He came into the game having lost his only decision against the Phillies that season.

The Phillies got off to a good start against Suppan, when Jimmy Rollins led off the game with a home run. Pat Burrell, who came into the game 0-for-8 in the series, added to the lead with a three-run home run in the top of third inning. The next batter, Jayson Werth, made it back-to-back homers to put the Phillies up 5–0. By the time Burrell added a second home run later in the game, the Phillies were already well on their way to an NLCS matchup with Los Angeles. Much like Game 2, the Phillies jumped out to an early lead and the starting pitching took care of the rest. Blanton gave up one run in six innings, and relievers Ryan Madson and Lidge finished off the series-clinching victory for the Phillies.

Shane Victorino was born on the island of Maui and later became a star athlete at St. Anthony High School in Wailuku, Hawaii.

Seen here with his mother Joycelyn, father Mike, and brother Mike Jr., Shane was a rambunctious child with an insatiable appetite for sports.

Shane and his grandfather, Chester Nakahashi, shared one of the future star's most cherished relationships.

Drafted by Los Angeles in 1999, Shane bounced between the Dodgers and San Diego Padres organizations before landing in Philadelphia. (Getty Images)

Shane silenced the Los Angeles crowd with his two-run game-tying home run against the Dodgers during the eighth inning of Game 4 of the 2008 NLCS. (AP Images)

Shane and the Phillies celebrate after beating the Tampa Bay Rays in Game 5 of the 2008 World Series to claim the team's first championship since 1980. (AP Images)

The Flyin' Hawaiian hit two homers and drove in 13 runs during the Phillies' 2008 postseason charge. (AP Images)

Shane later commemorated Philadelphia's World Series title with fellow Hawaiian President Barack Obama during a visit to the White House. (AP Images)

Being chosen to represent the United States in the 2009 World Baseball Classic cemented Shane's status as a rising major league star. (Getty Images)

After a brief return to the Dodgers organization, Shane signed a three-year, $39 million contract with the Red Sox in 2012. (AP Images)

Shane acclimated quickly to his new team and city, though his friendship with former teammates such as Ryan Howard remained as strong as ever. (AP Images)

One of the most memorable moments in Red Sox history, Shane's go-ahead grand slam in Game 6 of the 2013 ALCS sent Boston back to the World Series.
(AP Images)

Shane's three-run double in Game 6 of the World Series was all the Red Sox would need, as they went on to win their third championship since 2004. (AP Images)

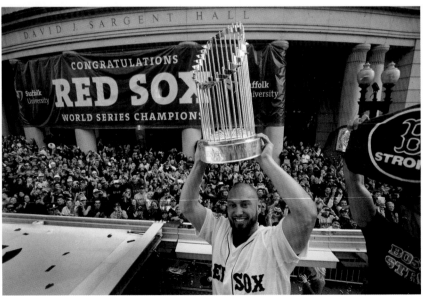

No stranger to victory parades, Shane raised another trophy over his head as the city of Boston celebrated its baseball heroes. (Getty Images)

"I like our chances," Manuel told reporters after the victory. "I think we can hold our own with [the Dodgers]. Actually, I think we can beat anybody in the National League, really."

IT HAD BEEN A WHILE, but Philadelphia and Los Angeles had a history on the diamond.

The 2008 National League Championship Series came three decades after the Dodgers bested the Phillies for the second straight year for the NL pennant, back-to-back defeats the Phillies at least somewhat avenged with an NLCS victory against Los Angeles in 1983.

But that was a long time ago.

Many had expected a Phillies-Cubs matchup in the NLCS, but the Cubs, who had the National League's best record in 2008, floundered in their attempt to break a 100-year championship drought.

Dodgers manager Joe Torre, in his first year at the helm in Los Angeles, felt his team's defeat of Chicago helped build confidence going into the NLCS.

"It was certainly good for our egos because of the fact they had led the league in wins," Torre said. "But I think we were still growing at the time. Everybody was getting to know each other and getting used to their new jobs as regular players."

The team's young core, all appearing in the playoffs for the first time, included 26-year-old right fielder Andre Ethier, 24-year-old first baseman James Loney, and center fielder Matt Kemp, the man whose potential had helped convince the Dodgers that Victorino was expendable four years earlier.

Since August, Kemp, Loney, and Ethier had been overshadowed by a major trade-deadline acquisition. The player whose name graced the marquee in the final months of the season was Manny Ramirez, formerly of the Boston Red Sox, who in 53 regular season games with Los Angeles hit .396 and incredibly averaged an RBI per game. In the NLDS against the Cubs, Ramirez went 5-for-10 with two home runs.

The Dodgers also featured a talented table-setter in shortstop Rafael Furcal, who had missed most of the season with a back injury but was healthy for the playoffs.

Leading L.A.'s pitching staff was crafty veteran Derek Lowe, a 14-game winner during the season with ample playoff experience. In the first years of his career, Victorino struggled most against sinkerballers like Lowe (2-for-24 through 2010) and the Rockies' Aaron Cook (1-for-16).

Arguably the Dodgers' best starter in 2008 had been 24-year-old Chad Billingsley, who won 16 games.

Dodgers pitching coach Rick Honeycutt knew his staff would have to elevate its game against the Phillies' potent lineup.

"The Phillies were almost at a different level," Honeycutt said. "I thought our pitching matched up well against the Cubs, but then you move on to the Phillies who had so many good left-handed hitters, switch hitters, and speed."

The series was not lacking in potential drama: Could Torre, who won four World Series titles as manager of the Yankees, win his fifth with the Dodgers? Could Manny, who left Boston on bad terms, end up facing his former team in the World Series? Or would the Phillies get a shot at their first championship since 1980?

No less compelling a subplot was the one involving Victorino, who had his first opportunity on a big stage to go up against the organization that drafted him out of high school and eventually decided to dangle him out to other teams. That had happened twice, with Victorino going as a Rule 5 Draftee in 2002 to the Padres and then again to the Phillies in 2004. When the Phillies were forced to offer him back to the Dodgers in 2005, Los Angeles declined to accept the offer. The decision by Los Angeles not to welcome him back amounted to a third slap in the face.

"Everybody thinks it must feel great to beat the Dodgers, but I don't hold a grudge against them," Victorino said. "One man's trash is another man's treasure. Not everyone gets to the majors with the team that drafted them. If the Dodgers hadn't picked me in 1999, I might not have had the chance to play pro ball at all. Is there a little more incentive when I play them? Yeah. Does it feel good to beat them? Yeah, it does, because I never got my shot, and that's all I wanted was one shot. Tommy Lasorda tells me all the time that he gives the Dodgers a hard time for letting me go. But if Tommy really loved me that much, I'm sure his word would have been enough to carry the day. He spent hours with us on the back fields watching us hit. Every time I see him, he says, 'I don't know how we let you get away.'"

Lasorda, in his role as special adviser to the Dodgers, watched admiringly as the former Dodgers farmhand tried to help vanquish the organization that cast him aside.

"He worked awfully hard to become the player he became," Lasorda said. "He did the same thing [former Dodgers and Mets All-Star] Mike Piazza did. No one thought either of those guys would make it, but both became very successful through desire and hard work."

Torre was very aware of the vital role Victorino played on the team.

"He's the type of player that really gets your attention," Torre said. "You spend a lot of time on Ryan Howard, Chase Utley, and Jimmy Rollins, but you can never take a guy like Shane Victorino lightly. The same goes for a player like Jayson Werth. These are the players that I have a great deal of respect for, the ones that grind at you and find a way to get the job done. Shane certainly fits that description."

Werth, like Victorino, had also previously been a member of the Dodgers organization, playing parts of two seasons in Los Angeles. But after a knee injury caused him to the miss the entire 2006 season, Werth signed as a free agent with the Phillies.

The Dodgers also had someone very familiar with Philadelphia. Larry Bowa, who was fired as Phillies manager near the end of the 2004 season, was in his first season as the Dodgers' third-base coach.

The Phillies and Dodgers had split eight games during the regular season, with the home team winning each contest. In the best-of-seven NLCS, the Phillies hoped to capitalize on home-field advantage. That meant Hamels needed to come out strong in Game 1 against Lowe.

As he had in the opener of the division series, Hamels helped spot his team to a one-game lead in the NLCS, pitching seven strong innings. A two-run home run by Utley and a solo shot by Burrell in the sixth inning accounted for all three Phillies runs in a 3–2 come-from-behind victory. Lidge closed out the game with a scoreless ninth inning for his third save of the playoffs. Victorino went 0-for-4 in the opening game but reached base on an error and scored on Utley's homer.

What happened the next day was another reminder that life does not stop for baseball.

Before Game 2 of the Dodgers series, Charlie Manuel learned that his mother, 87-year-old June Manuel, had passed away in Virginia. But amid his grief, he was in the dugout that night managing his ballclub in its 168th game of the year.

The Phillies did everything they could early in the game to provide their manager with a pleasant distraction. By the third inning, Philadelphia had an 8–2 lead, with Victorino knocking in four runs on a single and a triple, becoming the first Phillies player since Gary Matthews in 1983 to have four RBIs in an NLCS game. Matthews' big game had also come against the Dodgers.

The other offensive hero of the night was pitcher Brett Myers, who followed up a couple pesky at-bats in the Milwaukee series with a three-hit, three-RBI explosion against Los Angeles. It was a near-miraculous performance considering Myers had just four hits in 58 at-bats during the regular season.

Ramirez helped keep the Dodgers close with a three-run home run off Myers in the fourth inning. In Manny's first at-bat of the game, Myers threw a pitch behind him, an act that would loom large later in the series.

"When something like that happens, there should be a response, and it should happen pretty quick," Honeycutt said. "There was some tension within our group that the situation wasn't addressed right away."

With the Dodgers down by three runs with two outs and two runners on base in the seventh inning, Victorino flashed his defensive skills, taking a hit away from Casey Blake by making a leaping catch in front of the center-field wall.

The Phillies hung on for an 8–5 win to take a 2–0 lead in the NLCS.

The win might have helped lift Manuel's spirits, but some more bad news was delivered after the game, and this time Victorino was the recipient.

"I did a press conference, and after I got back to my locker, Frank [Coppenbarger], our clubhouse manager, said he had to speak with me in his office," Victorino said. "I walked in the office and saw my dad standing there. Frank closed the door behind him. My dad congratulated me on the game, and then I saw tears in his eyes. I said, 'Don't tell me what I think you're going to tell me.'"

Victorino's paternal grandmother, Irene Victorino, whom he called Vovo, had been sick for several months. It had appeared she would pull through, but earlier that day, before the first pitch of the game, she passed away at the age of 82 on the Big Island of Hawaii. Mike Victorino Sr. waited to share the news of his mother's death with Shane until after the game.

"I went from absolutely being on cloud nine to feeling so devastated," said Victorino, who had already lost both of his maternal grandparents.

No one could understand what he was going through more than his manager.

"I could definitely relate to how Shane felt, and vice versa," Manuel said. "To be able to block things out and have the kind of series he had was really special. I feel like some of the things we went through during the playoffs, especially with the passing of my mom and Shane's grandmother, showed something about our team. I think the guys definitely rallied behind that."

For Victorino, the catch he made on the Blake fly ball in Game 2 took on new meaning. "When I left the ground, I didn't think I had a chance to catch the ball. It was almost like something was helping me get a little higher," he said. "I think Vovo and Charlie's mom were both there to lift me."

Manuel and Victorino remained with the team as the series moved to Los Angeles for the next two games. Manuel's plan to fly to Virginia for his mother's funeral later that week would not require him to miss any games. The Victorino family, meanwhile, was trying to make arrangements to delay the burial of Irene Victorino until after the playoffs.

The simmering tension from the Myers-Ramirez incident in Game 2 in Philadelphia escalated when the teams met again on the West Coast.

In the first inning of Game 3, Phillies starter Jamie Moyer, hardly a flamethrower, hit Dodgers catcher Russell Martin with a pitch. Moyer was already out of the game, having surrendered six earned runs in just $1\frac{1}{3}$ innings, when Martin came to the plate again in the second inning. With the Dodgers leading 6–1, Phillies reliever Clay Condrey sent Martin diving for cover with another inside pitch.

The Dodgers had evidently seen enough.

With Japanese right-hander Hiroki Kuroda on the hill, the Phillies' half of the third inning opened with a groundout by Geoff Jenkins and a strikeout by Jimmy Rollins. That brought Victorino to the plate. The first pitch out of Kuroda's hand, clocked at 94 miles per hour, sailed over the Flyin' Hawaiian's head. Umpire Mike Everitt sprung out from behind home plate to warn both managers against engaging in a beanball war, but the admonition mattered little at that moment. As players from both teams inched up the dugout steps toward the field, the situation threatened to get out of hand.

But in what became a signature moment of the series and of Victorino's career to that point, he stood his ground and shouted at Kuroda while emphatically gesturing to his head and rib area. His message to the non-English speaking pitcher was clear: if you want to throw at me, fine, but do not aim for my head.

"I was yelling at the guy, but then I came to grips and realized he probably didn't understand what I was saying," Victorino recalled.

From his seat in Dodger Stadium, which was hosting the biggest crowd in its history, Mike Victorino Sr. recognized his son's body language. "Shane's grandpa [Chester Nakahashi] always told his grandsons never to punch anybody in the head or face. He didn't want them to fight, but if they did, he wanted them to never hit somebody where they could really get hurt," he said.

Victorino, who struggled immensely during high school to control his explosive outbursts on the playing field, kept his cool this time. "Myers had thrown behind Manny at our place. [Myers] wasn't the smartest of guys when it came to throwing at guys and stuff like that. I think the Dodgers wanted [Chad] Billingsley to throw at one of our guys in that game, but he didn't," he said. "Everybody knew something was coming. When we hit Russell Martin in the first inning of that game, I remember seeing Derek Lowe looking back into their dugout. I think he was looking for Kuroda to make sure he did something. My whole thing was, if you're going to throw at me, I understand that, just don't throw at my head. I have no problem with you drilling me if you throw low. If you hit me in my head, it could be career-ending."

Joe Torre viewed the act of retaliation as necessary. "When we threw close to Victorino, it reminded me of old-time baseball," he said. "I don't want to say you're getting even by doing that, but you're taking care of your own. You make sure the message is loud and clear. Then you move on and play baseball. Any time you let getting even with someone interfere with what you're there to do, then it doesn't serve its purpose."

After Victorino grounded out to end the inning, he and Kuroda had words near first base, which was more than enough provocation for players from both benches to spill onto the field. The situation quickly settled down, and no one was ejected from the game. Major League Baseball later fined Victorino $2,500 and Kuroda $7,500 for their actions.

As far as Victorino was concerned, the episode raised the stakes of an already hugely important series. "My feeling was, 'Let's play now,'" he said. "The best way to make a team upset is to beat them. And that's what we planned on doing."

It was too late to salvage Game 3, however. Moyer's rough start did the Phillies in, and the Dodgers went on to win 7–2 to climb back into the series.

In the Phillies' first seven games of the postseason, the starting pitcher for both sides had picked up the win or loss. By the sixth inning of Game 4, however, starters Joe Blanton and Derek Lowe had already hit the showers. This game would be decided by the relief corps.

The Dodgers led 5–3 in the top of the eighth inning, and with star closer Jonathan Broxton ready to pitch an inning or more, they appeared poised to even the series.

But in the blink of an eye, that all changed.

First, Victorino tied the game at 5–5 with a two-run homer off reliever Cory Wade, solidifying his status in Los Angeles as the most despised member of the Phillies.

"It was a great feeling to tie the game with that home run," Victorino said. "But we still had some work to do with Broxton waiting in the wings."

A Carlos Ruiz single off Wade resulted in a call to the bullpen. In came Broxton to try and blow away pinch hitter Matt Stairs, who had made a living during 11 major league stops at catching up with fastballs and hitting them a long way.

Stairs, a gruff-looking Canadian, was loved by many Philadelphia fans because he looked like a lot of guys who played in their recreational softball leagues. His outward appearance suggested he might not take kindly to a mischievous motormouth like Victorino, who, ironically, actually *did* play in a slow-pitch softball league in the off-season. But in actuality, the two were buddies.

"Our personalities are the same," Stairs said. "We'd go get our Starbucks together during the season, and we'd ride to the ballpark on the road together. During spring training, he drove with me to all our games. We became good friends."

Among the things Stairs and Victorino have in common is a fondness for the phrase, "Yada, yada, yada," a shorthand way of describing the details of a story, immortalized in the television show *Seinfeld*.

They also both have an affinity for coming through in the clutch.

"After I heard my name announced as a pinch hitter, my mind went blank and I couldn't hear anything," Stairs recalled. "I watched Broxton warm up, and when I got in the batter's box, everything felt perfect. I was fired up when Vic hit the home run. Then Ruiz got a hit, and all of a sudden, it felt like it was my turn to do something special."

On a 3-1 count, Broxton came in with a fastball that Stairs put in the right-field stands to give the Phillies a 7–5 lead.

J.C. Romero and Brad Lidge shut down the shell-shocked Dodgers the rest of the way. The comeback victory on the road put the Phillies one win away from the World Series. Victorino's two RBIs in the game gave him 11 for the playoffs, breaking the Phillies postseason record of 10 set in 1993 by Lenny Dykstra.

In an online journal he kept for MLBlogs.com, Victorino described his emotions after his team won Game 4:

> Last night was one of the most exciting games I've ever been involved in, and Matt Stairs put an exclamation point on it. My home run just tied the game. His put us over the top.
>
> It just goes to show how we're never out of a game. That said, this series is far from over. It's seven games for a reason. They're going to come out strong and try and take it. We can't let them.
>
> As you guys know, this has been a crazy month for me. I've had a lot of emotions, but playing games has been great therapy. It's about winning. All the off-the-field stuff is forgotten on the field. I'm glad I'm able to play in the postseason and turn my focus on baseball. I know my grandmother is helping me.
>
> We're enjoying this. We'll be ready to go Wednesday.

Victorino's hitting during the series left an impression on Casey Blake, who played third base for the Dodgers in the 2008 NLCS. "He really can do it all," Blake said. "He's really a thorn in your side with all his weapons. He's a good guy and hard-nosed, but I really can't stand playing against him because he has such a complete game. Somebody with his size doing what he's doing at the big-league level, you have to have a little swagger, a little cockiness, and I appreciate that in him."

As he had against CC Sabathia in the NLDS, Victorino had delivered a pressure-filled hit in Game 4 of a postseason series. In a short span of time, Victorino had gained a reputation as a player who elevated his game in big situations. He was clutch and would continue to be in the coming years.

But what does it take to be clutch, and what separates the players who have the ability to do well in big situations from those who do not?

Former major leaguer Pat Tabler was an astounding 43-for-88 with the bases loaded during his 12-year career with the Cleveland Indians and several other teams. Tabler believes the secret to clutch hitting lies with the thoughts that flash through a player's mind while standing at home plate. "In those big situations, I could feel my concentration level go way up," he said. "A lot of guys melt in those situations because they let outside things interfere with their thought process. They let negative thoughts enter their minds, even if it's for a split second. For me, it was about positive thoughts winning out over negative thoughts. I was locked in, and my concentration level was almost like an out-of-body experience. It was like I was looking down and seeing myself doing the things I was supposed to do. The guys who can do that over the course of 500 or 600 at-bats in a season are the ones who are heads above everybody else."

Victorino had that ability to channel positive energy in big situations. "I want to make the headlines," he said. "I want to be the guy who gets the game-winning hit or the guy who makes the big catch. I have friends who say I often have big games when we're on ESPN or Fox or in the playoffs, but I don't change my game for the postseason. I just like to be known as a clutch player."

Between Games 4 and 5, Victorino found out the price of making headlines when he got embroiled in "Spam-gate," an attempt by an animal-rights group to draw attention to the alleged misconduct of the canned meat's pork suppliers. Victorino became a public target of scorn by the People for the Ethical Treatment of Animals after publicly declaring he consumed large amounts of spam musubi, a sushi-like snack made with the meat that is popular in Hawaii. In the middle of the playoffs, PETA shot off a graphic letter to Victorino urging him to become a vegetarian. He ignored the advice.

With the Phillies on the verge of clinching a trip to the World Series, Hamels took the hill again in Game 5 against Billingsley, the loser of Game 2.

In a repeat of the NLDS-clinching game against the Brewers, Rollins led off the game with a home run. Singles by Howard and Burrell plated two more runs in the third inning. A pair of errors by Furcal at shortstop in the fifth led to two unearned runs, pushing the Phillies' lead to 5–0. Victorino, hitting sixth for the second straight night, was issued two intentional walks in the game, one of them by surefire future Hall of Famer Greg Maddux, who had come on in relief of Billingsley. They were the second and third free passes given to Victorino in the playoffs.

"There's no way I ever thought I'd be intentionally walked in the postseason," Victorino said.

A lot of things had happened in the past two weeks that once seemed unimaginable for the player many doubted could ever be a major league player. There had been euphoria at winning the division and the first-round playoff series, grief at the death of his grandmother, anger at a pitcher who threw a ball near his head, and, ultimately, the unmatched feeling of triumph in the National League Championship Series.

The Phillies beat the Dodgers 5–1 to clinch the pennant. Hamels was named MVP of the NLCS on the strength of a 2–0 record and a 1.93 ERA in 14 innings pitched.

As champagne flowed in the visitors' clubhouse, the Dodgers were collectively left with an empty feeling.

"You sit there knowing you had a successful season, but it almost doesn't feel like that because it's such a letdown in the end," said Blake DeWitt, the Dodgers' second baseman in that series. "What I most remember is walking off the field after that last loss and thinking, *Man, I don't want to have this feeling again.*"

The Phillies did not yet have to contemplate an end to their magical journey. The only question to ponder at that moment was who they would face in the World Series—the Tampa Bay Rays or the Boston Red Sox.

The answer came a few days later when the Rays wrapped up a seven-game-series win to lock in a date with the Phillies in the Fall Classic.

The fun was just starting.

BREAKING THE CURSE

IT HAD BEEN A WHILE. FIFTEEN YEARS TO BE EXACT.

And as good as the 1993 pennant-winning season was for the Philadelphia Phillies and their fans, the cringeworthy way in which it ended largely overpowered the special memories that came before it.

That was the nature of October baseball. Teams play 162 games and only a select few qualify for the playoffs. Within a couple weeks, two of them make it to the World Series. And the teams that come up short, no matter how good a season they had, conclude things on a sour note, making baseball the only sport where a team can win 100 games in a season and still feel like a failure.

The 1993 Phillies won 97 games during the regular season and another six in the playoffs, but a ragtag group that included Lenny Dykstra, Darren Daulton, and John Kruk still came up short.

In a famous comedy bit that contrasts baseball and football, George Carlin riffed on the symbolic difference between sudden-death overtime and extra innings, the point being that football games end abruptly, while baseball games tend to linger. But the conclusion of the 1993 World Series was about as close to sudden death as you will find in baseball. That year's Fall Classic between the Phillies and the Toronto Blue Jays was only the second in history to end on a walk-off home run. The Phillies entered the bottom of the ninth of Game 6 with a 6–5 lead. But with two runners on base, Joe Carter deposited a low-velocity Mitch Williams fastball into the left-field seats at SkyDome to give the Blue Jays their second consecutive World Series victory.

Sports talk radio in Philadelphia that night took on the feel of group therapy as moribund hosts urged callers to recall their favorite moments of the season rather than dwell on its abrupt and heartbreaking end. There was always next year, they reminded listeners. No one knew at the time that it would be so long before the Phillies would make it back to the World Series.

In fact, going into October 2008, none of Philadelphia's major professional sports teams had won a title in 25 years. The last team to do it was the 76ers, led by Moses Malone and Julius Erving, who beat the Los Angeles Lakers for the 1983 NBA crown. The Phillies' most recent championship was way back in 1980. The Flyers last skated to a Stanley Cup victory in 1975, and the Eagles had never won a Super Bowl. For Philadelphia fans, watching losing teams had become a year-round activity.

After Smarty Jones, a horse bred in the Philadelphia area, won the Kentucky Derby and the Preakness Stakes in 2004, some wondered whether the city could celebrate a championship if the thoroughbred completed the Triple Crown with a victory at the Belmont Stakes. The two-legged creatures had let the city down time and again, the thinking was; maybe a four-legged one would get the job done. Alas, Smarty came in second at Belmont Park.

The City of Brotherly Love's championship drought even had a name: the Curse of Billy Penn. According to the tongue-in-cheek legend, Philadelphia's sports misery was the founding father's revenge from the grave for the 1987 construction in Center City Philadelphia of a building that supplanted the statue of Penn atop city hall as the highest point of the Philly skyline. In an attempt to break the curse, a smaller version of the Penn statue was put on the top of an even taller building that went up in 2007.

Could the 2008 Phillies end the dry spell?

In 1993, the Phillies' World Series opponent was a veteran-laden offensive juggernaut from north of the border. In 2008, the foe was an upstart group of youngsters from sunny Florida.

The Tampa Bay Rays had been anything but an elite franchise since joining the major leagues in 1998 as the "Devil Rays." In fact, they had been about as miserable as a team could be. In 2006 and 2007, Tampa Bay posted the worst record in baseball, in part due to the unfortunate circumstance of playing in the same division as the talented Boston Red Sox and New York Yankees. But then suddenly in 2008, the year they became just the "Rays," a young group of players excelled under manager Joe Maddon, then in his third year leading the team. In the case of the Rays, just making the playoffs for the first time had been a major accomplishment. But they had no intention of stopping there. En route to the Series, the Rays knocked off two teams that had combined to win three of the previous four world championships: the Red Sox and the Chicago White Sox.

It had been a surreal journey to the Fall Classic.

"How far the Rays had come in such a short period of time was kind of phenomenal, actually," Maddon said. "If there had been a videographer following us in '06, '07, and into '08, you would have thought that you were seeing fiction more than reality. It was that far-fetched."

The headline of a *Rocky Mountain News* article previewing the 2008 World Series encapsulated the matchup: "Loser-friendly Philly, Tampa earn chance to end exercises in futility."

The Phillies had waited a long time to make it back to the World Series; as it turned out, they would have to wait just a little bit longer until the games began. The Phillies polished off the Dodgers on October 15. The Rays became American League champs four days later, beating the Red Sox in seven games. Three days after that, the World Series finally got underway, meaning the Phillies had nearly a week off without competition.

"That was kind of different," Victorino said. "We don't get anywhere near that many days off during the season. I think there was a lot of anticipation to just get out there and play."

Between series, Victorino worked out, took batting practice, and found time to make an appearance in South Jersey for a local charity. He also sent off a couple boxes of Phillies World Series T-shirts to students in Maui.

The American League's 15-inning win in that summer's All-Star Game meant the Rays had home-field advantage in the World Series. If the same rules that governed other sports applied to baseball, Tampa Bay would have had the extra home game anyway, having finished with a 97–65 regular season record, superior to the Phillies' mark of 92–70.

All sorts of numbers could be crunched while waiting for the first pitch of the World Series on October 22.

On paper, it appeared Tampa Bay would have a big edge playing the first two games at Tropicana Field. The Rays had gone 57–24 at home during the season, the best record in the major leagues. On the road, meanwhile, they lost more games than they won.

In 2008, the Phillies had the second-worst record in the majors in interleague play, while Tampa Bay had the second-best mark. Head to head, the Rays held a 10–5 advantage over the Phillies in interleague play since 1998.

Furthermore, the previous two teams to endure long layoffs before the World Series had lost to teams coming in with less rest.

For these reasons, most prognosticators, as well as the Las Vegas oddsmakers, made Tampa Bay a slight favorite to win the championship.

Both teams had a lot of what Maddon described as "Stage 5" players, guys who had evolved from being happy just to be in the majors, to hoping to stick around, to feeling like they belonged, to looking to make a lot of money, and finally to wanting to reach the peak of their profession.

"The Phillies reminded me a lot of us at that time, only they had more experience than we did," he said.

He was definitely not taking the Phillies' lineup lightly.

"I've always been a big fan of their MVP guys, but I liked Victorino also," he said during the ALCS against the Red Sox. "He made a big impression on me in spring training."

Mike Vaccaro of the *New York Post* had this to say about Victorino before the Rays and Phillies did battle in Game 1: "[The Phillies] have the biggest pest in baseball playing for them, a 28-year-old outfielder who was twice exposed to the Rule 5 Draft by the Dodgers and returned to haunt them like those old apparitions from Amityville, and who also has the coolest nickname in baseball. Without Shane Victorino, someone else is playing here, representing the National League. Without the Flyin' Hawaiian, Philly would be chilly and would have long ago reverted to its default state as a football town. Instead, the Phillies sit four wins away from the franchise's second title in 125 years of business."

In preparing for the Phillies, Rays pitching coach Jim Hickey studied the tendencies of every hitter in the Philadelphia lineup.

"With Shane, it was really difficult to go anywhere," Hickey said. "He's a very aggressive hitter, and when he gets on base, he can steal. Apart from Utley, I'd say he provided the most difficult assignment for us as a whole."

No one played a bigger role in getting the Phillies to the World Series than Cole Hamels, who accounted for three of the team's seven wins in the playoffs. He faced off against Scott Kazmir of the Rays in the World Series opener.

The game got off to a great start for the visitors with Utley smacking a two-run home run in the first inning. The Phillies added to their lead when Victorino led off the fourth with a single and later scored on a Carlos Ruiz groundout.

The early runs helped quiet the cacophony of cowbells being rung by the standing-room-only crowd at Tropicana Field, which had not seen many full houses during a regular season in which the Rays drew an average of about 22,000 fans.

Again, Hamels came up big. His pitching compensated for the fact that the Phillies were 0-for-13 with runners in scoring position in Game 1. Hamels scattered five hits in seven innings to win his fourth game of the postseason. Lidge came on in the ninth to notch yet another save in the 3–2 victory.

Victorino, hitting in the sixth slot which he would occupy for the entire series, chipped in with two hits and a run scored.

After the game, an exuberant Victorino shared his post-victory thoughts with ESPN Radio during an on-the-field interview. "Cole came in and did his job and kept them to a minimum," he said. "And then he handed the ball to the bullpen. The bullpen's been lights out all year long with a guy named Lights Out. No questions asked, it's nice to get Game 1, especially on the road the way [the Rays] have been playing."

The World Series opener also had special meaning for a father and son who got to broadcast an inning of the game on the radio together. The father was legendary broadcaster Harry Kalas, who had been calling Phillies games for nearly 40 years. His son, Todd, had been on the Rays' announcing team since the team's first season.

"We knew that some time in the near future Dad was probably going to have to contemplate retirement," Todd Kalas said. "If the Phillies and the Rays played in the World Series, we realized it might be our one shot to be together for this kind of event. It was great to be around him that whole time."

THE PRESSURE WAS SQUARELY ON THE RAYS going into Game 2. If they lost again, they faced the daunting prospect of leaving St. Petersburg, possibly without returning, to play a middle set of games in Philadelphia.

Brett Myers, who won a game in both the NLDS and NLCS, got the start for Philadelphia against James Shields, who came in with a 1–2 record in the postseason.

Myers dug himself an early 3–0 hole, and the Phillies' bats went dead for the second game in a row. A pinch-hit home run in the eighth inning by Eric Bruntlett and an unearned run in the ninth accounted for all the team's scoring.

Shields pitched shutout ball into the sixth inning, and the Rays' bullpen kept the Phillies from clawing back. The final score: Rays 4, Phillies 2.

A night after going hitless with runners in scoring position, the Phillies went just 1-for-15 in clutch situations. The only hit they got with a runner on second or third base was a Victorino infield single in the fourth inning that did not produce a run. Victorino was 2-for-4 in the losing effort.

"That might be one of our sloppiest games all year," Charlie Manuel said afterward. "I'm concerned about us hitting with guys on base, because it looks like at times we might be trying a little too hard. But we can fix that."

By winning one of two games in St. Petersburg, the Phillies had accomplished the unspoken goal of teams that start a best-of-seven series on the road. Their sudden hitting woes aside, they had a lot to look forward to in returning to Citizens Bank Park for the first home World Series game in Philadelphia since 1993.

MUCH WAS MADE OF THE GAME 3 pitching matchup between 24-year-old Matt Garza of the Rays and 45-year-old Jamie Moyer of the Phillies. Garza was less than a year old when Moyer was drafted by the Chicago Cubs in the sixth round of the 1984 amateur draft. But despite being at radically different points in their careers, both were making their first World Series starts.

His chance to pitch for the Phillies in such a big spot had extra meaning to Moyer, a Philadelphia-area native who grew up going to games at old Veterans Stadium. Moyer had been with a lot of teams in his career, but he regarded the Phillies teams he played on as special.

"We have a bunch of professionals who like to have some fun, share some jokes, and dig on each other," Moyer said in 2010, his last season with the team. "I think that's a great way to get away from the stress of the game. We've all been raised in this game somewhat differently, but we had the same goal of trying to win a championship."

The Phillies and Rays had ample opportunity to get to know their teammates during the 162-game regular season and the playoffs, but the weather in Philadelphia gave them a chance to spend that much more time together before Game 3 of the World Series.

The first pitch of the game was scheduled for 8:35 PM local time, but there had been steady rain and blustery winds in the Delaware Valley throughout the day. The weather gods seemed to have it in for Philadelphia fans who also had to wait out a 72-minute rain delay before the start of the Phillies' first home game in the 1993 World Series. By the time the 2008 storm front passed, the Saturday night game had been delayed 90 minutes. The fans returned to their seats as Moyer strode out to the damp Citizens Bank Park mound a few minutes after 10:00 PM. He got Rays second baseman Akinori Iwamura to fly out on the second pitch of the game. Die-hard fans, night owls, and folks in the Pacific Time Zone were rejoicing at the late start time, even if network executives were not.

In case the home fans were feeling at all sluggish after the long delay, the Phillies helped energize them by putting runners on second and third with nobody out in the first inning. But an RBI groundout by Utley produced their only run that frame.

The teams traded scores in the second inning, as the Phillies got theirs on a go-ahead solo home run by catcher Carlos Ruiz. The score remained 2–1 until the sixth inning when Chase Utley and Ryan Howard hit back-to-back, post-midnight home runs. It was Utley's third home run and ninth RBI of the postseason. For Howard, who slugged 48 homers during the season, the long ball was his first in 43 at-bats during the 2008 playoffs. It would not be his last.

Moyer put aside his two rocky starts earlier in the playoffs and rose to the occasion in his most important start of the season, if not his career. He left the field to a standing ovation in the top of the seventh inning with a runner on third base who eventually came around to score to cut the Phillies' lead to 4–3.

In the eighth inning, B.J. Upton did everything he could to steal the game from the home team. He led off with an infield hit to shortstop against Ryan Madson and, with one out, he stole second base. In a classic example of small ball, he then swiped third and came home when Ruiz's throw went into right field. As quickly as that, the Rays had tied the game.

Tampa Bay had momentum on its side. A win would guarantee them at the very least a return trip to Tropicana Field for Game 6. The Phillies needed a last dose of good fortune on this late night/early morning to keep the Rays from regaining the edge in the series.

The bottom of the ninth inning started with Rays reliever J.P. Howell hitting Bruntlett, who had come in as a defensive replacement in left field for Pat Burrell. Grant Balfour entered the game in relief of Howell and uncorked a wild pitch. Bruntlett took off for second and continued around to third when Rays catcher Dioner Navarro's throw went into center field. Still with nobody out, Balfour intentionally walked Victorino and Greg Dobbs to load the bases. That brought Ruiz to the plate and prompted Maddon to summon in his right fielder Ben Zobrist to form a five-man, softball-style infield.

The Rays would have likely needed another few infielders to prevent what happened next. Ruiz followed up his earlier home run with a well-placed cue shot down the third-base line that brought Bruntlett home with the winning run.

Ruiz's crucial hit summed up the series for Rays pitching coach Jim Hickey.

"Every time they needed the big hit, they got it, whether it was a jam shot that eluded a defender or whether it was a resounding double," Hickey said. "And every time they needed the big out, they got it, whether they [struck] a guy out or the guy hit the line drive and it found somebody's glove."

Ruiz's single at 1:47 in the morning was not a thing of beauty, but it did the job as well as a towering home run. The most exciting game of the Fall Classic to that point drew a record-low TV audience for a World Series game, and it prompted a question that would be asked again a couple nights later: should the game have even been played?

The soggy conditions did not dampen the enthusiasm of the fans that packed Citizens Bank Park, a raucous group that included several dozen of Victorino's friends and family from Hawaii who flew in to share the moment with him.

"Seeing him in Philly, a lot of us noticed he had grown up from being that little rascal kid," said Lyle Cummings, a childhood friend who took in the World Series games. "He ain't the joker anymore. He's all business."

THE TEMPERATURE MADE IT ALL THE WAY up to 54 degrees for Game 4 as Joe Blanton sought to extend his record to 6–0 since joining the Phillies in a midseason trade. Andy Sonnanstine, pitching on 11 days' rest, opposed him.

The first three games of the series had been decided by a total of four runs. They had featured stolen bases, swinging bunts, and good pitching. This game would follow a different script.

A two-run home run by Howard in the fourth inning of Game 4 gave the Phillies a 5–1 lead. Eric Hinske of the Rays went deep in the top of the fifth, and all of a sudden, Game 4 had become a home run derby. The Phillies made two quick outs in the home half of the fifth, bringing Blanton to the plate. If a runner had been on base, Manuel might have considered pinch hitting for his pitcher. Blanton came to the Phillies from Oakland with a grand total of 10 major league at-bats. He batted only 16 times for them during the 2008 regular season and registered just one hit. But something was in the air that night when he came up to face Rays pitcher Edwin Jackson, a former minor league teammate of Victorino's. Up in the count 2-1, Jackson threw a fastball that Blanton smacked over the left-field wall for the most improbable home run of the postseason.

Blanton pitched a scoreless sixth inning and left the game with his team up by four runs. Any doubts that this game was going the Phillies' way were erased when Jayson Werth and Howard each hit two-run home runs in the eighth to extend the lead to 10–2. That would be the final score.

The Phillies were one win away from the world championship.

Two losses in Philadelphia had left the Rays reeling, but they felt they would be in the driver's seat if they could find a way to take the final game at Citizens Bank Park.

"Every guy in a blue jersey felt like if we got back home for Games 6 and 7, we were going to win," Hickey said. "And I don't think there was anybody on [the Phillies'] side that was looking forward to going back to the Trop."

A couple of the most important guys in blue jerseys were just looking to get a hit. Evan Longoria and Carlos Peña, who had helped carry the Rays this far, were a combined 0-for-29 through the first four games of the World Series.

GAME 5 WAS SCHEDULED FOR THE NEXT EVENING, a Monday, and the weather forecast again called for showers. The day started dry, but as game time approached, the skies darkened and a light rain started falling.

Victorino saw the condition of the field and fully expected the game to be called off. "I thought there was no way we were playing," he said. "You knew the field was going to be wet from the beginning and that it was going to be an ugly night."

Victorino and dozens of other amateur meteorologists had firm opinions on whether the game should be played, but the decision was not theirs to make. It instead rested with Major League Baseball commissioner Bud Selig, and after holding a meeting with the teams' managers and general managers, the umpiring crew, and the head groundskeeper, Selig concluded the weather forecast was favorable enough to try to get the game in. The temperature at first pitch was a damp 47 degrees.

Play ball!

If you can, that is.

The pitching matchup mirrored Game 1, with Hamels going against Kazmir. For the second straight game, Victorino, who entered Game 5 hitless in his last nine at-bats, came up in the first inning with the bases loaded. He was in a minor slump at a major time. But just when he needed to, he came out of it. On a 2-1 pitch from Kazmir, Victorino stroked a single down the left-field line to plate Werth and Utley and give the Phillies an early lead.

Every game in the 2008 World Series featured a first-inning score, with the team that jumped out to an early lead going on to win each time. Game 5 was no different, even though the first run of the game crossed the plate 48 hours before the last would.

By the fourth inning, Victorino was convinced the game was going to be stopped at any minute. A hard rain was falling, and puddles of water were now collecting on the field.

"As we're going through the game, I'm thinking, *They've got to call this at some point. It's getting out of control*," he said. "I still wondered why we even started the game in the first place. The conditions were horrible. It was cold and it was rainy and it was windy. The visibility was horrible."

But the game went on.

Seeing a steady diet of fastballs from Hamels, the Rays scored a run in the fourth on back-to-back hits by Peña and Longoria, both players' first hits of the series.

The Phillies led 2–1 when the game became official at the end of the fifth inning. By regular season rules, that would have meant a Phillies victory if the game got called because of rain. But could a rain-shortened game end up deciding the World Series? The best option for Selig at the time was to put off addressing that question by keeping the players on the field.

No one questioned that the weather was adversely affecting the quality of play. From Hamels' inability to grip pitches to Jimmy Rollins' fifth-inning adventure in pursuing a pop-up that hit off his glove for an error, these were hardly conditions befitting a game played by the boys of summer, especially one of such magnitude.

In the top of the sixth inning, Hamels retired the first two hitters, but Upton reached base on a soggy infield single. He stole second and scored on Peña's second hit of the game, and suddenly the game was tied 2–2. After Victorino squeezed a fly ball from Longoria for the third out, the tarp came out and play was stopped.

A far-from-ideal situation was at least now a bit more manageable. An official game that was tied would be suspended and resumed from the point at which play was stopped.

But when would that be?

Selig decreed the game would continue "when weather conditions are deemed appropriate."

"We'll stay here if we have to celebrate Thanksgiving here," he told a mass of reporters the night the game was put on hold.

For the record, he added the game would have been suspended and resumed whether or not the Rays had tied the score.

Both teams questioned the decision to play a game in conditions that almost certainly would have led to the postponement of a regular season game.

"It was probably the worst conditions I've ever seen on a baseball field," Hickey said. "I'm really shocked we continued to play that game as long as we did. There was standing water all over the infield dirt. They were playing in slop."

The weather in Philadelphia on Tuesday showed no improvement. Rather than make the teams sit around and wait to see if they would play, Selig called the game off early in the day.

Victorino spent the most unusual of off-days visiting friends and family, trying at once to stay relaxed and focused.

"There was never a point when we were behind in the series, so being up 3–1 at that point helped give us confidence," he said. "But then you start thinking how big a game it is and how you want to celebrate at home. You think, *Okay, let's make this happen*. But you can't make it happen until you can take the field again."

On Wednesday night, the teams got set to play the final innings of Game 5, or Game 5½ as it became known to many. The Hawaii contingent was smaller by the time the game resumed. Some had booked trips to Philadelphia with an extra day on the back end in case of a rainout, but no one foresaw needing to factor in *two* extra days for bad weather.

Speaking of travel, Victorino had no intention of returning to Florida. He came to Citizens Bank Park on Wednesday afternoon looking to wrap up the World Series then and there. While every other player packed a suitcase in case the team would have to board a plane for Tampa, Victorino just had the clothes on his back.

Though the whole situation had been a royal mess, there was still something exhilarating about the truncated game the two teams were about to play.

"When we resumed Game 5, it was kind of like one of those NASCAR sprints to the finish where you have a 10-lap sprint after running 400 miles," Hickey recalled. "Grant Balfour was the pitcher coming into the game. I'm out there with him in the bullpen before the game starts up again. You never get a chance to watch a relief pitcher warm up. I wasn't even going to go out there and do it because I didn't want to do anything differently."

The first order of business for Manuel was to pinch hit for Hamels, who threw the first pitch two nights earlier and was still officially in the game. Off the bench came Geoff Jenkins, who promptly delivered a double. After the onslaught of home runs in Game 4 back on Sunday night, the Phillies showed they too could play small ball. Rollins sacrificed Jenkins to third base, and Werth followed with a single off Balfour that brought home the go-ahead run.

Ryan Madson took over for Hamels and yielded a game-tying home run to the second batter he faced, Rocco Baldelli. After a one-out single by Jason Bartlett, Manuel turned to J.C. Romero, who finished off the inning with no further damage. The half-inning ended with Bartlett being thrown out at the plate trying to score from second on an infield hit.

The last innings of Game 5 featured both teams matching each other move for move and score for score.

"I felt like that game was so fast," Victorino said. "They hit and then we hit, and it came down to who was going to race to the finish line to win this game. It seemed like one of the most fast-paced games ever. From the time I ran out onto the field, I couldn't believe how loud the crowd was. The stadium was definitely adrenaline-rushed."

Burrell led off the home seventh with a double and was replaced with pinch runner Bruntlett. With Victorino due up, the Rays brought in their third pitcher of the night, Chad Bradford. Victorino had a productive at-bat, advancing Bruntlett to third base on a groundout. Pedro Feliz then came through with a run-scoring single to put the Phillies ahead again 4–3.

Romero came back out for the eighth and gave up a leadoff single to the fleet-footed Carl Crawford. With another speedster in B.J. Upton coming up, it had all the makings of a big inning for the Rays. But a swiftly executed Rollins-to-Utley-to-Howard double play erased both Crawford and Upton. A lineout by Carlos Peña ended the top of the eighth.

The Phillies got a runner to second in the bottom of the eighth, but that was all.

Game 5½ of the 2008 World Series went to the top of the ninth inning with the Phillies leading the Rays 4–3.

Brad Lidge, who had been perfect in 41 regular season and six postseason save opportunities, came striding in from the bullpen to try and shut the door one last time.

Longoria opened the inning with a pop out, but catcher Dioner Navarro singled to put the potential tying run on base. Navarro was lifted for pinch runner Fernando Perez. With a 1-2 count on Ben Zobrist, Perez took off for second base, beating the throw by Ruiz for a crucial steal. The Rays now had the tying run in scoring position with only one out.

Zobrist followed with one of the hardest-hit balls of the night, but his line drive wound up in the glove of right fielder Jayson Werth for the second out of the inning.

All that stood between the Phillies and their first championship in 28 years was pinch hitter Eric Hinske, whose entire 2008 postseason consisted of one at-bat and one home run, a pinch-hit shot off Blanton in the Phillies' Game 4 victory.

Before facing Hinske, Lidge met on the mound with pitching coach Rich Dubee.

"Dubee ran out and asked me if I remembered what I was doing with this guy," Lidge said. "I told him I faced him before, and he had rifled a fastball off the wall. I don't know if that seemed like a funny answer to Dubee, but he said, 'Okay, throw him some sliders.' We got into a favorable count, and Carlos Ruiz came out and said, 'What do you wanna do here?' I said, 'Let's throw a slider down and away.' We looked at each other an extra second longer because we knew what was on the line."

In center field, Victorino bounced on his toes in anticipation of the 0-2 pitch to Hinske. He had a perfect view as the ball was released, as it dipped toward home plate, and as Hinske swung and missed. As the ball landed in Ruiz's glove, Lidge fell to his knees.

"Next thing I knew, I was on my back with Ryan Howard on top of me," Lidge recalled.

Victorino could not wait to join the mob.

"I remember thinking, *This is the longest run in the history of sports,*" he said of his dash from center field to join his teammates on the mound. "I was like, *Oh my god, am I ever going to get there?*"

The former high school sprint champion finally made it to the mound on one of the biggest nights in Philadelphia sports history. In one of the iconic images of the celebration, the Flyin' Hawaiian is seen literally vaulting through the air and onto the pile of jubilant champions.

In his online journal for MLBlogs.com, Victorino summed up the feeling of having just won a World Series in—and for—the city of Philadelphia.

I almost lost it when the door opened in the ninth and Brad Lidge ran out. It was so loud. You could tell the fans were hungry and ready. I can imagine what it's going to be like on Broad Street. We'll celebrate with them on Friday. I have 50 text messages already, and that was 20 minutes ago.

I remember watching Sid Fernandez in 1986 when he won with the Mets, and how cool that was. I was six, but Sid was one of my idols, being from Hawaii. You always dream of being a part of a team that wins a championship. Lo and behold, 2008 here we are.

I guess the curse is gone. William Penn is happy, now.

Cole Hamels was named MVP of the 2008 World Series, becoming only the fifth player ever to win the MVP award for the League Championship Series and World Series in the same year.

As Hickey noted, the Phillies' offense came up big when it needed to against the Rays. Ruiz went 6-for-16 with a home run and a timely hit in Game 3. Howard found his power stroke at precisely the right time. Utley's two home runs and five runs scored and Werth's .444 average also helped buoy Philadelphia's attack. Victorino's performance against the Rays paled in comparison to his heroics in the earlier postseason series, but he saved his best game for last, knocking in two of the Phillies' four runs in the decisive Game 5 victory.

The Phillies gave the home fans a lot to cheer for during the 2008 postseason, posting a 7–0 record at Citizens Bank Park in the three playoff series.

The championship meant a lot to Phillies who had played on the 1980 World Series–winning team.

"When my career ended [in 1986], I stayed in Philadelphia," Garry Maddox said. "I've been here since I was traded here in 1975. I've gone through all the ups and downs of the organization from that point until they won in 2008. I was not happy when I heard all the teasing about the organization having lost 10,000 games. You're looking for those moments of pride, and to see the team come on the way they did, was unbelievable."

THIRTY-SIX HOURS AFTER LIDGE'S STRIKEOUT, the Phillies, members of their organization, and, of course, the Phillie Phanatic, boarded flatbed trucks at 20th and Market streets for a three-hour parade through town to share the accomplishment with hundreds of thousands of fans. Pat Burrell, his then-wife, and his dog, Elvis, led the procession on a horse-drawn beer wagon.

Philadelphia mayor Michael Nutter chose not to cancel school that day, but quite a few youngsters found their way to the parade anyway, just as Jamie Moyer had when the Phillies won the World Series in 1980.

"When I was in high school, I went to the parade and witnessed it from curbside," Moyer said. "In 2008, I was at the parade on a float. It was pretty cool to witness it from both sides."

Ruben Amaro Jr., who was named general manager of the team a few days after the festivities, also attended the only previous Phillies victory parade. As a 15-year-old clubhouse helper, he joined his father, Ruben Sr., a coach on the 1980 team, on a parade float. In his life, Amaro Jr. had experienced Phillies baseball from a variety of angles: as a batboy, as a player in the 1990s, and as a front office executive.

"When we were on the floats working our way down Broad Street and through Center City, it struck me what kind of impact this had on people," Amaro said. "It is something I'll never forget. The emotion I felt with the fans was indescribable."

Victorino, who shared a float with Jayson Werth, Matt Stairs, and their families, savored every moment of that day. At one point, he tossed soft pretzels to fans along the parade route. Some of the people they passed reciprocated with cans of beer and other gifts for the players.

"I've never seen so many people in my entire life," Victorino recalled. "There was a point when we got to Broad Street and Oregon Avenue, as we got close to the stadium, where there were grown men on their knees thanking us for winning a championship. There were a lot of people with tears in their eyes. That's what touches me so much about that city, and it's why I wanted to play there. I love their passion for the game."

Later that afternoon, Victorino climbed on top of a portable toilet in the flatbed truck that doubled as a float. The potty was less than sturdy, especially after bearing the weight of the Phillie Phanatic, who had shimmied to the top much to the delight of the crowd below.

"That was the 'look at me' Victorino making an appearance," Stairs recalled with a smile. "The Phillie Phanatic got up there and did that, so he figured he would, too."

When the team reached Citizens Bank Park, it was speech time. Chase Utley stole the show with his proclamation that the Phillies were "world champions, world [bleeping] champions!"

Victorino took to the podium and expressed his appreciation to the fans. "I just want to say thank you for all that you've done for us this year," he said. "You guys have been with us from day one! Hey, we brought this championship! We're going to celebrate tonight! Have a safe one! I want to say thank you again from me and all my team. Thank you!"

After the festivities were over, Victorino flew home to Hawaii for the funeral of his grandmother, who had passed away during the National League Championship Series.

"When I got there, I said, 'Vovo, thank you for waiting. I'm a World Series champ now. I'm sure you were watching me from above. You helped me with my playoffs,'" he said.

While in Maui, Victorino learned he had won his first Gold Glove Award.

A few days after the funeral, a letter addressed to Shane's parents arrived at the Victorino family home in Maui. It was from a woman named Marilyn Avila, one of Shane's former teachers at St. Anthony High School in Wailuku. The letter read:

> I want to congratulate you on Shane's success. And although it came in the form of a World Series championship and Gold Glove Award, what I really mean is the young man of outstanding character that he has become. When I watch him play and see the focus I remember that little squirrely freshman who had such a difficult time sitting still, and oh how he used to drive [teacher] Ms. Collins crazy. When I see him interviewed and he is polite, humble, filled with Aloha spirit, my spirit just beams. To this day, when I have a student with ADD or ADHD and when we have a conference with the parents, I always tell them that together we can make it.

The Phillies had made it. Shane had made it. Together.

ANOTHER RUN AT THE TOP

THE CELEBRATION THAT BEGAN ON THE STREETS of Philadelphia continued for Shane Victorino all over the country. In Las Vegas, his off-season home, Mayor Oscar Goodman, a Philadelphia native, presented him with a key to Sin City. In Oahu, he was honored by the Hawaii Winter Baseball League. Back home in Maui, he hosted the inaugural Shane Victorino Celebrity Golf Tournament, a benefit that raised $100,000 for the local Alzheimer's Association.

On January 1, 2009, a group of entrants in the Mummers Parade, one of Philadelphia's most hallowed traditions, honored Victorino and the Phillies on a frigid New Year's Day by creating a movable luau with hula dancers waving Phillies pennants.

Later that month, the Phillies recognized Victorino's accomplishments by giving him a major pay bump. He avoided salary arbitration by signing a one-year contract worth $3.1 million, more than six times what he earned in 2008. He viewed his new contract as a step toward his goal of landing a multiyear deal after the 2009 season, by which time he would be eligible for salary arbitration.

"No questions asked, I want to play here for a while," he told *The (Allentown, Pennsylvania) Morning Call* after coming to terms on the one-year deal. "It's definitely my goal. But, hey, why can't I revisit it? I'm happy with what I got, but I want to keep moving forward. This is a great bunch of guys. Why wouldn't I want to play in a city like this where the fans are great and it's a fun place to be?"

Before the start of the new season, Victorino got the call to play for Team USA in the second-ever World Baseball Classic. His chance to represent his country came after Cleveland Indians center fielder Grady Sizemore left the team due to an injury. Just three years earlier, Victorino was fighting to win playing time at Phillies spring training while All-Star right fielder Bobby

Abreu was playing for Venezuela in the inaugural tournament. Now Victorino had been recognized as one of the best players in the game at his position.

"It was an honor to put on the USA jersey and to play alongside guys like Derek Jeter, David Wright, Dustin Pedroia, Ryan Braun, Curtis Granderson, and a lot of other guys you'll probably never get a chance to play with again," Victorino said. "When you play opposite them, you marvel at what they do, but when you're on the same team, you get to see up close how they go about preparing for a game and playing the game. It's not like an All-Star team, because you're there over a period of time sharing a clubhouse, traveling together, and going to dinner together. The whole thing was just an amazing experience."

The team's first official workout took place at Bright House Field, the Phillies' spring training home in Clearwater, Florida. Jimmy Rollins, also a member of the national team, served as unofficial host to the assembled stars. Victorino and Rollins had the unique opportunity to play against their own ballclub when Team USA beat the Phillies in a tune-up game.

Over the course of the 18-day tournament, reliever Heath Bell of the Padres got to know the Phillies' center fielder and shortstop.

"On the USA team, I was like, 'I want to be a Phillie,'" Bell said. "Victorino and J-Roll always seemed to be having such a good time. They are great guys, and it seems like they have a lot of fun in Philly, in addition to winning a lot of games."

Victorino wore No. 50 for Team USA to honor Hawaii, the 50th state admitted to the union. In eight games, Victorino went 6-for-19 before the U.S. team was eliminated by eventual champion Japan in the semifinals.

The tournament gave Victorino an opportunity to observe different styles of baseball.

"I think Asian countries have an advantage in the tournament, because they play the right kind of baseball," he said. "Team USA had so many great hitters that we couldn't really play small ball. Even in 2006, when the team was loaded with almost every big name out there, they still couldn't win it."

Victorino enjoyed playing for the national team but had doubts about the future of the World Baseball Classic.

"I don't think something like the WBC will ever take off in terms of popularity," he said. "There's really no ideal time to play it. You're not in the best shape to play baseball at the beginning of the season. At the end of the season, you're exhausted. And obviously you can't do it in the middle of the season."

TWO WEEKS AFTER THE INTERNATIONAL TOURNAMENT, the regular season major league schedule was slated to begin.

The 2008 Phillies were going to be a tough act to follow.

The swapping of longtime left fielder Pat Burrell for veteran Raul Ibañez represented the only significant difference between the Phillies team that won the World Series and the team that took the field on Opening Day 2009. Under new general manager Ruben Amaro Jr., who replaced the retiring Pat Gillick, the Phillies let free agent Burrell walk in favor of signing Ibañez to a three-year, $31.5 million contract. Burrell ended up inking a two-year, $16 million deal with the Rays.

The team had not changed much, but the mood of Phillies fans certainly had. In a city whose identity is so tightly bound with sports, a championship team meant a better self-image.

"I think for the first time in a long time, Philadelphia didn't feel like it was playing second fiddle to anyone," Rollins said. "It was no longer that city whose teams had always tried but couldn't quite make it. There was this sense of hope that this is a city of winners. You see it driving down the streets. People are wearing Phillies jerseys and wearing them with pride. They can choose anybody on the team, and as long as it has the Phillies and a name and number on it, that's all that matters."

The World Series victory had meant so much to the city, which made the loss of a man synonymous with Phillies baseball that much harder to take.

A week into the 2009 season, legendary radio and television announcer Harry Kalas collapsed and died in the broadcast booth before a game in Washington against the Nationals. Kalas had narrated the baseball-playing months in Philadelphia for nearly 40 years. His distinctive call of "That ball is outta here!" for home runs and references to "Michael Jack Schmidt" never felt like contrived catchphrases. His deep, rich voice and chemistry with longtime color commentator Richie Ashburn, who passed away in 1997, led to his induction into the broadcasters' wing of the Baseball Hall of Fame in 2002. Kalas was 73 at the time of his death.

"We lost our voice today," Phillies president David Montgomery said at a press conference after Kalas' passing.

The day preceding Kalas' death, the Phillies defeated the Rockies in Colorado on a pair of late-game two-run home runs by Chase Utley and Matt Stairs. The pinch-hit shot by Stairs in the top of the ninth inning, which gave the Phillies a 7–5 lead, turned out to be Kalas' last home run call.

"I talked to him the morning he died," Stairs said. "We talked about the [previous season's] playoffs and how things were going with the season so far. It was two great honors to be part of a world championship in Philadelphia and to have the last home run he called be mine."

On that sad day in Washington, the Phillies had a game to play. But on the fly, the team conceived of ways to honor the longtime announcer. Victorino, Ryan Howard, and reliever Scott Eyre took puffs from a cigarette in the visiting dugout. Kalas' son, Todd, said the players were aware that his dad "was always running outside the stadium to grab a smoke right before a game." The gesture was criticized by some who observed that years of smoking may have contributed to Kalas' health problems.

But everyone agreed that Victorino's tribute during the Nationals game itself was spot-on perfect. In the top of the third inning, after hitting a home run off Daniel Cabrera, Victorino made the sign of the cross and then pointed up to the broadcast booth as he touched home plate.

The Phillies had been scheduled the following day to meet with President Barack Obama at the White House to receive congratulations for winning the World Series, but that visit was postponed until the team's next trip to Washington.

Todd Kalas, a broadcaster for the Rays, said his dad's ties to Hawaii gave him a special bond with Victorino. "His first minor league broadcasting job was with the [Triple A] Hawaii Islanders, and that's when he met my mom, who was born and raised in Hawaii," Todd said. "He felt a connection with anybody from Hawaii, so I knew there was a good chance he and Shane would hit it off."

Victorino made sure the tributes to Kalas carried through the rest of the season.

"When he passed away, I wondered if we could get something from Harry to put in the dugout," Victorino said. "I thought it would be fitting to get the powder-blue jacket and white shoes he wore, so we reached out to his wife and got them. It had a lot of meaning to walk out every day and see that stuff. The city is still embracing what Harry has done for us as players, as fans, as citizens of Philadelphia. I remember when I was a kid hearing him on NFL Films and thinking how much I loved that voice. When I got called up to the Phillies in 2005, I heard that voice and thought, *Why does that sound so familiar?* It took me a little while, but

I finally figured out it was the guy I grew up listening to on NFL Films. Then I found out he had ties to Hawaii. I've been told Harry was one of my biggest supporters. People said he loved the way I played the game, and that meant a lot to me."

The way the Phillies came together to remember his father moved Todd Kalas. "It was really neat that they kept him a part of their celebrations all year, because Dad loved being around the team," he said. "The 1993 team that went to the World Series was the one he was probably closest with. They were a bunch of different characters, and they'd go out and share some cocktails with him. But the 2008 team gave him a chance to do something he had never gotten to do before because they weren't allowed to [locally] broadcast World Series games [when the Phillies won the World Series] in 1980. He always had a special place for the 2008 team because of that."

For the rest of the 2009 season, the players wore "HK" patches on their uniforms.

Harry Kalas would have enjoyed a late April game at Florida that turned into one of strangest the Phillies played all year. After falling behind the Marlins 3–0 in the first inning, neither team had scored again before the game went to the top of the ninth. Then Florida closer Matt Lindstrom had a meltdown for the ages. Lindstrom had yielded three walks and two runs when Victorino came to the plate with the bases loaded and two outs. At the rate he was going, it appeared Lindstrom might walk in the tying run, especially after his errant 1-1 pitch forced Victorino to scurry to get out of the way. But when Lindstrom came back with another fastball, Victorino knocked it into the right-field stands for his first regular season grand slam. The Phillies went on to win the game 7–3 en route to a series sweep of the division-leading Marlins. The grand slam extended a hitting streak for Victorino that eventually reached 16 games. Then he plummeted back to earth, going 1-for-27 on a six-game homestand against the Braves and Dodgers.

The Phillies won the 2008 World Series less than a week before the election of President Obama, and the following May they were the first major sports team to visit him at the White House. In his remarks on the South Lawn, Obama jokingly wondered whether his Delaware-born campaign manager, David Plouffe, cared more about his victory or the Phillies' victory. He also mentioned that Vice President Joe Biden, a former Delaware senator, was a fan of the team.

"This is a team made up of guys who don't quit," the president said. "Cole Hamels, the unbelievable playoff ace. Chase Utley, a throwback who plays hurt and plays hard and never complains. Brad Lidge, who came to the Philly organization looking for a fresh start and who went a perfect 48-for-48 in save opportunities all season long and who wiped away 28 years of near-misses and heartbreak with that final strikeout."

The commander-in-chief later singled out Victorino, a fellow Hawaiian, for his role in the Phillies' World Series victory.

"Shane, we don't get that many baseball players from Hawaii in the majors. Where did Shane go? He was around here somewhere. He was pointing out the Hawaiian flag on the carpet in there," he joked.

The shout-out from the president showed that regardless of whether Victorino was in the clubhouse or the White House, he was always on the move.

On the return trip to Washington, Victorino broke out of his slump with five hits in a four-game sweep of the Nationals. The Phillies finished May with a home sweep of Washington to cap a 17–11 month that put them eight games over .500 and in first place, half a game ahead of the New York Mets.

The Phillies and Mets both struggled in interleague play in June, allowing the Marlins to make a move back toward the top of the NL East. But the Phillies won nine out of 10 before the All-Star break to put some distance between themselves and the rest of the division. One of those wins came against the Reds on a walk-off single by Victorino in the bottom of the ninth.

After a streaky first half, Victorino went into the break hitting .309 with six home runs and 42 RBIs, to go along with 15 stolen bases. Those were All-Star caliber numbers, but he finished only fifth among National League outfielders in fan voting. He got another chance to make the team, however, when he was one of five players chosen to compete in an extra round of online voting to pick a final player for each league's roster. To secure his first All-Star appearance, Victorino had to garner more support than Pablo Sandoval of the Giants, Mark Reynolds of the Diamondbacks, Matt Kemp of the Dodgers, and Cristian Guzman of the Nationals.

In an attempt to mobilize Victorino's base, the Phillies concocted a plan to have him spend an afternoon going door-to-door in Philadelphia to personally appeal to his constituents. Philadelphia mayor Michael Nutter hit the streets with him to share the art of campaigning.

"Mayor Nutter and I went around to a bunch of neighborhoods," Victorino said. "I was definitely hesitant to do it at the beginning, but it turned out to be a great idea. He did most of the knocking and talking. I kind of sat back and listened to him as he went into campaign mode."

The idea of neighborhood canvassing was familiar to Victorino, whose father, Mike, was elected to the first of three terms on the Maui County Council in 2006. Victorino did not mind asking for All-Star votes, but he drew the line there. "You can't keep everybody happy in politics, so it's not something I ever want to be involved in," he said. "But going around with Mayor Nutter was definitely an interesting way to get a first-hand look at campaigning."

The Phi Delta Theta International Fraternity, which earlier that year had given Victorino its annual Lou Gehrig Award for his work in raising money for ALS, also urged members to throw support behind the Flyin' Hawaiian.

After four days of voting, Victorino emerged victorious, becoming the first Mauian and fourth Hawaiian ever selected to an All-Star Game. All the other All-Star Hawaiians—Charlie Hough, Ron Darling, and Sid Fernandez—had been pitchers.

The National League squad in St. Louis was heavy on Phillies. Charlie Manuel managed the team. Second baseman Chase Utley and left fielder Raul Ibañez were voted in as starters. Victorino, first baseman Ryan Howard, and right fielder Jayson Werth got picked as bench players. But an injury to Carlos Beltran of the Mets took Victorino from last man in the All-Star Game to starting center fielder.

Before the game, Victorino again got some face time with President Obama, who was in town for the festivities. The president made the rounds in the National League clubhouse, giving firm handshakes to several players as the cameras rolled. But when he came to Victorino, the two hugged like old friends. Victorino then presented him with a jar of macadamia nuts and other gifts. "Aw, that's what I'm talking about!" Obama exclaimed. "That's the Aloha spirit right there."

Later, Victorino explained the gesture. "It was a nice thing to be able to give the president a taste of home," he told MLB.com. "It was nice to see him again."

That prompted Werth to quip, "I told Shane he didn't have to campaign anymore. He already made the All-Star team."

The good vibes carried over to the game. In the second inning, Victorino stroked a single off Roy Halladay, then of the Toronto Blue Jays, and came around to score. The American League, however, won the game 4–3.

Back in Philadelphia, Amaro Jr. was busy working the phones in an attempt to make the Phillies stronger for the second half of the season. Over the All-Star break, the Phillies added depth to their pitching rotation by signing three-time Cy Young Award winner Pedro Martinez to a one-year, $1 million contract. Martinez, a free agent, had not appeared in a game since the previous September with the Mets.

"I don't expect to be the same Pedro that I was when I was 26," the 37-year-old right-hander told reporters before being sent to the minors for a few tune-up starts. "There's a lot of innings I've pitched since then. It's not the same, but I still feel like I can still bring something to the table."

Not content with picking up just one pitcher, the Phillies then traded four minor leaguers to the Indians for 2008 AL Cy Young winner Cliff Lee and outfielder Ben Francisco. The deal left no doubt that the Phillies' front office was serious about getting back to the World Series. Unlike the season before, when CC Sabathia went to the Brewers before the trade deadline, the Phillies landed the best available pitcher in 2009.

Victorino, who had four three-hit games and two four-hit games in July, was pleased that management took aggressive steps to make the team better. He noted that the new acquisitions did not come at the expense of team cohesiveness. "When Pedro came, he brought the utmost personality to the clubhouse," he said. "He fit right in. Cliff Lee was the same way. They came from teams where they were *the* guys, but they fit right in here. That is also a credit to the upper echelon of our management. Ruben's done a great job. Pat Gillick did a great job. Dave Montgomery's done a great job. They haven't brought in anybody who's created any kind of imbalance.

"We're with each other from mid-February through October, and there is a lot going on. There might be troubles at home or something else serious going on. But guys don't snap, because there is always somebody around to pick him up.

"We are men, and we all have our ego and personalities. Jimmy [Rollins] has the radio next to his locker. He's the radio guy. Jimmy plays a certain CD before the game, and everybody buys into it. Everybody knows it's a team thing. That sounds like a small thing, but it's the kind of thing that matters when you're around guys for all those months."

A 20–7 RECORD IN JULY put the Phillies six games in front of second-place Florida. The two-time defending NL East champs were cruising.

A good team that wins is fun to watch. But a few side dramas during a long season help keep things interesting. In the dog days of August, Victorino provided fans with a lot to talk about around the water cooler and on the blogs.

The first incident occurred while the Phillies were trying to avert a sweep by the visiting Marlins, their closest competitor in the NL East. A win in the final game of the three-game series would mean the difference between a six-game lead and a four-game lead over Florida. The Marlins were up 3–1 in the sixth inning when Ryan Howard was called out on strikes by home-plate umpire Ed Rapuano with two outs and two runners on base. The Phillies bench grumbled at the call.

In the top of the seventh, Rapuano took umbrage with Victorino's body language in center field. After a close pitch was called a ball, the center fielder raised his arms in protest. When Rapuano thought he saw Victorino gesture a second time, he booted him from the game. That prompted Victorino to storm in from the outfield to confront the umpire. The sellout crowd chanted Victorino's name and heartily booed Rapuano for the remainder of the game.

Werth replaced Victorino in center and committed a two-base error that allowed three unearned runs to score. The Marlins went on to a 12–3 rout, a win that tightened the division race, at least for the time being.

Afterward, Rapuano explained his rationale for ejecting Victorino.

"I gave him the chance to not do it again," Rapuano said. "He's right in the line of sight and he's out in front of everybody, waving his arms in disgust of a pitch that I called. It is very simple."

Victorino denied he was trying to show up the umpire. "I love Ed. He's a great umpire," he said. "But when Ryan struck out on a close pitch, things were being said from the dugout. In the top half of the next inning, there was another close pitch that went against us. The fans were really riding him. He said later he saw me throw my arms up twice, but I just did it once."

Charlie Manuel chalked up the incident to Victorino's fiery personality.

"Shane likes to joke and kid around, and there's nothing wrong with that," Manuel said. "The umpire who threw him out is someone with a bubbling personality, someone who likes to talk. Before the game, he was joking with Jimmy Rollins and Shane. When he threw Shane out, it was without a doubt a little bit of an overreaction."

Lost in the shuffle of the memorable and unique ejection was that it was Victorino's first in more than three years in the majors. For someone who battled self-control problems his entire childhood and got kicked out of numerous games in high school, his ability to keep his cool was a sign of real maturity.

"I definitely lost my temper a few times in high school, and maybe that's a time you can get away with stuff like that," he said. "But part of growing up was coming to understand that I'm responsible for my actions. I didn't want to be known as somebody who had a hard time controlling himself. I wanted to be known as someone who played the game the right way."

Victorino experienced another adventure in center field a few days later in a game at Wrigley Field against the Chicago Cubs. The nationally televised night game was Pedro Martinez's first chance to show Phillies fans how much he had left in his tank. His addition to the rotation prompted Manuel to send a struggling Jamie Moyer to the bullpen.

Martinez looked like his old self through the first few innings, and he got a ton of offensive support from Victorino and the rest of the team. By the end of the fourth inning, the Phillies were pasting the Cubs 12–1, thanks in part to a Victorino triple and two-run home run.

The game seemed destined to be remembered as a successful start to Martinez's tenure with the Phillies. Then something happened that forced Pedro to share the headlines with Victorino.

In the bottom of the fifth inning, the Cubs had the bases loaded with one out when Jake Fox lifted a Martinez pitch toward the warning track in left-center field. Victorino raced back, got under the ball, and prepared to make the catch. But as the ball landed in his glove, he experienced something unusual.

"I felt an object hit me, and then I was all wet," Victorino said. "I didn't know what was going on. I had to get the ball in because there were runners on base. After I threw it in, I looked around and tried to figure out what happened."

The answer was that a denizen of the Wrigley Field bleachers had doused Victorino with a cup of beer, the type of act that many thought only possible in hardscrabble Philadelphia, New York, or Boston. But a century of losing had apparently made at least one Cubs fan as ornery as his East Coast counterparts.

"He had the most unbelievable timing," Victorino said of the fan's ability to drench him just as he made the catch. "If he had to do it again, I guarantee he wouldn't have timed it that perfectly."

Immediately after the incident, left fielder Raul Ibañez pointed out a man in the bleachers who was yelling at Victorino as the likely perpetrator behind the beer shower. Security officers swooped in and escorted the fan from the stadium. They had the wrong guy, however. The real culprit had not stuck around to taunt his victim; he had instead disappeared into the crowd.

Fortunately, he could not escape technology.

As soon as videos of the incident popped up on the Internet, 21-year-old college student Johnny Macchione of Bartlett, Illinois, realized he was a wanted man and turned himself in to police. Based on a criminal complaint by the Cubs and Victorino, Chicago police cited Macchione for battery and illegal conduct in a sports facility, both misdemeanors.

Macchione apologized to Victorino and to Cubs management for acting in a way that reflected poorly on fans of the team. And Victorino forgave.

"It was a situation where somebody made a simple mistake," Victorino said. "Nobody got hurt, and I hope he learns from the mistake. I didn't want to press charges, but Major League Baseball wanted me to so they could teach him and other fans a lesson. Just because a fan's behind a fence and I'm on the field doesn't mean he can throw beer at me. If he did that to me on the street, I might have gone ballistic.

"I love Wrigley Field. It's one of my favorite places to play. I love the fact that the fans there are loud and so into the game. After the incident, I got so many letters of apology, and a security person for the Cubs took me aside and told me what an embarrassing moment it was for Cubs fans. The guy got caught up in the moment. It was as simple as that."

The Phillies swept the three-game series at Wrigley before moving on to Atlanta to face the Braves, where Victorino dashed around center field as if he was trying to outrun a tidal wave of beer. In the first game of the Atlanta series, he made no fewer than three spectacular catches. He sprinted after and caught up with a drive by Yunel Escobar in the second inning. He robbed Brian McCann of extra bases in the fifth. And he banged into the wall to take a hit away from Garret Anderson in the sixth. Victorino's defense propelled the Phillies to a 3–2 win and helped his case for a second consecutive Gold Glove Award.

Garry Maddox, the former Phillies center fielder and a successful businessman in Philadelphia who regularly attended games at Citizens Bank Park, enjoyed watching Victorino roam center field. "I watch the games from right field, so I'm behind him a little bit. I notice the jumps he gets on the ball," Maddox said. "A good jump is about recognizing very quickly where the ball is going and then taking the best path to the ball. He is fearless out there, and by that I mean he comes in really close and isn't afraid that the ball will be hit over his head or in the gap."

With Cliff Lee living up to his billing as a top-of the-rotation starting pitcher, the Phillies were beginning to zero in on another division title. Lee won his first five starts with his new team, a stretch that included two complete games.

Unlike the previous two seasons, the Phillies did not need a late push to win the NL East. The slimmest their lead ever got in September was four games, and that was with just six games left in the season.

The Phillies all but wrapped up the division on September 13 when they swept a doubleheader against the Mets. In the second game of the twin bill, Martinez pitched eight scoreless innings against his former team in a 1–0 victory. That same day, the second-place Marlins fell to the Nationals. Those results gave the Phillies a 6½-game lead with just 16 to play. Barring a collapse of the same magnitude as the Mets' in 2007, the Phillies were on their way to a third straight division title. They officially clinched the NL East after the 158th game of the season on September 30.

A dry spell in the final weeks of the season deprived Victorino of a .300 batting average, but 2009 featured career highs for him in hits, RBIs, doubles, triples, and games played. It was the second straight season he led the team in batting average and scored more than 100 runs.

Kevin Towers, who as general manager of the Padres took a chance on Victorino in the 2002 Rule 5 Draft, observed Victorino evolving into a star during the 2009 season.

"I think that ballpark's perfect for him," said Towers, who became general manager of the Arizona Diamondbacks late in the 2010 season. "What power he does have really plays at Citizens Bank Park. He can hit home runs in that park, he puts pressure on the 'D,' he puts pressure on the pitcher, and when he gets on base, he can very easily turn a walk into scoring a run. He's one of those guys who can drive you crazy. He's a big man in a little body and he plays like a big man and has the confidence of a big man."

Most players hit for a higher average in games their teams win, but Victorino's numbers in 2009 suggested that his performance and the success of the team were even more closely linked than normal. In the 90 games in which he played that the team won, he hit a staggering .354. In the 66 appearances he made in losing efforts, his average was a dismal .197.

Howard had another huge year, slugging 45 home runs and knocking in 141 runs. Werth had a breakout year with 36 homers and 99 RBIs. And Ibañez, who cooled off after a torrid start to the 2009 season, more than made up for Burrell's absence.

Only the Yankees, Angels, and Red Sox scored more runs than the Phillies during the 2009 season.

Three Phillies pitchers tied for the team lead in wins: Joe Blanton, Moyer, and one of the most pleasant surprises of the season, rookie J.A. Happ. With the addition of Lee and Martinez, the pitching staff appeared more formidable than the year before. The big question mark for the Phillies was Hamels, who had failed to build upon his successful 2008 campaign. In 2009, he won only 10 games, and his ERA was more than a run higher than the season before.

One of the most marked differences between 2008 and 2009 was Brad Lidge. In 2008 he had come through on every save opportunity. In 2009, his first blown save came in April, and he finished with a major league–leading 11 for the season. Lidge, who spent time on the disabled list in 2009 with knee inflammation, finished the regular season with an 0–8 record and a 7.21 ERA. His poor performance led Manuel to take the closer's role away from him in September.

Despite the struggles in the bullpen, the team was playoff-tested and had more depth than the year before.

It would be hard to top the 2008 postseason, but the Phillies were going to give it their best shot.

CHASING HISTORY

ENTERING THE 2009 POSTSEASON, THE NEW YORK YANKEES were the last team to repeat as World Series champions, having won three straight titles from 1998 to 2000. The last National League team to win back-to-back Fall Classics was the Cincinnati Reds in 1975 and 1976.

Now it was the Phillies' turn to try.

The first task at hand was getting past the Colorado Rockies, the team that had steamrolled them in the 2007 National League Division Series. At that point, the Phillies were playoff newbies. This time around, they were defending champions.

The Phillies' regular season record of 93–69 was only a game better than the wild-card Rockies, who after an 18–28 start under former manager Clint Hurdle went 74–42 with Jim Tracy at the helm. Colorado featured a balanced offensive attack and three starting pitchers who won 15 or more games. Tracy's club had won 20 of 31 games to finish the season, a hot streak that rivaled the one they had going into the 2007 postseason. In short, the Rockies were no pushovers.

At the start of the NLDS, Charlie Manuel faced a dilemma every major league manager would have loved to have. The question: who should get the ball in Game 1—2008 postseason hero Cole Hamels or 2008 AL Cy Young Award winner Cliff Lee? Lee, who was injured the only other time his team made the playoffs, had been terrific since joining the Phillies in early August. Hamels had struggled for much of the 2009 season, but his four wins in the 2008 postseason, which earned him National League Championship Series and World Series MVP honors, showed he was capable of winning the big game.

Whatever Manuel decided, the Phillies had a potentially formidable 1-2 punch in the rotation.

From his view in center field, Victorino had seen both pitchers master opposing lineups.

"It was fun to watch," he said. "I'd be out there and think, *How does Cole throw the changeup the way he does? How does Cliff throw the curveball that way?* I just enjoyed watching them pitch."

Manuel opted to go with the hot hand, sending Lee to the mound in the opener to face the Rockies' Ubaldo Jimenez at Citizens Bank Park.

In retrospect, it was a very good choice. On a day that featured gusts of wind up to 40 miles per hour, Lee pitched a complete-game gem and every player in the Phillies lineup, Lee included, got at least one hit as the defending champs coasted to a 5–1 win over Colorado. Victorino contributed a double and a stolen base in the win. In addition to throwing a masterpiece, Lee picked up his first career stolen base in the game. It appeared base-running guru Davey Lopes could work his magic on just about anyone.

The Phillies, playing in front of a record crowd of 46,452, had picked up where they left off the previous October.

Already up a game in the best-of-five series, Hamels looked to put the Phillies firmly in control with a win in Game 2. History, however, was not on his side. The only postseason loss of his career had come against the Rockies in Game 1 of the 2007 NLDS. In his lone career regular season outing against Colorado, which came in his first start of 2009, he was touched for 11 hits and seven runs in just 3⅔ innings.

In Game 2 of the NLDS, the Rockies again enjoyed success against Hamels, jumping out to a 4–0 lead and fending off a late Phillies rally to win 5–4. Victorino, who had three hits in the game, lined out with runners on first and second to seal a frustrating loss.

With the NLDS deadlocked 1–1, the Phillies traveled to Coors Field for the pivotal third game of the series. During the previous year's playoffs, the Phillies had not trailed in any series. To keep that from happening in 2009, Manuel chose to send playoff veteran Pedro Martinez to the mound in Denver for Game 3. But snow and record-low temperatures in the teens prompted Major League Baseball commissioner Bud Selig to postpone the game 12 hours before the scheduled first pitch. By calling it off, he hoped to avert the type of criticism he got when he let the Phillies and Rays start Game 5 of the 2008 World Series in cold and rainy conditions.

While the Phillies and Rockies got the night off, the Los Angeles Dodgers finished off a sweep of the St. Louis Cardinals in the other National League Division Series.

With an extra day of rest, Manuel scratched Martinez in favor of rookie J.A. Happ, whose 12–4 record during the season convinced his manager he could handle the playoff spotlight. The game-time temperature in Denver was 30 degrees. Undaunted by the cold, Victorino trotted out to center field in the bottom of the first inning in short sleeves.

The broadcasters on the nationally televised game commented on the Flyin' Hawaiian's choice of summery apparel. He shrugged it off, however, as merely a personal preference.

"I just don't like wearing sleeves if I can possibly help it," he explained. "I'll wear them if it's rainy and cold like it was at home in the '08 World Series. But other than that, I'm not a big sleeves guy."

Both starters, Happ and Jason Hammel of the Rockies, were long gone by the time Game 3 was decided. The seesaw battle was tied 5–5 in the top of the ninth inning when the Phillies manufactured the go-ahead run. Jimmy Rollins singled, advanced to second on a Victorino sacrifice bunt, and came in to score on a Ryan Howard sacrifice fly. Brad Lidge, who did not inspire the kind of confidence in 2009 that he had in 2008, recorded the save, getting the final out of the game with the potential tying and winning runs on base.

Another Phillies win would set up a National League Championship Series rematch with the Dodgers.

The Phillies and Rockies both returned to their Game 1 starters for Game 4 at Coors Field.

The Phillies got out to a lead in the top of the first inning when Victorino jumped on a 99-mph fastball from Jimenez and sent it into the Rockies' bullpen for a solo home run. It was Victorino's second career postseason home run against Jimenez, one of the rising stars of the game.

The game remained 1–0 until the sixth inning when the teams traded runs. With one out and a runner on in the bottom of the eighth, Manuel lifted Lee, whose pitch count had reached 117. Before Ryan Madson could close out the inning, the Rockies scored three runs to take a 4–2 lead.

Huston Street, the Rockies' closer who had given up the winning run the night before, came in to try to close out the win and force a deciding

Game 5 in Philadelphia. But for the second night in a row, he failed to get the job done. Ryan Howard hit a two-out double to score Victorino and Chase Utley, tying the game. On the play, Victorino initially missed third base and had to scramble back to touch the bag. Due to the mishap, Utley came within a few feet of passing Victorino on the base paths, which would have made Utley the third out and given the Rockies the win. Catastrophe averted, Jayson Werth then singled to bring Howard home and give the Phillies a 5–4 lead.

If the Phillies' bullpen could do what the Rockies closer had failed to do, the defending champs would be on to the next round.

Manuel did it by committee. Scott Eyre started the ninth but gave way to Lidge with two outs and two runners on base. Lidge then struck out Troy Tulowitzki to end the game.

It had been another good playoff series for Victorino, who went 6-for-17 with four runs scored in the four games. Utley, Howard, and Werth also provided key hits against the Rockies. And the Phillies' bullpen, a weakness of the team during the season, came through by winning two of the three games. Now, the only obstacle remaining in the team's quest for a second straight World Series appearance was the Los Angeles Dodgers.

THE 2009 NATIONAL LEAGUE CHAMPIONSHIP SERIES was a sequel of the year before. For teams on opposite coasts that played each other only a handful of times during the regular season, the Phillies and Dodgers had in a two-year span developed a dynamic postseason rivalry.

Jimmy Rollins suggested several Phillies harkened back to their childhoods when they played L.A. "We have so many guys on the team from Southern California who grew up in San Diego or Los Angeles," he said. "They want to beat the Dodgers because that's their home team. And guys like me from Northern California, even though I was an A's fan, when it came down to Dodgers-Giants, I wanted the Giants. Now it's my chance, and I want to beat the Dodgers."

Maybe Rollins had a point. In the 2008 NLCS, Utley and Greg Dobbs, both from the Los Angeles area, went a combined 9-for-23. Hamels, a San Diego native, beat the Dodgers twice and was named MVP of that series. And Madson, who hailed from Long Beach, won a game and pitched five scoreless innings. Rollins, who struggled for much of the series, awakened in the series-clinching game, hitting a home run.

This time around, the two teams had swapped roles. In 2008, the Phillies were the club coming off a playoff defeat the season before. They played like a team on a mission until there were no more games left to win. In 2009, it was the Dodgers who hoped to build upon recent playoff failure.

"I certainly believe we grew a lot from '08 to '09," Dodgers manager Joe Torre said. "We had a little better idea going into the series of what to expect, as opposed to not really knowing what the whole playoff stuff is all about. We had high expectations of ourselves."

Another difference in 2009 was that the Dodgers finished two games ahead of the Phillies during the season, which gave them home-field advantage. In 2008, the Dodgers never recovered after beginning the series with two losses in Philadelphia.

Dodgers third baseman Casey Blake was optimistic going into the rematch. "We swept the Cubs in '08, and nobody expected us to do that," he said. "Then we swept the Cardinals in '09 and that surprised everybody, too. I felt like we belonged there. It helped that everybody was familiar with that atmosphere from the year before. I thought it was just as good, if not a better Phillies team. It was going to come down to who played better baseball during those few days."

Familiarity between playoff foes can breed contempt, especially when the teams in question nearly came to blows the previous year. But Victorino, who found himself in the middle of the benches-clearing incident in the 2008 NLCS, saw no reason for the tension to carry over.

"It was a totally different atmosphere in 2009," Victorino said. "There was no friction between the teams."

Any lingering hard feelings were expressed in the first inning of the series opener. Victorino singled but made the final out of the inning when he broke too soon for second on a stolen base attempt. As the Dodgers left the field, catcher Russell Martin taunted Victorino.

"Martin started running his mouth, but that was okay," Victorino said. "We were going to let our play do the talking."

And that is exactly what they did in Game 1. The Phillies scored five runs in the fifth and three in the eighth to outslug the Dodgers 8–6 in a four-hour contest at Dodger Stadium. Hamels was less than sharp but pitched well enough to win a playoff-series opener for the fourth time in his career. Victorino collected two of the Phillies' eight hits, but the biggest offensive contributions came from Carlos Ruiz and Raul Ibañez, who each blasted three-run home runs.

Pedro Martinez got a chance to make his first playoff appearance as a Phillie in Game 2. He had thrown only seven innings in the final three weeks of the season, raising the question of whether he would be rested or rusty when he took the mound in Los Angeles to try and give his team a 2–0 series lead against the Dodgers for the second straight year.

Pedro did everything he could to help make that happen, throwing seven innings of two-hit, no-run baseball. When Manuel lifted him for a pinch hitter in the top of the eighth inning, the Phillies led 1–0. But five relievers could not hold the lead and J.A. Happ, coming out of the bullpen after his start in the NLDS, forced in the go-ahead run with a bases-loaded walk to Andre Ethier. Dodgers closer Jonathan Broxton shut down the Phillies in the ninth to secure a 2–1 win that evened the series at a game apiece.

The Phillies had lost a chance to take a commanding series lead with two road wins, but by taking one game at Dodger Stadium, they were in a position to avoid having to go back to Los Angeles if they could take the middle three games of the series at Citizens Bank Park.

Game 3 pitted Lee against Hiroki Kuroda, whose pitch over Victorino's head in the 2008 playoffs created the moments of high tension between the teams. Coming into the game, Lee had yielded just two earned runs in 16⅓ innings in the postseason.

The Phillies' offense staked Lee to a 6–0 lead after two innings. The team's four-run bottom of the first featured a little bit of everything the team had to offer: Victorino singled and stole a base; Howard grooved a two-run triple; and Werth hit a bomb to center field.

Lee pitched eight scoreless innings, giving up just three hits and striking out 10. A three-run home run by Victorino in the bottom of the eighth came long after the game had been decided but it provided the runs that made Game 3 of the 2009 NLCS the most lopsided win in Phillies' postseason history.

It was now up to Torre and the Dodgers to bounce back from a loss that put them in a 2–1 series hole.

The Phillies picked up where they left off the night before by scoring two runs in the first inning of Game 4 off former Phillie Randy Wolf. But another laugher was not to be. Wolf kept pace with Joe Blanton as the Dodgers pulled in front 4–2, and when the late innings rolled around, so began a battle of the bullpens reminiscent of the previous year's NLCS Game 4. In that game, Victorino's two-run home run off Cory Wade in the eighth inning tied the game, and Matt Stairs' two-run shot off Broxton gave the Phillies a lead they would not relinquish. In the 2009 rematch, a sixth-inning triple by Victorino helped draw the Phillies a run closer, but the Dodgers held a 4–3 lead entering the bottom of the ninth inning. Once again, out came Broxton to face Stairs, who came up to pinch hit for Pedro Feliz with one out.

Four pitches and no swings later, Stairs was on first base. "People talked about it like he pitched around me, but I think he just didn't want to make a mistake," Stairs said. "He was trying to pinpoint fastballs. Pitching around somebody means throwing four sliders in the dirt."

Eric Bruntlett pinch ran for Stairs. Broxton, apparently rattled by such a quick base on balls, hit Ruiz with a pitch. Dobbs, pinch hitting for Lidge, lined out to third for the second out of the inning. It was up to Rollins, who had only three hits in the series to that point, to prolong the game. And he did more than just that. He ended it with a sharp double that plated Bruntlett and Ruiz for a 5–4 victory. The Phillies had come from behind to steal Game 4 and take a commanding 3–1 series lead.

Through four games, Phillies pitchers had done a good job of keeping the Dodgers' best hitters in check. Outfielders Manny Ramirez and Matt Kemp both entered Game 5 just 4-for-16 with a home run apiece. Ethier picked up three hits in Game 1 but had been hitless since then. Blake and shortstop Rafael Furcal were a combined 4-for-31.

In the first inning of Game 5, however, it appeared the Dodgers' bats were ready to come alive. Ethier put L.A. on top 1–0 with a solo home run off Hamels. But one mighty swing of Werth's bat in the home half of the first gave the Phillies a 3–1 lead.

With the score 4–2 in the fourth inning, the Phillies broke through for two more runs, the latter of which came the hard way for Victorino. Hitting with the bases loaded and two outs, he was plunked, unintentionally, by George Sherrill, forcing in a run that gave the Phillies a 6–2 lead.

The Dodgers refused to quit, however. Entering the bottom of the sixth inning, the Phillies' lead had been trimmed to 6–3. To keep the Dodgers close, Torre brought in Clayton Kershaw, a 21-year-old starting pitcher who had shown flashes of brilliance in his second season in the majors. Kershaw got two quick outs in the inning but then hit Rollins with a pitch. Up came the Flyin' Hawaiian, hitting right-handed against the lefty Kershaw, and he wasted no time jumping on what the young hurler had to offer. First-pitch swinging, he drove a ball to left field that sailed over the fence for a two-run homer that gave the Phillies a commanding 8–3 lead.

"After he hit Jimmy, I was like, 'You know what, I'm going to try and swing at the first pitch,'" Victorino said. "I thought he would try to run one in there, so I got ready to swing at a first-pitch fastball."

Werth's second homer of the day in the seventh further sealed a 10–4 victory that ended with Victorino gloving a Ronnie Belliard pop fly to center field.

For the second straight year, the Phillies were bound for the Fall Classic.

In 2008, Victorino's clutch hitting made him one of the offensive heroes of the first two rounds of the playoffs. In his team's march back to the World Series, he had been just as good. In nine games against the Rockies and Dodgers, he hit .361 with three home runs, seven RBIs, and eight runs scored. But Howard, who hit .333 with two homers and eight RBIs against the Dodgers, was named MVP of the National League Championship Series.

The Phillies were in a familiar situation, going back to the World Series for the second consecutive year.

THREE DAYS AFTER THE PHILLIES ELIMINATED THE DODGERS, the Yankees finished off the Los Angeles Angels in six games in the ALCS to set up a duel between two of baseball's oldest franchises. The 2008 World Series had pitted two teams, the Phillies and the Rays, with a history of losing. The 2009 matchup had other overtones. No team in professional sports was as closely identified with winning as the Yankees, but the franchise that owned 26 World Series titles had not won one since 2000. By Yankees standards, especially in the free-spending 2000s, this constituted a major drought. Now they faced the Phillies, a team with only two championships in its 100-plus-year history but one that entered the series as king of the hill. Adding to the allure of the series was that it would be the first world championship played in the new $1.5 billion Yankee Stadium.

The Phillies and Yankees had not played each other in the World Series since 1950, the year the Bronx Bombers swept the Whiz Kids in four straight games. That, in fact, was the last time teams from Philadelphia and New York met in any kind of major sports championship, mainly because the Yankees and the NFL's New York Jets are the only Big Apple teams not in the same division as their Philadelphia counterparts.

"At a number of levels, this will be a fascinating confrontation," William C. Rhoden wrote in *The New York Times.* "You get the sense that Philadelphia—the fans, not the team—has been looking forward to taking on a glamour franchise that routinely fields the best team that money can buy. New Yorkers and Philadelphians regularly commute to, and hang out, in each other's backyard. Now they get to battle over a World Series championship."

Victorino took the World Series hype in stride. "Even though we were playing the Yankees, I felt like it was just another series," he said. "You can't let yourself think too much about the history of the team you're playing, or you risk beating yourself mentally."

Victorino certainly had enough to occupy his mind. He had experienced flu-like symptoms for several days, and during the break between the NLCS and the World Series, he went to see a doctor.

The diagnosis: a mild case of swine flu.

At the time, the H1N1 virus and its potential to affect millions of Americans was the subject of much media attention.

"My symptoms were starting to go away by the time they figured out what it was," Victorino said. "The people who suffered the most from it were kids and elderly people who couldn't fight the sickness. I had it all through the Dodgers series."

Nothing was going to keep him off the field against the Yankees.

A Philadelphia–New York World Series was likely to produce good baseball, but it was even more certain to generate memorable headlines, stories, and columns from the tabloid press. The New York papers struck first and struck hard a day before the teams faced off in the first game of the series. The target was Victorino, whom the *New York Post* pictured on its back cover. From the waist up, the photo appeared normal, with Victorino wearing a Phillies jersey and his double ear-flap batting helmet. But the paper doctored the bottom half of the photo so that Victorino was seen wearing a cheerleader skirt. The accompanying headline sarcastically read, "Gotham Trembles—The Frillies are Coming to Town!"

Good morning, Mr. Victorino. Have you read the morning paper yet?

"I was getting texts all morning from people asking me if I had seen it," Victorino said. "Finally somebody sent me a picture of it. I was like, 'What!' So I went out and got a copy. I never thought I'd be on the cover of the *New York Post* and definitely not in a skirt! But any press is good press, I guess. Why did they pick me? Maybe I bring something to the table that concerns them. Maybe they were thinking, *He's a guy who might bring excitement or energy to his team, so let's try to make a mockery of him.*"

Asked later by a *Post* photographer to pose with a copy of the paper for the next day's edition, Victorino tersely responded, "No, I'm not holding that up, bro."

That same day, Joanna Malloy of the *New York Daily News* took a shot at the City of Brotherly Love and its fans. "Believe it or not, people down here in Silly-delphia actually think the Phillies will beat the Yankees in the World Series, which starts tomorrow," she wrote.

The editors of the Philadelphia papers did not return fire, instead filling their pages with sober analyses of the two teams that would meet to decide a champion.

Jimmy Rollins, however, helped nudge the tabloid wars along with a bold, serio-comic prediction similar to the one he made prior to the 2007 season when he said the Phillies were going to unseat the Mets as division champs.

"Of course we're going to win," Rollins said on *The Jay Leno Show.* "If we're nice we'll let it go six [games], but I'm thinking five. Close it out at home."

For Rollins to be right, the Phillies needed strong performances from just about everyone. The Rays team they faced in 2008 was full of pluck and potential, but in terms of talent and experience, it was hard to match the 2009 Yankees. New York's lineup featured Derek Jeter, Jorge Posada, and Hideki Matsui, who had all been in pinstripes since New York's last World Series appearance in 2003. Alex Rodriguez and Mark Teixeira, two of the game's best hitters, were gearing up for their Fall Classic debuts. On the mound, CC Sabathia, A.J. Burnett, and Andy Pettitte formed a strong one-two-three punch. And if the Yankees got to the late innings with a lead, they could call on Mariano Rivera, perhaps the greatest closer of all time. With the possible exception of a shaky middle-relief corps, this was a team without discernible weaknesses.

IN GAME 1, LEE MATCHED UP AGAINST LEFT-HANDER SABATHIA, his former Indians teammate and a 19-game winner during the season. Sabathia brought an unblemished 3–0 postseason record into the World Series. The Phillies had reason for confidence, however. In 2008, when Sabathia was with Milwaukee, Philadelphia roughed him up for five runs in 3⅔ innings in the division series, the decisive blow coming when Victorino hit a grand slam.

The duel between Sabathia and Lee, the two immovable forces of the 2009 postseason, looked to be one of the best pitching matchups in recent World Series history.

As expected, Sabathia was good, surrendering only two runs in seven innings of work. But Lee was phenomenal, slicing through the Yankees' lineup and completely confusing and defusing the Bronx Bombers on their own turf. In going the distance at Yankee Stadium, Lee yielded just one unearned run, which came after the game was already out of reach in the ninth inning. He also displayed some nifty glove work, making a behind-the-back snare of a ground ball hit back up the middle by Robinson Cano. Lee's mastery of the Yankees lifted his record in the 2009 postseason to 3–0 and lowered his ERA to 0.54. At the plate, Chase Utley homered twice and Victorino added an RBI single in the ninth as the Phillies beat up on the Yankees' bullpen and cruised to a 6–1 victory. The loss was the Yankees' first at home in the 2009 playoffs.

A victory by the Phillies the following night would send a resounding message that the defending champions had no plans to relinquish their title.

For Game 2, the Fox network took advantage of Victorino's loquaciousness by having him wear a microphone on the field.

"They kind of know who likes to talk a lot during a game," Victorino said. "I did it for them in 2008, and they had fun with it. I remember in the '08 NLCS, when [I was miked and] Rafael Furcal made an error. I looked at him and told him to keep his head up. It was his second error of the inning and you could tell he was a little distraught about what was going on. So I just told him, 'Keep your head up, bro.' A father came up to me later and told me he and his son saw that and thought it was a nice moment."

The second game of the series started off well for the Phillies when designated hitter Matt Stairs knocked in the first run of the game with a single off Burnett. The Yankees knotted the score in the fourth inning on Teixeira's home run off Pedro Martinez. The Bronx Bombers then added single runs in the sixth and seventh innings to take a 3–1 lead. The Phillies had an opportunity to get back in the game in the eighth, but with Rollins on second and Victorino on first, Rivera got Utley to ground into a controversial inning-ending double play. Instant replays showed Utley beat the throw to first, but Major League Baseball rules at the time allowed video review to confirm or overturn only a home run call. The umpire's decision stood. Rivera survived another minor jam in the ninth, striking out Stairs to end the game.

So far the World Series was playing out the same as the National League Championship Series, in which the Phillies split the first two games on the road.

Game 3 was part of a massive sports Sunday for Philadelphia and New York. That Halloween afternoon, the Eagles and Giants squared off at Lincoln Financial Field, with the home team thrashing their NFC East rivals 40–17. Would the day-night, baseball-football doubleheader result in a Philly sweep, or could the Big Apple salvage a split in the nightcap? The answer would have to wait until after Mother Nature played a little Halloween trick on the fans, many decked out in costumes for the occasion. For the second year in a row, a World Series Game 3 at Citizens Bank Park was delayed by rain, this time for more than an hour. It was already past 9:30 PM when Cole Hamels delivered the first pitch of the game, which was played in wet but unseasonably warm conditions.

Hamels, the MVP of the 2008 World Series, had not pitched past the sixth inning of any of his three starts in the 2009 postseason. His counterpart, Andy Pettitte, had already won twice in the playoffs, bringing his career postseason wins to a major league–record 16.

The Phillies got to Pettitte early, taking a 3–0 lead in the bottom half of the second inning on a Werth home run, a bases-loaded walk by Rollins, and a sacrifice fly by Victorino.

The Yankees' first hit of the game came from Alex Rodriguez in the fourth inning. The only question was what kind of hit it was. Rodriguez stood on second base, suggesting a double, but Yankees manager Joe Girardi thought otherwise. He believed the ball had struck an object after going over the fence for a home run, causing it to return to the field of play. Unlike the close play at first base involving Utley in Game 2, this was precisely the type of call that instant replay could decide. The umpires went into the recesses of the stadium to take another look. What they saw on a monitor was that the ball had in fact struck a television camera above the right-field fence. When the umpiring crew re-emerged, Rodriguez was awarded a home run. The Yankees had cut the lead to 3–2.

One of the disadvantages the Yankees faced playing in the Phillies' home ballpark, other than the festive partisan crowd, was the fact that they could not play with a designated hitter as they could in the American League. That meant Pettitte, who was hitting less than .150 for his career, had to swing the bat. In the fifth inning, after yielding a leadoff double to Nick Swisher, Hamels struck out Melky Cabrera, bringing Pettitte to the plate. It appeared that with the light-hitting pitcher coming up, Hamels would get one step closer to working his way out of the jam. But in the latest chapter of Hamels' poor 2009 postseason, Pettitte blooped the first pitch he saw into center field for a hit, scoring Swisher. Following a Jeter single, Johnny Damon doubled in two runs to put the Yankees on top 5–3.

New York went on to win 8–5 to take a 2–1 lead in the series. The highlight of the game for the Phillies was a pair of home runs by Werth, which gave him a record-tying seven for the postseason.

With the loss, the Phillies trailed in a postseason series for the first time since being swept out of the playoffs by the Rockies in 2007.

Rather than risk having Lee pitch on three days' rest, Manuel opted to give Joe Blanton his second start of the postseason in Game 4. He matched up against Sabathia, New York's Game 1 starter who was accustomed to pitching on short rest.

The first two Yankees batters of the game reached base, and both came around to score, giving the visitors an early two-run lead. The Phillies countered with a run in the home half of the inning on back-to-back doubles by Victorino and Utley. A Pedro Feliz single tied the game in the fourth, but the Yankees quickly retook the lead 4–2 with two runs in the fifth. The Phillies fought back to tie the game again on solo home runs by Utley in the seventh and Feliz in the eighth. Though it was not a save situation, Manuel turned to Brad Lidge with the score tied 4–4 in the top of the ninth inning. Lidge's strong playoff outings to that point made a convincing case that he had put his stomach-churning regular season behind him. He entered his first game of the 2009 World Series having not yielded a postseason run since Game 1 of the 2008 National League Division Series, a streak that spanned 13 games and 12⅓ innings.

His Game 4 appearance started off strong, as he retired Hideki Matsui and Derek Jeter in order.

Then came calamity.

Johnny Damon singled and stole second and third bases, putting the go-ahead run 90 feet from home. After Lidge hit Mark Teixeira with a pitch, Alex Rodriguez doubled sharply into the left-field corner to put the Yankees up 5–4. The Yankees had the lead and, with runners on second and third, were a hit away from giving closer Rivera considerable margin for error. They got that hit from Jorge Posada, whose single to left-center field plated Teixeira and Rodriguez.

The Phillies went meekly against Rivera in the bottom half of the ninth, as Victorino grounded out to end the game.

Down 3–1 in the series, the best the Phillies could hope for was a win at home in Game 5 and a return to Yankee Stadium for two more must-win games. The Fightin' Phils had no intention of packing it in, but in retrospect, the frustrating Game 4 loss severely affected their chances of repeating as World Series champs.

"I think that game was a turning point, but we knew we had Cliff on the mound in Game 5, so we felt confident," Victorino said. "All we could do was look at the next game we had. We weren't looking past that."

The Phillies fought back quickly in Game 5 after the Yankees darted in front with a run in the top of the first inning. Utley delivered a three-run homer in the bottom of the inning that gave the Phillies a 3–1 lead. Utley homered again in the seventh inning to become just the second player in major league history to have two multiple–home run games in the same World Series. The only other player to accomplish the feat, Willie Aikens, did it against the Phillies in 1980. Utley also joined Reggie Jackson as the only player to hit five homers in one World Series.

A defining moment in Victorino's 2009 World Series came right before Utley's first home run, when he squared to bunt and was hit in the right index finger by a Burnett fastball. Victorino, who had just recovered from the flu, was now dealing with a hand injury. If he had gotten his way, he would have played all of Game 5, but with the Phillies leading 8–2 in the eighth inning, Manuel pulled him as a precaution. Victorino watched from the bench as the Yankees brought the potential tying run to the plate against Ryan Madson in the top of the ninth. But Madson struck out Teixeira swinging to secure an 8–6 win.

In Game 5, Victorino went hitless for only the fourth time in the playoffs, grounding out twice and popping out. After the game, Victorino confessed that his hand was bothering him. He told reporters it had stiffened up as the game went on, which made it hard to grip the bat.

"I couldn't find my grip, but that still isn't any excuse for me stinking it up at the plate," he said.

Victorino insisted he would be healed in time for Game 6 at Yankee Stadium. The X-rays on his finger came back negative, giving him further reason to shrug off the pain. Nothing was going to keep Victorino out of a hugely consequential World Series game. He was a "gamer." His teammates knew it, and so did his opponents.

"He busted up his finger pretty good," Yankees right fielder Nick Swisher said a few months after the series ended. "For a guy like that to keep going out there and play hard, that's a tough dude, no doubt."

The Phillies had the odds stacked against them, but history proved anything was still possible. Against the Yankees in 2004, the Red Sox had rallied from a 3–0 series deficit to win the American Championship League Series, a comeback capped by two wins at Yankee Stadium, which was exactly what Philadelphia now needed.

Pedro Martinez had pitched well in losing efforts in both his previous starts in the 2009 playoffs. On a chilly 47-degree night in the Bronx, Martinez, who was on the Red Sox team that stunned the Yankees in 2004, looked to help the Phillies stay alive in the 2009 World Series.

Despite his sore hand, Victorino was in the lineup for Game 6.

So was Yankees designated hitter Hideki Matsui, who had been relegated to pinch-hitting duties in the three games played in Citizens Bank Park.

Matsui, who would later be named World Series MVP, almost single-handedly assured that the Phillies would be fighting from behind all night. His two-run home run in the second inning and two-run single in the third propelled the Yankees to an early 4–1 lead. New York struck again for three runs in the fifth, two of them courtesy of a Matsui double.

Howard's two-run blast off Andy Pettitte in the sixth brought the Phillies within striking distance at 7–3, but the Yankees' bullpen kept the visitors at bay the rest of the game.

The 2009 baseball season ended on a harmless grounder to second base by Victorino. The final out of Game 6 set off a raucous celebration in baseball's shiniest new cathedral; the Yankees were champions for the 27th time in their illustrious history.

The man with the injured hand who made that final out would see replays of his last swing the entire off-season. But Victorino had nothing to be embarrassed about. In fact, except for its outcome, his 10-pitch battle against Yankees closer Mariano Rivera was a tense display of stubbornness, which Phillies fans had to respect.

"I made the last out on the biggest stage, but when the game was done, I looked in the mirror and knew I gave it my best shot," Victorino said. "I wasn't going to go down easy. We would have loved to win again in '09, but during that week, the Yankees played better than us."

The old adage is true: you win some, you lose some, and the victories are as sweet as the defeats are bitter. But as Shane Victorino learned at a young age, you always fight until the end.

THE MEASURE OF THE MAN

TEN DAYS AFTER THE WORLD SERIES LOSS TO THE YANKEES, Shane Victorino and about 400 friends and family gathered on a Maui beach to celebrate a joyous occasion. Victorino and his fiancée, Melissa, had intended to wed the previous fall, but to make sure every detail of the special day was exactly right, had postponed the event for a year.

"When you're married to a Major League Baseball player or just trying to get married to one, you have such a small window to plan things," Melissa Victorino said.

The special moment had finally come for the couple who had been together since meeting in Las Vegas in the summer of 2004.

On a beautiful Saturday, Shane and Melissa exchanged vows at St. Anthony of Padua Catholic Church in Victorino's hometown of Wailuku.

Jimmy Rollins, who had a wedding of his own scheduled for January 2010, was a member of the wedding party. Victorino's brother, Mike Jr., served as best man. Ryan Howard attended the event, as did mixed martial arts fighter Chuck Liddell.

After the ceremony, the bride and groom joined their guests for a sunset reception on a white-sand beach.

The nuptials garnered extra attention because another of the invited guests was Jon Gosselin, the star of the reality show *Jon & Kate Plus 8*, a cable television hit that documented a Pennsylvania couple's rearing of eight young children. Shane and Melissa had befriended the Gosselins, and invited both to Maui for the wedding. Before the wedding day arrived, however, Jon and Kate's marriage hit the skids amid allegations that both were having extramarital affairs. The story created a tabloid furor, and the celebrity press began tracking the Gosselins' every move. If Jon was attending a wedding in Maui, dozens of photographers would not be far behind.

Victorino, a celebrity himself who knew a thing or two about invasions of privacy, could have gotten angry at the sight of strangers carrying cameras equipped with telephoto lenses. Instead he decided to have fun with it.

"There were paparazzi on the other side of the bay shooting pictures," said Victorino's childhood friend Lyle Cummings, another of the groomsmen. "Shane was just laughing. He ran down near the water and started jumping up and down and yelling, 'I see you guys, I see you guys!' He didn't care that they were there. He thought it was a big joke."

It was another busy off-season for Victorino.

A few days before his wedding, he learned he had won his second consecutive Gold Glove Award. And a week after he got married, he hosted the Shane Victorino Celebrity Golf Classic in Maui, benefitting the Hawaii Children's Cancer Foundation.

Victorino reconnected at the tournament with Julian Rimm, a Maui teenager he got to know a year earlier during Rimm's battle with bone cancer. As the Phillies were fighting to win the 2008 World Series, Julian was in a fight for his life. He had beaten the cancer, but as a result of losing circulation to his foot during surgery, he had to have two toes amputated. By late fall 2009, he had regained use of his foot and was close to being able to compete in sports again.

"He was feeling great," said Gabi Galler-Rimm, Julian's mother. "Shane looked at Jules and said, 'Okay, let me see it.' So Julian showed him a scar on the outside of his ankle going up his leg from where they removed the bone that had cancer. Shane says, 'No, no, no! That's not what I want to see. Show me the foot.' So Julian sits down and takes off his shoe and sock and shows him his foot. Shane takes a look and says, 'Cool, man, you got a foot!'"

As he had during a visit to the hospital following Julian's surgery, Victorino again put a smile on the young man's face.

Back in Las Vegas in January, Shane took a few weeks to decompress by spending time with his family, playing golf, and attending his stepson Keenan's middle school basketball games.

"It's definitely an adjustment in the off-season," Melissa Victorino said. "During the season, he's in the 'single guy' role a lot of the time, staying in hotels by himself, getting to go out to dinner with the boys every night. It takes some time for him to get back in the swing of things when he gets home. For us, it was about coming up with a parenting system that was both his and mine."

Later in the off-season, Victorino went to the Cayman Islands for Rollins' wedding. The reception featured a favorite dessert of the groom, deep-fried Oreos à la mode, a delicacy Rollins asserts cannot be eaten in moderation. As Rollins made the rounds at the reception, shaking hands and thanking guests for coming, he realized he had yet to sink his teeth into one of the treats. He gazed longingly at the deep-fried Oreos stand where a long line had formed. Then he noticed Victorino on the other side of the stand with the chef, furiously serving ice cream to those in line.

"Shane, what are you doing?" he yelled over.

"I'm trying to get the line to go faster so I can get me some more!" Victorino responded, never looking up from what he was doing.

The memory makes Rollins laugh. "He just wanted to help and wasn't going to stop serving until everybody got theirs," he said. "That's just Shane. He's a very giving and caring person. It comes across in everything he does. And he always wants to be part of something. That's why we call him 'the Mayor.'"

Victorino also entered the fashion world in early 2010 by collaborating on the design of a T-shirt with a company that outfits mixed martial arts fighters. The eye-catching shirt featured everything from a skull to the Hawaiian flag.

In March 2010, the Phillies and New York Yankees matched up again, this time in an exhibition game at the Phillies' spring training facility in Clearwater, Florida. Though nothing was really at stake this time, the spring weather brought both teams' faithful out in force.

Among the standing-room-only crowd of 10,700 at Bright House Field were several dozen people in Phillies jerseys emblazoned with Victorino's No. 8 on the back. In terms of volume, the No. 8's could not compare with the No. 26's (Chase Utley) or the No. 6's (Ryan Howard), but the fans who opted to wear the Flyin' Hawaiian's jersey number made up for their smaller numbers with great enthusiasm.

One of those fans was Sean Cahill, a 30-year-old lifelong Phillies fan who met his wife in South Florida while attending spring training games in 2007. Cahill got a unique and up-close look at the World Series celebration in 2008. A Philadelphia police officer, he was on duty patrolling an area in Northeast Philly the night the Curse of Billy Penn was broken. "It was a little nuts," Cahill said. "They almost flipped my police car over. We were just as happy as they were, but we didn't want anybody to get hurt."

Cahill took a liking to Victorino shortly after Shane's rookie season with the team. "When he first came and was playing, he'd always wave to the fans," Cahill said. "He just seemed like an all-around nice guy. My wife and I are big fans, and we come down to Clearwater every year now. She got me a Victorino jersey for Christmas."

Lisa Baumhauer, a physical therapist from South Jersey, also came to the Phillies-Yankees game to cheer on her favorite player. "I've been wearing his No. 8 for three or four years," she said. "The thing I like about him is how into the game he gets. Every time something good happens, he's the first one out there cheering."

In the Phillies' spring training clubhouse, a catcher and native Hawaiian fighting for a spot on the roster discussed how Victorino's success in the major leagues has had a ripple effect in his home state.

"When you reach that status, kids in Hawaii look up to you," said Honolulu-born Dane Sardinha, who spent part of the 2010 season with the Phillies. "It gives them something to strive for. It's a great thing for a guy like Shane to pave the way."

By Opening Day 2010, three players from Maui—Victorino, catcher Kurt Suzuki of the Oakland Athletics, and relief pitcher Kanekoa Texeira (a distant cousin of Victorino's) of the Kansas City Royals—were on major league rosters. Texeira was in his first season; Suzuki had been in the majors since 2007. Especially because of Victorino, baseball is now a big deal on the island.

"Having three guys from here in the major leagues has promoted baseball," said Craig Okita, who coached Victorino in high school and now manages a Little League team in Wailuku. "It was a lot more popular today than it was before. More and more kids come out and at least try to play."

At St. Anthony High School, Victorino's alma mater, the number of kids coming out for the team has held steady as enrollment at the school has dropped dramatically.

On a warm summer day in 2010, a group of kids and teenagers gathered near the 50-yard line at War Memorial Stadium in Maui to participate in group fitness drills. It was the same football field on which Victorino starred in high school and the same stadium where he set records at track meets.

Kekoa Turbeville, a recent graduate of Kamehameha Maui High School, was getting in some last workouts before heading off to Whitworth University in Spokane, Washington, on a football scholarship.

Like many young athletes on the island, he looked up to Victorino.

"A lot of people here followed his career after he got drafted, and we saw how he didn't achieve everything overnight," Turbeville said. "It was small steps. And he had a lot of adversity along the way. That told me that adversity is something you have to deal with, no matter how good you are. He set a good example for us. Our football coach showed us tapes of Shane playing in high school. To see him back then and to see him now on *SportsCenter*, it's pretty cool."

Lilyana Koa, a social studies teacher at St. Anthony, has used Victorino to help inspire her students to strive for greatness, whether on the ballfield or in other endeavors.

"I do current events with students, and they always want to write about Shane," Koa said. "He gets them pumped up and makes them excited about their community. I make sure they know how hard he worked to get where he is. When he went off to play professional baseball, he was a small fish, and he struggled in the beginning. But he's a role model now, because he shows that no dream is out of reach."

Those looking to emulate Victorino might take another lesson from the way he approached sports long before he reached the professional level.

Fred Engh, a nationally recognized expert on youth sports, believes Victorino's enjoyment of many sports as a child likely helped him develop a healthy relationship with athletics.

"Before the age of 12, kids should be exposed to as many sports as they can, just like Shane," Engh said. "Suppose Shane's parents had been like so many others today that push their children into specializing in one sport and for Shane that sport had been football. He might have failed at football, and the world of baseball might never have heard of Shane Victorino."

For former teammate Jayson Werth, who played four seasons with Victorino before signing a lucrative deal with the Washington Nationals after the 2010 season, the Flyin' Hawaiian was part of what made his time in Philly so special.

"You're not going to find too many Shane Victorinos in the world, if any," Werth said. "We were talking about it the other day. It seems like everybody on this team is like someone you'll never meet again. I think that's what makes our team unique. It makes for good times on and off the field. Everybody gets along great, and Shane's a big part of that. His personality is one of the stronger ones, and I couldn't imagine this place without him."

For as long as he plays baseball, Victorino plans to take nothing for granted.

"I play the game today the same way I played in high school and Little League," he said. "My family always told me it never hurts to hustle. That's still what's embedded in me today. At the end of the night, you might go 0-for-5, but fans can look at you and say, 'He's playing the game hard. He's trying to win the ballgame.' I'm doing something I love, and I'm doing it with passion. Getting the opportunity to play at the highest level is a dream come true, and I love the fact that people recognize me, not so much for my accomplishments but for the way I play the game."

15

STAYING ON TOP

THE TWO-TIME DEFENDING NATIONAL LEAGUE CHAMPION Philadelphia Phillies entered the 2010 season with expectations as high as they had ever been. A fourth consecutive division title and another deep run into the playoffs would elevate the current era to the greatest in Phillies history.

Between the 2009 and 2010 seasons, the Phillies rewarded several current members of the team, including Victorino, with contract extensions. Victorino signed a three-year, $22 million agreement, which bought out his final two years of arbitration and his first year of free agency.

Victorino was thrilled to have his first long-term contract with the Phillies.

"The player that I am is meant for a city like Philadelphia," he said. "The fans there know the game. They love their players. But you have to earn their respect. If you slip up, they'll let you know."

The front office believed Victorino had earned the multiyear extension that represented a raise over his $3.1 million salary in 2009.

"We felt like Shane showed he was a bona fide major leaguer who would be a complementary piece to the core guys that we have," said general manager Ruben Amaro Jr. "He's a guy we felt could help propel us forward and bring home a couple more rings.

"He likes to be the town jokester from time to time. He likes to try and keep things loose in the clubhouse, which is a good thing. I think all in all the guys know when to be serious. We try to create a winning atmosphere here, and I think Shane's pretty aware that his energy is an important part of that."

The new contract also paved the way for Shane and his wife, Melissa, who was pregnant with the couple's second child, to start a charitable foundation, a venture they had planned to undertake the moment it became feasible. Already, Victorino had sponsored two charity golf tournaments, the first for the Aloha Chapter of the Alzheimer's Association and the second for the Hawaii Children's Cancer Foundation. Now the Victorinos were prepared to expand their philanthropic efforts. The foundation's focus would be on the recreational and educational needs of children in Philadelphia, Hawaii, and perhaps eventually, Melissa's native Alaska.

"Philly has a lot of underprivileged areas that are in desperate need of more healthy activities for children to participate in," Melissa Victorino said. "Growing up in the places we did, both Shane and I could relate to how important it is to have these types of things to get involved with."

Garry Maddox, a former Phillie whose civic involvement in Philadelphia dates back more than 30 years, was impressed by Victorino's generosity. "The Phillies organization encourages that players give back to the community," he said. "Some guys do it monetarily, and some do it by giving their time. What I see with Shane is a willingness to do both." After the season, the Philadelphia Sports Writers Association honored Victorino for his philanthropy by naming him its 2010 Humanitarian of the Year.

Gone from the pennant-winning 2009 team was ace Cliff Lee, who got dealt to the Seattle Mariners on the same day the Phillies worked out a separate trade that brought former Cy Young Award winner Roy Halladay from Toronto to Philadelphia. Whether the Phillies could have held on to Lee after acquiring Halladay and signing him to a three-year, $60 million contract extension would be the subject of considerable discussion among fans. The fact that such a debate was even taking place was in itself remarkable. It showed that for the first time in recent memory star players like Halladay were seeking out Philadelphia as a preferred destination.

A move that brought Lee back to the Phillies after the 2010 season was further proof of this new reality. Almost a year to the day that Philadelphia dealt him away, the baseball world was stunned when Lee, a free agent, chose to rejoin the Phillies for less money than the Yankees and Rangers were offering.

"Players want to play in Philly now," Victorino said in 2010. "They see what we've built as a team, the personalities we have, and the enjoyment we have on the field. You see other teams that bump heads or are on edge. Our team's not like that. Everybody goes on the field with the same purpose in mind—to win ballgames and have fun."

Before the 2010 season, Phillies manager Charlie Manuel announced he was dropping Victorino from his customary second slot in the lineup to seventh, a move prompted by the team's off-season signing of second baseman Placido Polanco, a former Phillie who had a successful run as the team's two-hole hitter from 2002 to 2005. Manuel said the shuffling of the batting order demonstrated his confidence in Victorino's ability. In the No. 2 slot, his job was to do whatever was necessary to get on base and to give hitters in the heart of the lineup a chance to knock in runs. Batting near the end of the lineup, he could be more of a free swinger and would likely have more RBI opportunities.

"I can hit him anywhere in the lineup," Manuel said. "He's that kind of player, very versatile. That's why he's such a big part of our team."

Victorino, who had never hit that low in the lineup on a regular basis, accepted the change with an open mind, if not with great enthusiasm.

"Going from two to seven, I won't change my game," he said. "Maybe it'll help me."

Milt Thompson, the Phillies' hitting coach for the first half of the 2010 season, had high hopes for Victorino. "He's one of the most exciting players in the game," Thompson said. "His game is to be a gap hitter. He should hit a lot of triples and doubles. I'm trying to convince him to try and bunt more this season. If he could get 10 or 15 bunt hits, he'd hit .300 easily."

Accordingly, Victorino vowed to work on his bunting. "If I was better at it, I'd probably do it more. It's something I used to do all the time, but I lost the touch for it. It's definitely something I need to do more often," he said.

For the team, 2009 was a lesson in how bad it feels to come up just short of a championship. The 2010 campaign was a chance to try to reclaim supremacy of the baseball world.

"Getting all the way there and losing in '09 left a sour taste in everybody's mouth," pitcher Joe Blanton said before the 2010 season. "Everybody wants to get back and be on top again."

The regular season was only a week old when Jimmy Rollins strained his right calf running out a ground ball, thrusting Victorino into the leadoff role during Rollins' prolonged absence.

Whether he was at the top or bottom of the lineup, however, Victorino struggled offensively in the first month of the 2010 season, hitting only .226.

But he did not allow his difficulties at the plate to affect his defense. In a game in late April against the Braves, he scaled the wall at Turner Field to rob Troy Glaus of a home run and preserve a Halladay shutout.

"I can be in a slump at the plate, but I can win a game on defense whether it be by throwing a guy out on the bases or running down a ball in the outfield," Victorino said. "You can't take your offensive problems with you when you go out to the field."

For the first several weeks of the season, the Phillies again set the pace in the NL East by scoring runs in bunches. The wins were piling up, thanks in part to the performance of Halladay, who won six of his first seven starts, going the distance three times. Those outings helped appease the segment of the fan base still unsure of whether the Phillies should have parted ways with Lee. Some still complained, however, that the Phillies should have had both Halladay *and* Lee on the roster, a lofty goal that would have to wait a season.

Victorino's early season offensive contributions came in spurts.

In two wins in early May against the Mets at Citizens Bank Park, he knocked in seven runs on a three-run home run off Mike Pelfrey and a grand slam off Johan Santana, against whom he was just 2-for-24 coming into the at-bat. Victorino's batting average and on-base percentage continued to disappoint, but his early power numbers put him on pace to shatter career highs in homers and RBIs. It was shaping up to be a different kind of season for Victorino, who to that point was known in baseball circles as a table setter and a spark plug, or in Sabermetric terms, as a guy who could be counted on to "create" a lot of runs.

For a stretch in May, it suddenly became a different type of season for all of the Phillies batters, and it was not the kind of change they might have hoped for. Over the course of a five-game tailspin, the team was shut out four times, including three times in a row by the Mets.

This head-scratching power outage against the Mets was quickly overshadowed, however, during the Phillies' next series against the Marlins. On May 29 in Florida, Halladay threw the second perfect game in Phillies history, blanking the Marlins 1–0. But then it was back to more of the same; the Marlins beat the Phillies 1–0 a day after Halladay's masterpiece.

Throughout the majors, 2010 quickly gained a reputation as the "Year of the Pitcher." Halladay's perfect game came a few weeks after one tossed by Dallas Braden of the Oakland A's. Three days after Halladay's feat, the Tigers' Armando Gallaraga nearly became the third pitcher in 2010 to retire 27 consecutive batters, but a blown call at first base on what would have been the final out cost Gallaraga his perfect game. By season's end, there had been a major league–record 27 games in which a team got one or zero hits. Phillies pitchers were responsible for six of these "low-hitters." The team's stellar pitching had added meaning in a season during which the team paid tribute to Hall of Famer Robin Roberts, a former Phillie who passed away at the age of 83 in early May.

By the end of May, the surging Braves had passed the Phillies to take over the top spot in the NL East. The Phillies played .500 ball in June, allowing the Braves to hold on to first place and the Mets to slip ahead of the Phillies into second.

Rollins missed most of the first three months of the season with his calf injury, and in late June, the team put Chase Utley and Placido Polanco on the disabled list, forcing Manuel to trot out a makeshift lineup. In a four-game span in late June, Manuel put Victorino in four different spots in the batting order—first, second, fifth, and seventh. Around that same time, Dane Sardinha got several starts at catcher, allowing the Phillies to boast two native Hawaiians on the same field.

Despite this nice moment for the Aloha State, the season was not going as planned.

A few days before the All-Star break, having lost two of three to the visiting Braves to fall six games out of first place, Victorino told reporters that Phillies fans needed to think twice before lashing out verbally at the players.

"If I'm a fan of a team and they're not doing good, I get frustrated, too," he said. "But don't throw in the towel. Get behind us. Find a way to get behind us and pick us up. We need them. That's what this game is about. It's not just us. The atmosphere that they've created, it's been awesome. They're still coming out, even though we are struggling. But to hear those things, it's like, 'Oh, really?' It's frustrating when you hear those things from your own fans."

Victorino's words bordered on ones uttered in 2008 by Rollins, who said Phillies fans were front-runners.

There are two types of media markets in baseball—those on the East Coast and those everywhere else in the country. If a player in Minnesota or St. Louis had said the same thing Victorino did, it would have been unlikely to kick up controversy. If anything, it might lead fans to figure out ways to be more supportive of their team.

But not so in Philadelphia, where a player's every move is under the microscope.

"The next couple games after that I heard some things from fans," Victorino said. "They were yelling things like, 'We sell this place out every night, and you're saying we're not fans of the team!' That's not what I was trying to say, but if I pick up a local newspaper or magazine and read a headline, I guess I'm going to believe what it says. And whatever it says becomes embedded in people's heads."

Later in the season, *Philadelphia Inquirer* columnist John Gonzalez jokingly thought up midseason awards for players on the team. He gave Victorino "The Jimmy Rollins F-word Award."

"Shane Victorino stopped just short of calling the fans front-runners for booing the team before the All-Star break," Gonzalez wrote. "The next day, he said he loves the fans here. Be sure to make a note of that next time you're at the old ballpark."

Victorino spent a long time on the phone with his brother, Mike, talking about how his words had been misinterpreted.

"He felt the media turned things around on him," Mike Victorino Jr. said. "He was so bent out of shape over that incident. He just wanted fans to support the team."

It had already been a tough year for Phillies fans. The national media jumped all over a story about a man who was arrested at an April game for emptying the contents of his alcohol-saturated stomach onto a family sitting in his section. Then in May, another "fan" was Tasered by police when he ran onto the field. The incidents helped reinforce the tired stereotype about the boorishness of people who root for Philadelphia teams.

With frustration bubbling to the surface for both players and fans, a four-game series at home against Cincinnati right before the All-Star break shaped up as the most pivotal of the first half of the season.

When Victorino came to bat in the opener of the Reds series, his first time up since his controversial comments, a smattering of boos could be heard from the crowd. But the jeers turned to cheers when Victorino promptly deposited a 1-1 pitch into the right-field stands for a home run, his 14th of the year, which tied a career high. The Phillies won the game in the 12th inning on a walk-off homer by catcher Brian Schneider. The next night Victorino sparked a six-run rally in the ninth that sent a game that had appeared lost into extra innings, where the Phillies promptly delivered another walk-off victory in the 10th.

The first two games of the Reds series were as dramatic as any the Phillies had played since Halladay's perfect game in May. The third game saw a pitcher nearly do to the Phillies what Halladay had done to the Marlins. Rookie Travis Wood, making only his third career start, held the Phillies without a base runner through eight innings. But thanks to a strong outing by Halladay, the game remained tied going to the bottom of the ninth. That is when catcher Carlos Ruiz broke up Wood's perfect game with a leadoff double, and the Phillies went on to beat the Reds 1–0 in 11 innings. In the final game of the series, Cole Hamels twirled a shutout and the Phillies won again 1–0, making it the first time in 97 years that the Phillies had won two consecutive games by that score.

The Phillies rode the high of an exhilarating four-game sweep into the All-Star break.

Had Victorino's words provided him with extra motivation?

"The booing pisses you off because you think, *What, I'm not playing the game hard?* But deep down inside, it wakes me up," Victorino said before the 2010 season. "It makes me look around and see if we're playing at the level and pace we should be. I might go back in the dugout and say, 'Let's go, let's pick it up.' Philadelphia fans help you see when you need to do things like that."

Victorino's actions off the field spoke loudly about his affection for Philadelphia and the city's residents. In early June, Victorino through his foundation donated $900,000 to the Nicetown Boys & Girls Club chapter in northwest Philadelphia. The money will be used to renovate one of the club's original buildings, which has stood since 1906.

"It's a special day, not only for me, but for my wife, Melissa," Victorino said at a press conference announcing the gift. "I'm definitely excited to give back to the community."

The opportunity to do something worthwhile for kids was a pleasant distraction from some of his occupational stresses. Rumors swirled at the break that the Phillies would make a trade to bolster their starting pitching or to obtain an infielder to fill in for the banged-up Utley and Polanco.

The name most commonly mentioned in these rumors was Jayson Werth, whose contract expired at the end of the 2010 season. But Victorino was never definitively ruled out as trade bait.

"There are a bunch of guys on our club who generate interest from other teams," Amaro said. "We pretty much have inquiries about all our players, every year."

Victorino tried to tune out the gossip.

"You pay attention to it because your name's involved, but it's really out of your control," he said in 2010. "Every year I seem to be the guy whose name gets brought up. It's never happened though, so you kind of just get used to it. You hear about it, but you can't let it influence what you do on the field. You understand that it's a business decision sometimes."

Unfortunately, his inconsistent play only fed into the what-have-you-done-for-us-lately mentality of some fans.

Perhaps because he had embraced the approach of a free-swinging seventh-hole hitter, Victorino offered at more pitches out of the strike zone than he had since his rookie season in 2006. As a result his on-base percentage hovered around .320 at the 2010 All-Star break. His OBP had been in the .350s in 2008 and 2009.

Amaro had a blunt midseason assessment of Victorino. "There's always a question of how a [multiyear contract extension] is going to affect a player's motivation and how they will react to having the comfort of that kind of deal," he said. "This has been a very strange year. Shane is a young man who had been overachieving a lot through his career. Now we're affording him a very significant contract. It was something we had to weigh. So far he's handling it okay.

"Shane is very committed to the community, which is fantastic. And I think there's a fine line between committing yourself to the community, which is important for his image and the organization, and making sure you spend an ample amount of time on your craft. Every once in a while, we have to remind guys that baseball still has to be No. 1."

AFTER THE PHILLIES OPENED THE UNOFFICIAL second half of the season with a blowout loss to the Cubs at Wrigley Field, veteran pitcher Jamie Moyer, who had nine wins at the All-Star break, shared his opinion of the team's struggles.

"I think we don't quite have the swagger we once had," Moyer told reporters after taking the loss against Chicago. "I don't think it was a cocky swagger, it was just a swagger. We have some new faces. That's not the reason, but as teams change I think it's the responsibility for those who remain to try to continue that swagger in the way that we play. We just haven't found a way yet to get running on all cylinders."

On a more positive note, in the second game of the Cubs series Victorino set a new career high with his 15th home run of the season, a solo shot in another tough loss.

The Phillies' losing ways continued in the next series in St. Louis. A 7–1 defeat on July 20 dropped the Phillies seven games back in the divisional race. It was the furthest the team had been from first place since September 12, 2007, the date the Phillies started an improbable run against the Mets to the first of a string of division titles. Adding to the pain of the loss to the Cardinals, Moyer left the game in the first inning with a strained left elbow, an injury that ended his season.

Having lost six of seven games since the All-Star break, the Phillies made a move but not one involving a player. The team fired Milt Thompson, replacing him as hitting coach with Greg Gross, a coach at Triple A Lehigh Valley, as well as a former Phillies player and hitting instructor.

Manuel said Thompson could not be blamed for the team's offensive woes, but he nonetheless had become the fall guy for them.

"The more I think about it and realize it, I felt like we had to do something," Manuel told reporters. "We have to do something to see if our guys can't react and start putting together good at-bats."

After Thompson's departure, the Phillies went on an eight-game winning streak in which they averaged nearly six runs per game. The surge helped them cut into Atlanta's division lead, but in the midst of that streak, Victorino became the latest member of the team to sustain an injury. In a game against the Diamondbacks, he strained his left abdominal muscle while sliding back to first base on a pickoff attempt. The next day, he was put on the 15-day disabled list, prompting the Phillies to call up touted outfield prospect Domonic Brown.

The season had reached a critical point: would the Phillies succumb to their injuries and fade from contention, or could they rebound to win the NL East for the fourth straight time?

Amaro felt the team could win the division again but likely needed another weapon to do so.

Two days before the non-waiver trading deadline, the Phillies made a significant move by acquiring 32-year-old right-hander Roy Oswalt from the Astros for pitcher J.A. Happ and two minor league prospects. It was similar to the deal a year earlier when the Phillies traded for Cliff Lee. They could only hope that Oswalt, a two-time 20-game winner, could provide his new team with the same bounce.

As someone who had been hearing his own name mentioned in trade rumors, Victorino felt bad for Happ, who had shown great promise since joining the Phillies' starting rotation in 2009.

"When he got traded, it was mentally tough for him," Victorino said. "I told him that he shouldn't look at it as a bad thing. He had a chance to go to the Astros and to be the go-to guy. He was someone who could make Houston better."

Hopes for a healthy August were quickly dashed when slugger Ryan Howard got bitten by the injury bug. Philadelphia's slugger hurt his ankle while running the bases in a game against the Nationals. His placement on the disabled list two days later meant that all four Opening Day infielders would miss substantial time due to injury in 2010. When Howard went down, he was helping to carry the Phillies' offense, leading the National League in RBIs and the team in hits, home runs, and runs scored.

If the Phillies hoped to stay in the pennant race while their big guns were out, they needed contributions from the likes of Ross Gload, Wilson Valdez, the newly acquired Mike Sweeney, and other players the team would never have imagined playing such important roles in the 2010 season.

And sometimes they needed a little luck, too. In an early August game against Florida, with the score tied 4–4, it appeared the Marlins had won the game in the bottom of the ninth when first baseman Gaby Sanchez scorched a ball down the third-base line with the speedy Hanley Ramirez on second base. But in what Marlins manager Edwin Rodriguez said was "the worst call I've ever seen in my 30 years of baseball," third-base umpire Bob Davidson called the ball foul. The game went into the 10th inning, where Carlos Ruiz's home run gave the Phillies a 5–4 victory, allowing them to keep pace with the Braves, who had won earlier that night.

With Victorino leading cheers from the bench, the Phillies started August on a five-game winning streak. After a brief rehabilitation stint at Triple A Lehigh Valley, the Flyin' Hawaiian was activated on August 12 for the finale of a three-game series against the Los Angeles Dodgers.

He returned just in time for what was the defining win of the season to that point, an incredible comeback victory that suggested the Phillies had a chance to rediscover the swagger Moyer had talked about earlier in the season. Trailing the Dodgers 9–2 in the eighth inning, the Phillies scored four runs in each of the final two frames to pull off an improbable 10–9 victory. Victorino watched from the bench most of his first game back on the active roster but contributed a pinch-hit walk and a stolen base in the seventh inning.

The win put the Phillies 14 games over .500, pulled them within two games of the idle Braves, and affirmed an observation made by Dodgers pitching coach Rick Honeycutt prior to the 2010 season.

"What the Phillies are able to do is create big innings," Honeycutt said. "You can shut them down for two, three, or four innings, but all of a sudden, they'll jump on you for three or four runs and take control of a game."

For Manuel, the win proved an old saying: "That's why you play 27 outs."

Nonetheless, the Phillies still had ground to make up in the NL East.

The Braves, whose longtime manager Bobby Cox had announced he would retire at the end of the season, showed no sign of fading even after they lost team leader Chipper Jones on August 10 to a season-ending knee injury. In the wake of Jones' injury, Atlanta traded for Cubs first baseman Derrek Lee, hoping Lee and recently acquired outfielder Rick Ankiel would provide added pop to the offense.

The Phillies followed up their dramatics against the Dodgers with a trip to New York to play the Mets, who had humbled the Phillies earlier in the season with three consecutive shutouts. The August rematch started poorly with yet another blanking, a 1–0 game that made a hard-luck loser of Hamels. The next night, the Phillies finally broke through for a run at Citi Field, ending a 38-inning scoreless streak against the Mets. Philadelphia went on to win the game with a 4–0 shutout of its own.

Utley, who missed nearly two months of the season with a thumb injury, returned to the lineup for the opener of a three-game set at home in mid-August against the Giants, with whom the Phillies were tied for the wild-card lead. The Phillies took the first two games of the series, but the Giants averted a sweep by taking the final game in front of the 100th straight sold-out crowd at Citizens Bank Park.

On an off-day before the Giants series, Victorino and wife Melissa held a celebrity fashion show to raise funds for the Nicetown Boys & Girls Club. Rollins, Howard, Hamels, and several other teammates walked down the runway to support the cause.

The Phillies took a big step toward getting back to full strength when Ryan Howard returned from the disabled list on August 21 after missing 16 games with his sprained ankle. Hitting in his customary cleanup spot, he squared off in his first game back against Stephen Strasburg, the Nationals' young phenom who was making his first career start against the Phillies. Howard went 1-for-4 with an RBI, but after getting Ibañez on the 92nd strikeout of his nascent 68-inning career, Strasburg left the game in the fifth inning with an injury that would require season-ending Tommy John surgery.

In the final game of the series, Oswalt won his third straight decision. He and Halladay, who had won six consecutive starts, had emerged as a force at the top of the rotation. Oswalt's contributions took on greater significance in light of the fact that Hamels was struggling to win games. Through August, Hamels, despite pitching well in several starts, had not won a game in his first eight starts after the All-Star break.

But things were generally looking up for the Phillies, and a home series against the Astros in late August appeared to be as good a time as any to finally kick things into high gear. Houston had long since abandoned hope of competing for anything but pride in the 2010 season. They had dealt Oswalt to Philadelphia and unloaded veteran first baseman Lance Berkman to the Yankees. Former Phillies general manager Ed Wade had nonetheless been able to put together a roster that had an air of familiarity to Phillies fans. All-Star center fielder Michael Bourn had come to the Astros in the Brad Lidge trade before the 2008 season. Utility outfielder Jason Michaels, whom the Phillies dumped before Victorino's first full year with the team, had also found his way to Houston. Then there were two of the starting pitchers the Phillies would face in the series: Brett

Myers, a member of the 2008 World Series team, and Happ, who went to Houston in the Oswalt trade.

The ghosts of Phillies past haunted Citizens Bank Park during the four-game set.

In the opener, the Astros rallied for a come-from-behind 3–2 win, giving Myers his first win against his former team. A turning point in the game came in the eighth inning when Bourn laid down a bunt and apparently went out of the base path to avoid being tagged by Howard but was called safe at first. The play was reminiscent of one earlier in the season when Victorino was called out for doing the very same thing.

Perhaps the most dispiriting—and bizarre—loss of the season came the next night when the Phillies fell 4–2 to the Astros in 16 innings. In the 14th inning of that game, Ryan Howard was ejected by third-base umpire Scott Barry for flipping his bat in disgust after Barry said he failed to check his swing on a two-strike pitch. The Phillies had already emptied their bench, forcing Manuel to bring Oswalt in to play left field and replace Howard in the cleanup spot. Oswalt came up to bat with two on in the 16th inning but grounded out to end the game.

Even Halladay could not stop the bleeding in the third game of the series, as Happ outdueled him in a 3–2 Astros win. The silver lining to an increasingly frustrating week was that the Rockies had rallied after being down 10–1 to beat the Braves and complete a three-game sweep of the NL East division leaders.

The nightmare series against Houston ended with a Thursday matinee that the Astros won 5–1, finishing off the first ever four-game sweep by a visitor in the nearly seven-year history of Citizens Bank Park. The Phillies scored a total of seven runs with the Astros in town.

The return of the team's offensive struggles brought attention to the fact that Victorino's average when batting right-handed was more than 100 points higher than his left-handed average.

Amaro, a switch hitter himself during his playing days, could identify with Victorino's situation. "When you're a switch hitter, you have to manage a couple swings," he said. "It's tough enough to manage one swing. I think it's a really a matter of constant maintenance, but you'll have years when you'll be a much better hitter from one side of the plate than the other. This is one of those years when Shane is struggling a little bit more from the left side."

Phillies bench coach Pete Mackanin attributed Victorino's up-and-down season to his difficulty in figuring out how opposing teams were handling him. For one thing, he was seeing fewer fastballs than in previous seasons.

"At this level, the pitchers see you constantly, and everybody is looking for weaknesses," Mackanin said. "It's a game of constant adjustment. That's one of the things Shane hasn't done as well as he could, making the adjustments to how pitchers are pitching him. They've been pitching him very well. They've pitched our whole team very well, and we've been slow to make adjustments. It's not an overnight thing where you say, 'Okay, I'm going to do this or that different.' You have to figure it out over time. That's the whole nature of the game. It's a thinking man's game."

It may be a thinking man's game, but the more thought a player gives to what is not working, the harder it becomes to get out of a slump.

"It's definitely been mentally frustrating for me," Victorino said after an August game. "I definitely don't want those splits, and I definitely don't want to be hitting .250. If I said I don't think about it, I'd be lying. It's just part of the game, I guess. I just have to keep plugging along."

Following the sweep at the hands of the Astros, the Phillies hoped to find redemption on the West Coast against San Diego and Los Angeles. The Padres owned the best record in the National League, which gave the defending league champions a chance to make a statement.

They did just that, proving the Houston series was the final low point of the regular season.

In the series opener against the Padres, the Phillies toughed out a 3–2 win in 12 innings after Brad Lidge balked in the tying run in the bottom of the ninth inning. The next afternoon, Manuel considered sitting Victorino, who was mired in a 1-for-23 slump against right-handed pitching. Some reports indicated he had to talk Manuel into letting him start, but Victorino acknowledged he would have reluctantly accepted a seat on the bench if that was the manager's choice.

He spent the morning before the game studying video of his swing.

"It's a great tool," Victorino said. "I can go back five years or three days and see how my swing looked at any given time. It helps me figure out why I was swinging the bat well during certain times and not so well during other times. It's absolutely miraculous how much research you can do."

As it turned out, the decision to put him in the lineup against the Padres was the right one. Victorino accounted for two of the Phillies' three hits in the game, a single and a triple, and drove in two runs. He also threw out a runner trying to score from second base on a two-out single. His contributions were decisive in a 3–1 triumph. In the final game of the set, Hamels pitched eight shutout innings to top his hometown team and vault the Phillies to a key sweep of a playoff-contending team.

The momentum from the Padres series was temporarily lost somewhere on Interstate 5 between San Diego and Los Angeles. Hiroki Kuroda, Victorino's old playoff nemesis, held the Phillies hitless for 7⅓ innings in the first of a three-game set at Dodger Stadium. A sharp single to right field by Victorino in the eighth was the team's first and only hit. It was the 11th time the Phillies had been shut out in 2010 and the third time they managed just one hit in a game. It also represented the 10th time in the last 12 games that the Phillies had scored three runs or fewer.

In each of the first five months of the 2010 season, the Phillies played at least .500 ball, preventing the Braves from building an insurmountable lead in the NL East. The division would be decided by how the two teams played in the final month.

The Phillies bounced back to usher in September by taking two out of three against the Dodgers. On their way back east for a six-game homestand, they stopped off in Colorado to play a makeup game against the surging Rockies. The Phillies fell behind early but put up nine runs in the seventh inning to beat the Rockies 12–11. The scoring explosion made the team look like the Phillies of old. Backed by six RBIs from Utley, the offense came through on a night when the pitching staff yielded 20 hits. It was only fair considering the pitching had kept the Phillies afloat for much of the season.

Twenty-three runs crossed the plate in the Phillies-Rockies game; only one was scored the following night when the Phillies returned home to face the Brewers, and one was enough. Victorino came home on a Ruiz groundout in the second inning, and Hamels pitched seven shutout innings to give the Phillies their fifth 1–0 win of the season.

In recent Septembers, the Phillies had been both the pursuer and the pursued.

"We've been on both sides of it," Mackanin said. "We've been ahead and behind. When you have a two- or three-game lead going down to the last couple weeks of September, your thought process is, *Okay, let's not blow this*. That can create problems. Other than having a 10-game lead and just coasting to the finish, it's almost like you're better off hanging around a game or two behind those guys because then the pressure's on them to maintain their lead."

On September 6, Labor Day, the Phillies won the back end of a doubleheader at home against the Marlins. The split, coupled with a Braves loss, pulled the Phillies within half a game of the Braves, the closest they had been since Memorial Day. The unofficial days of summer had started and ended the same way. Now it looked like it would be another dash to the finish line, with the six games between the Phillies and Braves in the final 10 days of the season likely to determine the NL East champion.

Melissa Victorino, eight months pregnant, watched every Phillies game from her Las Vegas living room.

"I was glued to the TV," said Melissa, who, in contrast to when she first met her future husband, was now a big fan of the game. "It was typical September baseball. They always make it interesting."

Manuel had juggled the lineup all season, and in the early days of September, he played a hunch and put Victorino back in the leadoff spot. In the days prior to the switch, Victorino had done two things to justify moving him up in the order: he had shown more patience at the plate and he was taking better cuts from the left side.

Manuel's decision paid early dividends. In the third game of the Marlins series, Victorino stroked his first left-handed home run in two months, made a nice running catch, and topped off his night by demonstrating how speed can help win games. With the score tied 7–7 in the eighth inning, he singled to center, stole second, and came around to score on a Polanco base hit. The 8–7 win, which came on the heels of a Braves loss, put the Phillies in first place. A three-hit night in the series finale, another Phillies win, made Victorino 8-for-16 since reclaiming the leadoff duties.

The season had been full of twists and surprises, and Victorino knew better than to ask too many questions.

"I just showed up one day and I was leading off," he said. "Now I show up every day and wherever I see my name is where I'm playing."

A lot of Phillies bats got hot at the same time. In the first 10 games in September, a stretch during which Victorino raised his average from .252

to .262, he rapped out 16 hits, scored nine runs, and stole seven bases. Utley knocked in 14 runs during that period, including a six-RBI game. Most impressive of all, Howard hit five home runs and had 11 RBIs to open September.

Victorino remained at the top of the lineup when Rollins pulled a hamstring during a September 8 game against Florida.

The Mets, a team the Phillies had battled for division supremacy in years past, were slogging through September. With a sub-.500 record, New York was out of playoff contention but in a position to play spoiler against their rival to the south. But the Phillies took two out of three at Citi Field to preserve a one-game lead over the Braves after the second weekend in September. Oswalt's complete-game shutout in the rubber game of the series was the team's 16th shutout of the year, the most for the franchise since 1965.

The Phillies warmed up for their key home series against the Braves with a three-game sweep of Washington at Citizens Bank Park. In the opener, Oswalt raised his record with the Phillies to 7–1. Victorino's 11-game hitting streak ended loudly in the series finale. He appeared to check his swing on a sixth-inning strikeout, but third-base umpire Angel Hernandez determined he went around. The call prompted Victorino to slam down his helmet and bat and storm in Hernandez's direction. The outburst earned Victorino his third career ejection. He was not around to see the Phillies mount a four-run ninth-inning rally that won them the game.

The Phillies entered the Atlanta series with a three-game lead and the intention to deliver a knockout punch.

With the rally towels waving at Citizens Bank Park, Hamels won his fifth consecutive start as the Phillies took the opener of the Braves series 3–1 to open a four-game lead over Atlanta. The next night Halladay became the first Phillies pitcher to win 20 or more games in a season since Steve Carlton in 1982. The 5–3 victory put the Phillies 30 games over .500 and lowered the team's magic number to win the division to six. A combined one-hitter by Oswalt, Ryan Madson, and Lidge, who recorded a save for the 16th time in his previous 17 opportunities, capped a sweep of the Braves.

In one month, the Fightin' Phils had completely turned around their season, thanks to stellar pitching; the return to form of Lidge and several position players, including Victorino; and the key contributions of unheralded players like Ruiz, who ended up leading the team in batting average and on-base percentage. After the Astros swept the Phillies at home in late August, the Phillies posted a 22–4 record, which took them from three games back to a comfortable six games ahead of Atlanta in the NL East.

Victorino's first career leadoff home run helped the Phillies continue their winning ways in the opener of a three-game set against the Mets. The 3–2 victory gave the Phillies 11 consecutive victories, their longest winning streak since 1991.

In a resurrected season, Victorino continued to say what was on his mind, remaining chatty and readily available to the press and public, a point made by Frank Fitzpatrick of *The Philadelphia Inquirer* in a September 2010 column.

"Chase Utley and Roy Halladay are intensely focused and reluctant interviewees," he wrote. "[Jimmy] Rollins, despite being the team's longest-tenured player, doesn't do many endorsements or make many postgame pronouncements. Ryan Howard does Subway commercials but is hardly the big cheese when it comes to publicity. Cole Hamels has cut back on his accessibility. Jayson Werth, as demonstrated in discussing his new agent on Monday, can be curt... And so, though he's almost certainly way down on the Phillies Q-Score [popularity ranking] list, it's the garrulous Victorino, who has become the face—and especially the voice—of this Phillies team."

On September 27, the Phillies clinched their fourth straight NL East title with a win at Washington. Appropriately, a complete-game shutout by 21-game winner Halladay, his fourth of the season, helped him lock up the Cy Young Award and guaranteed his team another trip to the playoffs. The Phillies celebrated this seemingly annual accomplishment with champagne in the visitors' clubhouse.

ANOTHER SEPTEMBER, ANOTHER PENNANT RACE, another scheduling challenge for Shane and Melissa Victorino. The couple's second child, a son, was due October 3, the last day of the regular season. Several weeks before the birth, Melissa sat at her kitchen table in Las

Vegas looking for possible dates when she could have her labor induced so that Shane could be present for the birth. He badly wanted to be there, having narrowly missed the arrival of their first child at the start of the 2007 season.

The early clinching of the division made that possible.

During an off-day before the last series of the season at Atlanta, Victorino flew to Las Vegas to witness the birth of Kingston Shane Victorino, a seven-pound, eight-ounce baby boy. The Phillies had already locked up the best record in the National League, assuring themselves of home-field advantage throughout the playoffs, which gave the proud new father some extra time with his wife, newborn son, and two other children.

On October 2, the second-to-last day of the season, Shane headed back to Atlanta to finish out the regular season schedule. The Phillies took two out of three in Atlanta, setting up a National League Division Series matchup with the Cincinnati Reds. By beating the Phillies on the last day of the season, the Braves salvaged the wild-card berth.

For the season, Victorino hit just .259 in 147 games but set career highs in home runs and RBIs.

Under the watchful eye of first-base coach Davey Lopes (who left the Phillies at the end of the playoffs), Victorino stole 34 bases in 40 attempts. In the process he became the only major leaguer to reach double digits in doubles, triples, home runs, and stolen bases in both the 2009 and 2010 seasons. He also led National League outfielders in assists, which helped him win a third consecutive Gold Glove Award.

It had been a tumultuous six months, but the Phillies, for the first time in team history, finished the season with the best record in the majors en route to a fourth consecutive division title, a franchise record.

"We're that good a team," Victorino said. "We never feel like we're out of it. The way we finished up the season says a lot about who we are."

The ups and downs for the Flyin' Hawaiian during the 2010 season mirrored those of his team, which overcame challenges and uncertainties to secure another division title. But neither Shane nor his teammates had any intention of stopping there.

BACK TO EARTH

THE 2010 PLAYOFFS STARTED WITH A BANG AND ENDED WITH A fizzle for Shane Victorino and the Phillies, who were seeking to become the first National League team since the St. Louis Cardinals in the 1940s to make three consecutive World Series trips.

That goal seemed very much in reach when the Phillies took the field at Citizens Bank Park for the opener of the National League Division Series against the Cincinnati Reds, who were making their first postseason appearance since 1995.

Looking to set a tone for the entire series, Philadelphia sent 13-year veteran Roy Halladay to the mound in Game 1. Making his first-ever playoff start, all Halladay did was make baseball history.

Philadelphia fans had witnessed a lot of stellar postseason pitching performances in recent years, but Halladay's no-hitter against Cincinnati on October 6 shot right to the top of the list. The team that finished the season with the best batting average in the National League never had a chance against the tall right-hander, who threw first-pitch strikes to 25 of the 28 batters he faced. Just one Red reached base the entire game, and that was on a fifth-inning walk. Nineteen balls were put into play by Cincinnati batters, but only two could be defined as hard-hit.

Halladay's gem, reminiscent of his perfect game in May only with much more at stake, was the first postseason no-hitter in the majors since Don Larsen of the New York Yankees tossed a perfect game against the Brooklyn Dodgers in the 1956 World Series. Nearly 1,000 playoff games had been played between the masterpieces tossed by Larsen and Halladay.

Following his first hit in Game 1, Victorino stole third base and scored on a Chase Utley sacrifice fly. An inning later, Victorino's two-RBI single gave Halladay a comfortable four-run lead with which to work.

In providing almost all the offensive support in the 4–0 Game 1 win, Victorino achieved a distinction of his own. His first-inning double off Edinson Volquez gave him 34 career postseason hits, eclipsing Hall of Famer Mike Schmidt's team record. During the course of the playoffs, several of his teammates also passed Schmidt, including Ryan Howard, who finished with 42 postseason hits, one more than Victorino.

"Setting a hit record is a great individual achievement, but I have no problem with it getting overshadowed by a teammate doing something amazing," he said. "To me [Halladay] is by far the best pitcher in the game. Doing what he did in his first-ever postseason game just adds to what he's already proven. It absolutely amazes me how good this guy is."

Roy Oswalt, who entered Game 2 with a career record of 23–3 against the Reds, tried to pick up where Halladay left off. But "Little Roy" could not keep the Reds hitless or scoreless for even one batter. Brandon Phillips led off the game with a home run, and Cincinnati built a 4–0 lead by the bottom of the fifth inning.

Then the kings of the National League Central started to bumble like jesters.

Thanks in part to four Cincinnati errors—including two on one play in the seventh inning—the Phillies scored seven unanswered runs to win 7–4, despite not tallying an extra-base hit the entire game. Aroldis Chapman, the rookie pitcher from Cuba whose fastball topped out at 105 miles per hour during the season, gave up three unearned runs and took the loss.

The first two games of the NLDS showed the dangers of inexperience in the postseason. In two road losses to the battle-tested Phillies, the National League's best hitting and fielding team saw its bats and gloves fail it.

The task of finishing off the Reds in Game 3 at Great American Ball Park in Cincinnati fell to Cole Hamels, the onetime ace of the Phillies who had dropped to third in the rotation behind the Roys.

Unfazed by the reshuffling, Hamels was brilliant against the Reds. Aided by Utley's solo homer and a run-saving catch by Victorino, the Phillies shut out Cincinnati 2–0 to earn yet another trip to the National League Championship Series. A day after the Phillies eliminated Cincinnati, they learned they would next play the San Francisco Giants, who defeated the Atlanta Braves in four games in the National League's other first-round series.

After the sweep of the Reds, Philadelphia had to wait nearly a week for the start of the NLCS, an unwelcome layoff for a team playing as well as the Phillies were.

"You relax, watch the other playoff series, and try to keep yourself fresh and mentally focused knowing the task you have ahead of you," Victorino said over the break. "We know what we want to accomplish and we're ready to keep plugging along."

THE NLCS MATCHUP BETWEEN THE PHILLIES AND GIANTS was fitting in the Year of the Pitcher, as the 2010 season had become known.

The Giants reached the postseason and won in the NLDS largely on the strength of an outstanding starting rotation. A day after Halladay no-hit the Reds, two-time reigning Cy Young Award winner Tim Lincecum blanked Atlanta on two hits, striking out 14 batters in a 1–0 victory. In four games against the Braves, San Francisco's starting pitchers—Lincecum, Matt Cain, Jonathan Sanchez, and Madison Bumgarner—had an ERA of 0.93.

The Giants had the arms to beat anybody, but the Phillies entered the series as a heavy favorite based on equally good pitching, playoff experience, and, at least in theory, the ability to score runs. The Giants' lineup, with the exception of standout rookie catcher Buster Posey, consisted of a cobbled-together group of veterans who helped the Giants eke out a playoff berth on the last day of the regular season. Outfielders Pat Burrell and Cody Ross and infielders Edgar Renteria, Juan Uribe, and Mike Fontenot were all midseason or recent acquisitions with previous playoff experience, while center fielder Andres Torres and infielders Aubrey Huff and Freddy Sanchez were journeymen making their October debuts. During the season, San Francisco pulled off an impressive feat, beating Halladay and Hamels one time each and Oswalt three times.

The first game of the NLCS had the makings of a classic, pitting Halladay against Lincecum.

Ross, who was claimed off waivers from the Florida Marlins in late August, broke a scoreless tie in the third inning with a home run into the left-field seats, his team's first hit of the night off Halladay. Carlos Ruiz, who like Ross was hitting in the eighth spot in the lineup, evened the score with a home run in the bottom half of the inning. But Ross again went deep in the fifth to put the Giants back on top 2–1. Burrell, a member of the Phillies' 2008 World Series championship team, doubled in a run off Halladay in the sixth. By the time Big Roy retired the side in that inning, the Giants led 4–1. The Phillies answered back with a two-run home run by Jayson Werth in the bottom of the sixth but could not push across another run the rest of the game.

The 4–3 loss to the Giants broke the Phillies' string of seven straight wins in postseason series openers, dating back to the 2007 NLDS against the Colorado Rockies. In franchise history, the Phillies had never rebounded to win a playoff series after dropping the first game.

Game 1 of the NLCS was one of Victorino's most frustrating playoff games to date. For the second time in his postseason career, he went 0-for-5, an off night at the plate in which he grounded into a double play and struck out twice. His second strikeout came against Giants closer Brian Wilson to end the game.

Fortunately for the Phillies, Oswalt got the series back on track in Game 2, pitching eight innings of one-run ball. After the Giants tied the game 1–1 in the fifth, Victorino led off the home half of the inning with a double off Jonathan Sanchez and came around to score the go-ahead run. The Phillies broke open the game with four runs in the seventh inning, three of them driven in on a bases-loaded double by Jimmy Rollins. Philadelphia coasted to a 6–1 win that evened the series at a game apiece. The only run for the Giants came on a homer by Ross, a friend and former minor league teammate of Victorino's who had emerged as the most unlikely of playoff hitting stars.

In San Francisco for Game 3, Ross continued to hurt the Phillies. His two-out single in the fourth off Hamels broke a scoreless tie. By the next inning, the Giants had a three-run lead, more than enough run support for Matt Cain, who threw seven scoreless innings and combined with two relievers to record the first postseason shutout of Philadelphia since 1983.

The Phillies again found themselves trailing in the series and flailing for runs. But Charlie Manuel did not panic, sticking with his plan to send Joe Blanton to the mound in Game 4 instead of Halladay, who would've been throwing on three days' rest. Though Blanton had pitched well in the last month of the regular season, he had not started a game in three weeks.

When the Phillies pounced for four runs in the fifth inning to take a 4–2 lead and chase rookie starter Madison Bumgarner from the game, it appeared the team that finished the season with the best record in the majors was finally ready to assert itself. But as happened time and again in the NLCS, the two-time defending National League champs just could not shake the pesky Giants. San Francisco scored a run in the fifth, knocking out Blanton, and two in the sixth off reliever Chad Durbin to take a 5–4 lead. A Werth double in the eighth tied the score. With the game still deadlocked in the bottom of the ninth, Manuel called on Oswalt to try to force extra innings. He got the first out of the inning before surrendering hits to Huff and Posey. Uribe then lifted a sacrifice fly giving the Giants the win and a commanding 3–1 lead in the series.

The Phillies' periodic table included H_2O (Halladay, Hamels, Oswalt), but in these playoffs, the Giants had created a powerful alchemic blend that was overpowering the elements Philadelphia relied upon.

If the Phillies hoped to make a third straight trip to the Fall Classic, they were going to have to do it by winning three straight NLCS games. The first challenge they faced was getting the series back to Philadelphia. To do that, Halladay had to accomplish something he failed to do five days earlier: beat Lincecum.

Halladay, who Manuel later revealed was pitching with an injured right groin, willed his team to victory in Game 5, pitching six innings of two-run ball. The Phillies meanwhile got just enough offense to hand Lincecum his only loss of the playoffs. The key play in the game came in the third inning when Victorino smacked a grounder off first baseman Aubrey Huff's glove, an error that allowed two runners to come home. Victorino later scored to give the Phillies a 3–1 lead. The Giants clawed within a run, but in the ninth, Werth's second homer of the postseason gave the Phillies an insurance run. Brad Lidge shut down the Giants in the bottom half of the inning to force a Game 6.

If the Phillies could win twice at home, they would exhale deeply and move on to the World Series.

But through a combination of missed opportunities, mental mistakes, and bad fortune, Game 6 followed the same script as the other agonizing losses against the Giants. The Phillies stranded the potential tying run on second base in both the eighth and ninth innings. The eighth ended when

Ruiz lined out to Huff, who then doubled Victorino off second base. In the ninth, Howard took a called third strike from Wilson, whose fifth save of the postseason clinched the pennant and set off a celebration by the visitors at Citizens Bank Park.

The Giants went on to beat the Texas Rangers in five games for the franchise's first championship since 1954.

Victorino's playoffs had some high points, but like most of his teammates, he struggled to find a consistent rhythm at the plate. Hitting mostly at the top of the order, Victorino finished the postseason just 8-for-37. As a team, the Phillies hit only .216 against San Francisco.

"Our pitching kept us in ballgames, but unfortunately we didn't hit like we should have," Victorino said after the NLCS and a few days shy of his 30th birthday. "Maybe it was destiny for us to come up a little bit short and to come back even hungrier and get back to the World Series in 2011."

Despite the disappointment of falling short of the World Series, the Phillies could take comfort in knowing that any team that consistently plays baseball deep into October is doing something right. On the strength of four consecutive playoff appearances and a World Series title, the Phillies were enjoying an extended period of success that would have been unimaginable just a few years earlier. A franchise that had seen a lot of failure over the decades was now a consistent winner with the talent in place to continue climbing to new heights.

The Flyin' Hawaiian, whose career took him from baseball castoff to World Series champion, hopes to help take them there.

Watch him race from first to third on a single. Keep an eye out for the clutch extra-base hit or game-saving catch. And never underestimate what can be achieved with big dreams and an even bigger heart.

EPILOGUE

FOLLOWING THE DISAPPOINTING END to the Phillies' 2010 season, the team and its fans had every reason to believe that 2011 would be another banner year. And it was—to a point. The team won a franchise-record 102 games during the regular season and finished with the best mark in the majors en route to a fifth straight National League East title. The team was built on pitching, and the formidable quartet of Roy Halladay, Cliff Lee, Cole Hamels, and Roy Oswalt didn't disappoint, winning a combined 59 games. Charlie Manuel's club also got major contributions on the mound from an unlikely source, rookie hurler Vance Worley, who won 11 times.

Shane Victorino's standout performance that season earned him another All-Star Game selection and even led to discussions in the local and national media about the Flyin' Hawaiian as a National League MVP candidate. Victorino led the Phillies in runs scored and notched the best wins-above-replacement value of his career to that point. Ultimately, he finished 13th in NL MVP voting. Off the field, he received the annual Branch Rickey Award in recognition of his foundation's community work in Philadelphia and Hawaii.

The rest of the Phillies' lineup was decidedly average in 2011. With Chase Utley battling injuries and Ryan Howard failing to match the lofty home run and RBI totals of previous seasons, the team finished near the middle of the pack in the National League in most offensive categories. In an attempt to increase run production and fill the void left by the off-season free-agent departure of right fielder Jayson Werth, general manager Ruben Amaro Jr. dealt four minor leaguers to the Houston Astros in July for All-Star Hunter Pence. The new acquisition gave the Philadelphia's offense a major boost in the final months of the '11 season.

With the best pitching rotation in baseball and a more potent middle of the lineup, the Phillies were the team to beat in the 2011 postseason. As the 162-game schedule drew to a close, the only question was whom they would have to overcome in order to book another parade down Broad Street. On a frantic final night of the season, the Phillies helped determine their first-round opponent by rallying in the ninth inning and then beating the Braves in 13, capping a three-game sweep and putting an exclamation mark on Atlanta's massive late-season collapse. The defeat of the Braves and a St. Louis victory over Houston that night vaulted the surging Cardinals, who won 18 of 26 games down the stretch, into the playoffs.

For the playoffs, Victorino, who hit 17 home runs and an MLB-leading 16 triples during the regular season, was dropped from second to fifth in the lineup, and Utley moved up to the second hole. The opening game of the National League Division Series at Citizens Bank Park was a perfect encapsulation of the Phillies' 102-win season. Behind a strong outing from Halladay—who gave up three first-inning runs before setting down 21 hitters in order—and a barrage of offense, Philadelphia coasted to an 11–6 victory. Victorino, showing no signs of the back stiffness that plagued him at the end of the season, aided the onslaught with three hits and a pair of RBIs.

The roles were reversed the next evening, with the Phillies jumping out to an early 4–0 cushion against Chris Carpenter, who lasted only three innings while starting on three days' rest for the first time in his career. But Lee couldn't preserve the lead. By the time he was removed for former closer Brad Lidge amid a jam in the seventh inning, the Phillies trailed 5–4. And thanks to the combined efforts of six Cardinals relief pitchers, that's how the game ended.

Though it meant little to the Phillies in the wake of the frustrating loss, the game offered a reminder of the extent to which five players had driven the team's remarkable run of success. For a record-breaking 40th consecutive postseason game, dating back to 2007, Victorino, Howard, Utley, Jimmy Rollins, and Carlos Ruiz were all in the Phillies' starting lineup.

"You can't take anything for granted in this game," Victorino reflected. "Getting to play in one postseason game is special, but to do it 40 times with the same group is unbelievable. I will never forget those memories. I will never forget that group of guys. You become like a family and live for the opportunity to go into competition together at that time of year."

In Game 3, the Phillies took back command of the series, edging the Cardinals 3–2 at Busch Stadium in a contest that featured the first on-the-field appearance of a pesky rodent that the Cardinals later anointed their "Rally Squirrel." With the squirrel still on the loose the next night, the Cardinals evened the NLDS at two games apiece, forcing a decisive Game 5 back at Citizens Bank Park.

After exploding for 11 runs in the series opener, the Phillies had scored just 10 runs in the next three games combined. Victorino was mired in a 1-for-12 slump entering the winner-take-all game in Philadelphia. Their bats had gone largely silent in recent days, but the Phillies still had reason for confidence. In addition to having the support of the hometown crowd, Philadelphia had arguably the best pitcher in baseball slated to start. Halladay was fresh off a 19-win season that nearly topped his Cy Young Award–winning performance from 2010. On paper, Halladay had a distinct edge over his friend and former Blue Jays teammate Carpenter, who was pitching on normal rest this time.

The Cardinals plated their first batter in Game 5, and for inning after agonizing inning, the score remained 1–0. Entering the bottom of the ninth, the Phillies had only three hits, and more importantly, no runs. Utley, Pence, and Howard were due up in the last of the ninth. And if the Phillies could muster a base runner, Victorino was in a position to play postseason hero.

He never got a chance.

Carpenter retired Utley and Pence before getting Howard to ground out to second to end the game. A few steps out of the batter's box, Howard fell to the ground in pain. He got back to his feet and limped another 30 feet up the baseline before collapsing again, having torn his left Achilles tendon with his final swing. The hulking first baseman remained crumpled on the ground as the Cardinals celebrated around him.

It was a bitter end to a season that had promised to end in glory. And though it wasn't abundantly clear at the time, the loss to the eventual World Series champion Cardinals also represented the end of an era for Victorino and Phillies baseball as a whole.

VICTORINO WAS UNCHARACTERISTICALLY QUIET in the hours following the Phillies' ouster from the 2011 postseason, but a few days after the loss, he shared his feelings about getting eliminated.

"To me, the most disappointing thing is that this was a special team," he told reporters. "We had one goal, and that was to get to the World Series. On the drive home [after the Game 5 loss], I called my mom, called my dad, talked to my family, told my brother, 'This is probably the hardest one to swallow.' I never look by anybody, but the image that was portrayed in everybody's mind was World Series or bust."

During the off-season, murmurs in the media about the Phillies' aging nucleus turned to full-blown hollers. But the team that took the field on Opening Day 2012 looked much the same as the one that fell in the first round of the playoffs the previous October, with two glaring exceptions. Utley and Howard spent the first half of the season on the disabled list, putting more of an onus on Victorino, who was eligible for free agency after the season.

With the likes of Ty Wigginton, Mike Fontenot, and Freddy Galvis plugging holes in the lineup, the Phillies hoped their pitching would keep them competitive. Though Oswalt hadn't re-signed with the team, its starting rotation was still considered tops in baseball. The addition of closer Jonathan Papelbon inspired hope that the Phillies could be virtually unbeatable with a lead in the ninth inning. And the return to Philadelphia of fan favorite Jim Thome gave Manuel a powerful bat off the bench. If the Phillies could stay competitive until Utley and Howard returned, there might be a chance at another division crown, or at least a spot in the postseason, which featured a second wild-card team in each league for the first time in 2012.

In retrospect, that was just wishful thinking on the part of Amaro and the organization.

A four-game losing streak heading into the All-Star break dropped the Phillies to 37–50 and deeper into the National League East cellar. Victorino's struggles mirrored those of the team; he went into the break hitting just .245.

The Phillies front office faced a grim reality: the team was on the decline and in need of an overhaul. They'd already dealt Thome to the Baltimore Orioles, and as the trade deadline approached, the question was not whether the Phillies would be sellers, but whom they were going to trade away.

Because of his expiring contract and desirability to contending teams, Victorino appeared among the most likely trade candidates.

Amaro waited until the deadline to consummate a deal that sent Victorino to the Dodgers for reliever Josh Lindblom, minor league pitcher Ethan Martin, and a player to be named later, who turned out to be rookie-league infielder Stefan Jarrin. Victorino wasn't the only Phillie going west; Pence got dealt to San Francisco the same day.

Amaro said the decision to part with Victorino wasn't easy.

"As far as Shane's concerned, there are great memories for our organization," he said on ESPN Radio. "Some of the things he did for our organization were special. We just felt like him being a free agent at the end of the year and the fact that we just were not performing very well during the course of the early part of the year, we felt like we had to make some moves to give us some flexibility."

His time in Philadelphia over, Victorino was going back to his professional beginnings, to the organization that selected him in the sixth round of the 1999 draft and left him unprotected so that the Phillies could claim him in the Rule 5 Draft nearly six years later. Two days after the trade, Victorino and his wife, Melissa, took out a full-page advertisement in the *Philadelphia Daily News* to express their appreciation for the city and its fans. It read, "Mahalo Philadelphia and to the amazing Phillies fans for all the GREAT memories!"

The ad didn't begin to express Victorino's sadness at leaving the Phillies and Philadelphia.

"It was really disappointing," he said. "After winning five consecutive divisions, there were still a lot of expectations for us, and seeing things hit rock bottom like that wasn't easy. I became the player I was in that city, and I made a lot of great friendships there. It was frustrating to see my tenure in Philly come to an end like that."

The most difficult part of the trade was telling his five-year-old daughter, Kali'a, that their family was leaving Philadelphia.

"Why are we going to Los Angeles?" Kali'a asked.

"Daddy has to go someplace else to play baseball, but he still gets to play the game he loves," her father tried to explain.

The Dodgers were 56–49 and one game out of first place in the National League West when Victorino played his first game for a team that already included center fielder Matt Kemp and right fielder Andre Ethier, both All-Stars and Gold Glove winners in 2011. With those two positions filled, Dodgers manager Don Mattingly announced that Victorino would primarily play left field.

An ownership group that included basketball legend Magic Johnson had designs on bringing a World Series title to Chavez Ravine for the first time since 1988. And a blockbuster deal with Boston at the end of August seemed to all but assure the Dodgers a spot in the postseason. The Red Sox, who were struggling through a historically lousy season, opted to plan for the future by shedding several enormous contracts. And the Dodgers, whose new regime embraced a win-now mentality, were the perfect trade partner. In sending first baseman Adrian Gonzalez, outfielder Carl Crawford, pitcher Josh Beckett, and infielder Nick Punto to Los Angeles, the Red Sox shed hundreds of millions of dollars in future salary obligations while also ridding themselves of a group of underachievers and malcontents.

Shockingly, the infusion of veteran talent to the Dodgers roster didn't yield the intended results. Rather than taking command of the division, or at the very least qualifying for a wild-card spot, Los Angeles played no better than .500 ball following the Red Sox trade and failed to make the postseason.

Victorino didn't help the Dodgers much down the stretch, again registering a .245 batting average in 235 plate appearances. The only bright spot to an otherwise subpar season was that his 15 stolen bases in a Los Angeles uniform gave him a career-high 39 for the season.

Victorino had no illusions about his future with the Dodgers. Crawford, who underwent elbow surgery shortly before coming over from the Red Sox, didn't suit up for his new team in 2012, but he was expected to be back in action in 2013. Mindful that Crawford was under contract for another five years, Victorino realized he'd likely be switching teams again.

"Once they picked up Crawford, I mean, how many outfielders can you have? The game is a business and I knew I'd be affected," he later told the *Boston Globe*. "I wanted to stay there because that's where I was. I had turned that chapter in Philly and I was in L.A. But when they made that trade, I understood what was going on."

Victorino's performance over the final months of the 2012 season did little to convince the Dodgers that he was worthy of a medium-term commitment, let alone a long-term one. He finished the season with the most strikeouts and, save for his 36 games with the Padres in 2003, the lowest batting average of his career to that point.

Victorino hoped to return to Philadelphia, but negotiations with his former team didn't get far. "We wanted to make sure the Phillies were involved very early in the process," said Victorino's agent, John Boggs. "His first choice was to go back to Philly, but they never made an offer worthy of consideration."

So recently a key piece for a perennial World Series contender, Victorino was now considered an afterthought. Assessing the free-agent market, Tom Verducci of *Sports Illustrated* ranked him behind six other available outfielders: Josh Hamilton, Nick Swisher, Torii Hunter, Michael Bourn, Melky Cabrera, and B.J. Upton.

Any chance of returning to Philadelphia officially disappeared when the Phillies closed on a December 2012 deal that brought young center fielder Ben Revere from Minnesota.

In mid-December, a couple weeks after his 32nd birthday, Victorino found a team that still believed in him. The Red Sox, who were fresh off of a last-place finish in the American League East, offered him a three-year, $39 million contract. Before accepting that deal, Victorino instructed Boggs to check in with Amaro one last time. The Phillies general manager declined to counter the Red Sox's offer.

In signing with the Red Sox, Victorino passed up a more lucrative four-year offer from the Cleveland Indians, who later entered into deals with Swisher and Bourn. There was an ironic twist to Victorino landing in Boston. By trading Crawford to the Dodgers the previous August, the Red Sox had indirectly made Victorino the odd man out in the crowded outfield in Los Angeles. Now, Red Sox general manager Ben Cherington was counting on Victorino to fill the void that Crawford had left. In Boston, where Gold Glover Jacoby Ellsbury played center field, Victorino would be called upon to patrol Fenway Park's sizable and idiosyncratic right field.

"I didn't look at the 2011 or 2012 seasons when I signed with the Red Sox," Victorino said. "All I looked at was Red Sox Nation. I was in the gym during the off-season and saw a segment on ESPN about the Red Sox–Yankees being the greatest rivalry in sports. I thought, *Wow, if I'm going to get the opportunity to sign with Boston, how can I not want to play there?* I played against the Red Sox in interleague at Fenway. Thinking about the history: the Green Monster, Babe Ruth, Ted Williams, Yaz, Jim Rice. And knowing what was still there: Jon Lester, Pedroia, Papi. The core of the team was still good. It was just a matter of finding a few pieces and putting it all together."

Both the signee and the signer had critics to hush. Victorino's deal with the Red Sox raised the eyebrows of some pundits who believed his best days were already behind him. Following the signing, Keith Law of ESPN.com concluded that Boston vastly overpaid for a player who was coming off his worst season in the big leagues: "Victorino is a platoon outfielder at this point, and paying him $13 million a year, even with the rapid salary escalation we're seeing this off-season, is mad as pants." In making his argument, Law rightfully pointed to Victorino's paltry .229 left-handed batting average in 2012, a sore point among legions of Philadelphia fans who felt that Victorino's erratic performance as a lefty should have prompted him to abandon switch-hitting. Not to be outdone, Joe Lemire of *Sports Illustrated* chimed in with his critique of the acquisition, calling Victorino the worst free-agent signing of the off-season.

"The naysayers pilloried him," Boggs said. "When you tell Shane he can't do something, he really takes that to heart. He realized he didn't set the world on fire in Los Angeles, and his goal going into the 2013 season was to prove that he was still a good player. The Red Sox believed in him and knew they were getting a player who was going to help change the culture of the clubhouse."

Cherington, then just 38-years-old, had just presided over the least successful Red Sox season since 1965. And while most of the criticism for the team's poor performance was directed at former manager Bobby Valentine, who was fired a day after the close of the season, Cherington knew Red Sox Nation would get restless if the team's fortunes didn't turn around. "I think I deserve to be criticized for the results on the field," Cherington told Dan Shaughnessy of the *Boston Globe*. "You can't be GM in Boston and win 69 games and be absolved of that. It is what it is, so I accept that, but I'm glad I have an opportunity this year."

Though most prognosticators believed the new-look Red Sox would again flounder in 2013, Victorino entered the season with hope and optimism.

"People talk about the storied franchise, talk about the history behind that ballpark, and when I was there doing that [introductory] press conference, I just started getting that adrenaline rush," he told the Associated Press. "I'm excited. I'm going to go out there and give 100 percent, and I'm going to let the fans make the decision on falling in love or not."

On a late March afternoon in Clearwater, Florida, the curtain went up on the latest act of his career. The Red Sox had traveled to Bright House Field for a spring training game against the Phillies. During warm-ups, Victorino was reunited with his former teammates, a few of whom had spent each of the previous eight spring trainings with him. He exchanged hugs with Utley, Howard, and Rollins on the outfield grass. When the reunion was over, Victorino jogged off the field and into the visiting dugout. The Phillies years were just memories now. He was now a member of the Boston Red Sox.

AS VICTORINO WAS WELL AWARE, a player cannot fully enjoy the Red Sox experience until he takes the field in a Boston uniform to face the rival Yankees. Victorino didn't have to wait long for his chance, as his team opened the 2013 season with a three-game series at Yankee Stadium. And in front of an Opening Day crowd of nearly 50,000 in the Bronx, he quickly left an impression on both fan bases with two hits and three RBIs in a Red Sox win.

When Boston returned home a week later for its opening series at Fenway Park, Victorino was hitting .360 with four runs scored and two stolen bases. The season was young, but a successful six-game road trip provided a marked contrast to the team's sluggish start the previous April. Then, on April 15, baseball suddenly and appropriately took a back seat.

The annual Patriots' Day game at Fenway was played in chilly conditions. But it ended well for the home team when Mike Napoli doubled home Dustin Pedroia in the bottom of the ninth inning to defeat the Rays.

Less than an hour after Pedroia crossed home plate with the winning run and just over four hours after the start of the Boston Marathon, two bombs detonated on Boylston Street, near the marathon finish line, killing three people and injuring hundreds more.

As the city and nation grieved over the tragedy, the Red Sox flew to Cleveland for a three-game set. "Wearing a Boston uniform has new meaning for me today," Victorino tweeted from the road. "Honored and proud to represent a city of heroes!"

"I lived a block away from the bombings," Victorino said after the season. "A day before it happened, my wife took our son for a walk in that area. Then we went for coffee. That's our neighborhood. My mom called me on the day of the bombings, and she was crying. When we left Boston to go to Cleveland, we knew we were leaving our families behind. We couldn't wait to get back, because we knew everybody in the city was in this together."

Later that week, Victorino and his teammates returned to a city under siege. Law enforcement officials had identified two brothers as suspects in the terrorist attack. The older of the two, Tamerlan Tsarnaev, had been killed in a shootout with police just after midnight on the morning of Friday, April 19. SWAT teams were still combing the Boston area for 19-year-old Dzhokhar Tsarnaev. On what normally would have been a busy work day in a major metropolitan area, police urged people to stay home and lock their doors during the search. The Red Sox game against the Royals was postponed. As the manhunt unfolded, the *Boston Globe* described the eerie scene: "Boston's streets resembled deserted canyons Friday. No honking cars or groaning trucks, no aggressive bicycle messengers or absent-minded pedestrians stepping off curbs into traffic. In a glimpse of the post-apocalyptic, office towers languished without workers. Sidewalks lay abandoned. Parking spaces were plentiful. Emptiness enveloped downtown and Government Center, it haunted the Back Bay and Kendall Square."

That evening, police captured a wounded Dzhokhar Tsarnaev in the backyard of a home in Watertown, Massachusetts. He was arrested without incident.

The immediate crisis had passed, but the process of coming to terms with the tragedy was just beginning.

With one bomber dead and the other in custody, the Red Sox returned to the playing field on Saturday, April 20. A pregame ceremony that afternoon honored the victims of the bombing and saluted the scores of people who aided the recovery efforts. As in the wake of the terrorist attacks of September 11, 2001, baseball became a means through which a community attempted to become whole again. After the crowd performed an a cappella version of the national anthem, David Ortiz, the longest-tenured member of the Red Sox, spoke on behalf of the team.

"This jersey that we're wearing today, it doesn't say 'Red Sox.' It says 'Boston,'" Ortiz told the fans, referring to the special home uniforms the team wore that day. "This is our f--king city. And nobody is going to dictate our freedom. Stay strong."

The Red Sox went out and beat the Royals 4–3.

Buoyed by Big Papi's speech, the phrase "Boston Strong" took hold as a post-bombing mantra of hope and recovery. And though the hardships of a baseball team pale in comparison to tragedies like the Marathon bombing, the Red Sox rallied around the notion that they, in some small way, could help the city heal.

"We hoped we could give people an escape for two, three, four hours a day, and we wanted to honor the victims of the bombings and pay respect to law enforcement and everybody else in the community who helped catch these guys," Victorino said.

If the Red Sox wanted to give the locals something to be excited about, new manager John Farrell couldn't have asked for a better first month of the '13 campaign. The team that ended 2012 on a 16–42 slide raced out to a 20–8 start to the new season and remained in first place into mid-May.

As his team attempted to reestablish its winning ways, Victorino embarked on a personal career revival. His most significant obstacle in the first part of the '13 season was injuries, the first of which he experienced during the emotional return to Fenway after the bombing, a game he left with lower back tightness. When the Red Sox visited Philadelphia for two days at the end of May for an interleague series at Citizens Bank Park, Victorino was on the disabled list with a left hamstring strain. During the first game of the series, the Phillies honored Victorino with a video montage that included many of his most memorable moments in Philadelphia, including his grand slam off CC Sabathia during the 2008 postseason. Following the tribute, Victorino came out of the Red Sox dugout to acknowledge the fans. Aware of Philadelphia fans' reputation for fickleness and realizing that his time in Philly hadn't ended on a high note, he wasn't sure how he'd be received. Would there be muted applause? Might he even hear a smattering of boos?

Not a chance. Victorino was greeted with a thunderous standing ovation. The ebullient reception he got from the Philadelphia fans was "the biggest individual honor" he'd experienced as a major leaguer, Victorino later said.

Breaking up is hard to do, and on that late May night in Philadelphia, Victorino and the hometown fans could be forgiven if they carried a torch for one another. Early in the season, Revere was struggling mightily in his attempt to replace Victorino as the Phillies' center fielder, and the Phillies as a team were leaving no doubt that their glory days were over. And here was Victorino getting a hero's welcome from a capacity crowd in the City of Brotherly Love.

However, he had yet to leave his mark on Boston fans. In fact, through early June, he had missed nearly half of his team's games due to injury. To that point in the season, outfielders Daniel Nava and Jonny Gomes had logged more playing time than Victorino.

Because of injury, not poor performance, he was at risk of living down to Law's expectations of him as a fourth outfielder. But that was about to change in a dramatic way.

THE SPRING REPRESENTED A PERIOD OF ADJUSTMENT for Victorino, not only to a new team, ballpark, and set of circumstances, but also to playing hurt. As fate would have it, an adjustment he made to cope with his pain ushered in a period of career-affirming success that coincided with the Red Sox taking command of the American League East.

Since his second season in the minor leagues, Victorino, a natural righty, had switch-hit. It was a skill he worked hard to master, and he took pride in having become at least a serviceable left-handed hitter. But as discomfort in his back and left hamstring lingered, he found himself unable to comfortably put weight on his back leg when hitting left-handed. As a result, in early August, he started taking swings exclusively right-handed. The move didn't get much attention at the time, but when Victorino started putting up torrid offensive numbers, the baseball world quickly took notice.

In August, Victorino blasted seven home runs and knocked in 22 runs while hitting .328. A stretch at the end of the month summed up his extraordinary hot streak: at Dodger Stadium for an interleague series against his former team, Victorino homered in an 8–1 victory; two nights later in a 13–2 romp of the Orioles at Fenway, he went deep twice and collected seven RBIs.

Victorino remained largely silent on when he would resume taking cuts from the left side, but his manager addressed the issue on his behalf. "He hasn't abandoned the switch-hitting situation in general," Farrell told NESN, "but I think he feels so confident from the right-handed side of the plate, why mess with success at this point? Hitting solely from the right-handed side of the plate of late, he's proven to himself that not only can he handle right-handed pitching, but he's handled them with power. I think it just goes into the complete player that he's shown for us. Base-stealing capability, well-above-average defender, and a good offensive player."

Red Sox television color analyst Dennis Eckersley went a step further in his praise of Victorino's fielding, remarking during a mid-September game that Victorino seemed to make an outstanding defensive play almost every night. "If this guy doesn't get the Gold Glove, I don't know what you need to get one," the Hall of Famer opined. Victorino's defensive numbers supported Eckersley's claim. According to Baseball-Reference.com, he saved 24 defensive runs in right field with his glove work in 2013. And he led all American League right fielders with nine assists. His fearless play in the Fenway Park outfield prompted NESN staff to comment that Victorino "never met a wall that he wasn't willing to crash into."

His huge game in Baltimore also featured an example of the bruising trend of a baseball meeting Victorino's body. By season's end he had been hit by pitches an AL-leading 18 times, and he incurred all but one of those bruises as a right-handed batter. His crowding of the plate led some pitchers to grouse that a few of the pitches that hit him would have been strikes.

As his team played winning baseball, they also grew close off the field. It was a common sight for 20 Red Sox players to join each other for dinner on the road. After eating together, they'd hang out back at the team hotel. "We had a lot of guys who loved country music," Victorino said. "[Jake] Peavy, [Clay] Buchholz, [Ryan] Dempster, and Lester would get their guitars out and play. Some were better guitarists than others. We'd sit around and talk baseball and have a good time."

During a season in which he went back to regularly hitting second in the lineup, Victorino reestablished himself as a valuable run producer and creator on a team that paced the league in on-base percentage and runs per game. In Philadelphia's championship season in 2008, Rollins and Victorino formed a strong one-two punch at the top of the lineup. In Boston, Ellsbury and Victorino did the same. Ellsbury scored 92 runs and stole 52 bases from the leadoff slot. And in contrast to the previous season, Ellsbury and Ortiz remained healthy for the vast majority of 2013. The 37-year-old Ortiz finished the season with his highest RBI total since the World Series–winning year of 2007. And Pedroia, steady as always, came to the plate more often than any American Leaguer, scoring 91 runs and knocking in 84 more.

While Victorino was helping to kick-start a potent offense, the Red Sox were also benefitting from the resurgence of two young starting pitchers, Lester and Buchholz, who went a combined 27–9 in 2013. Buchholz missed three months of the season with bursitis in his right pitching shoulder. Before the injury, he was 9–0, and upon his return in mid-September, he reeled off three wins in four starts. In Buchholz's absence, Lester shook off a disappointing 2012 season to win 15 games.

The Red Sox also solved their closer problem, replacing injured Joel Hanrahan and Andrew Bailey with Japanese veteran Koji Uehara, who finished the season with 21 saves and a 1.09 ERA.

After Boston led the division from May 26 to July 24, the Rays briefly knocked them from their perch. But Boston took back possession of the top spot on July 31 and didn't relinquish it for the rest of the season. The month of September served as a countdown for the clinching of a postseason berth. As the players' trademark beards grew longer, so did the team's lead in the standings. On September 20, the Red Sox clinched the division crown at Fenway against the Blue Jays. With hip and thumb problems now added to his list of maladies, Victorino watched the first eight innings of the game from the bench. But in a nod to how much he had contributed to the team's turnaround, Farrell put him in as a defensive replacement in the ninth inning. And when closer Uehara struck out Brett Lawrie to end the game, Victorino joined his teammates in celebration.

Despite missing a sizeable portion of the season, Victorino finished with a wins-above-replacement value of 6.2, the ninth-highest figure among American League position players. The other six free-agent outfielders who *Sports Illustrated*'s Verducci ranked ahead of Victorino? They finished the 2013 season with a *combined* WAR of 7.9. In addition to 15 home runs and 61 RBIs, Victorino stole 21 bases in 24 attempts. His last hit of the season was the 1,200[th] of his career.

Victorino prepared for his sixth postseason trip in seven years, firm in his knowledge that strong regular seasons are all well and good but that legends are made in October.

A 97-WIN REGULAR SEASON VALIDATED Cherington's acquisitions of Victorino, Napoli, Gomes, Peavy, and Stephen Drew. But how would the new-look team fare when the games counted most?

In the American League Division Series, the Red Sox matched up against the Rays, who had stayed alive by winning three elimination games on the road. But any momentum Tampa had on its side entering Game 1 at Fenway Park quickly vanished in the wake of a 12–2 drubbing by the Red Sox. Victorino helped fuel a 14-hit attack with three singles and two RBIs. Boston beat 17-game winner Matt Moore to take a lead in the series. Next up was defending Cy Young Award winner David Price, who had pitched a complete game in Tampa's victory over the Rangers in a wild-card tiebreaker earlier that week. The Red Sox got to Price early with two runs in the first inning, the second on a home run by Ortiz, who capped a 7–4 Red Sox victory with a second blast off Price in the eighth.

With two wins at home, the Red Sox were just a victory away from wrapping up the best-of-five series. The Rays staved off elimination in Game 3 at Tropicana Field, scoring a tie-breaking run in the bottom of the ninth off Uehara to win 5–4. But the next night, Victorino played a sizeable role in ensuring that the series wouldn't return to Fenway for a decisive Game 5. With two outs in the seventh inning, he legged out an infield single that knocked in the go-ahead run. Then, in the ninth, his hit-by-pitch loaded the bases and was followed by a Pedroia sacrifice fly that gave the Red Sox an insurance run.

For the series, Victorino went 6-for-14, picking up at least one hit in every game. He reached base another four times by being plunked. Mike Cardillo of TheBigLead.com took note of Victorino's workmanlike effort against the Rays, writing after the series, "With each passing game this month, we learn there isn't an exact formula to winning games in October no matter what everyone writes or opines from afar. Having guys like Victorino—a World Series winner in 2008 with the Phillies—certainly helps."

After the Tigers vanquished the A's in five games in the other division series, two American League teams were left standing.

In a year of outstanding pitching across the majors, the Tigers boasted arguably the best rotation in baseball. In 2013, Justin Verlander, Max Scherzer, and Anibal Sanchez became the first trio of teammates in more than 40 years to each record at least 200 strikeouts in a season. Scherzer entered the postseason as the presumptive Cy Young Award winner. Sanchez had the best ERA of any American League starter. And Verlander, despite being only the third-best pitcher on his own team in 2013, was still capable of throwing a no-hitter every time he took the mound.

From April through September, the Red Sox had demonstrated the ability to light up the scoreboard, but this was the pressure-packed postseason. And these were the Tigers, a hungry bunch looking to make a second consecutive trip to the World Series. Not only did manager Jim Leyland's team seemingly have an edge in pitching, it also featured a Miguel Cabrera–led offense that was second only to the Red Sox in runs scored during the regular season.

If the Red Sox were going to advance to the World Series, they would need Lester and Buchholz to hold their own against the formidable Tigers rotation. And if either faltered, a third pitcher needed to step up to keep the team's championship hopes alive.

Lester came through with a strong outing in Game 1 of the ALCS, pitching 6⅓ innings and giving up just one run. Under normal circumstances, he would have departed the game with a chance of earning a win. But Game 1 was anything but normal. Sanchez, whom the A's roughed up in his first outing of the postseason, regained his form against

Boston. When Leyland removed him from the game after six innings, the Red Sox were still without a hit. Sanchez's stat line included six walks, 12 strikeouts, and 116 pitches. A parade of Tiger relievers preserved the no-hitter into the ninth inning, when, with one out, Daniel Nava lined a single to center field. Nava's hit put the potential tying run on base, and pinch runner Quintin Berry stole second, but the Red Sox came no closer to scoring. Detroit had eked out a 1–0 victory on the road.

As Victorino knew from the Phillies' abbreviated postseason run in 2011, a team with bats that suddenly go dormant in October can make a quick exit. Having already dropped a game at home, the Red Sox needed a win the next night to avoid going to Detroit down 2–0 in the series.

The Fenway faithful who saw their team nearly no-hit in the series opener had reason to panic after watching the first five innings of Game 2. As good as Sanchez had pitched the previous night, the Tigers were getting an even better outing from Scherzer, who didn't allow a hit until Victorino singled to left with two outs in the bottom of the sixth. Pedroia followed with a double that allowed Victorino to score with Boston's first run of the series. The scoreless streak was over, but Detroit still held a 5–1 lead. The prospects for a Red Sox comeback grew dimmer in the seventh when Scherzer resumed his mastery of the Boston lineup, setting down the side in order and capping his 13-strikeout performance.

With Verlander slated to pitch Game 3 at Comerica Park, the Tigers were six outs away from assuming complete control of the ALCS.

Then, as can only happen in the fall, an indelible baseball moment took place, one that fundamentally transformed the series.

After retiring the Red Sox in the seventh, Scherzer's pitch count stood at 108. Though Scherzer had exceeded that number of pitches in nearly half his regular season starts, Leyland decided to take him out and trust a bullpen that had turned in three solid innings in Game 1.

Following a Drew groundout, Will Middlebrooks, a strikeout victim in his first two at-bats, stroked a double off Jose Veras. With the left-handed Ellsbury coming to bat, Leyland lifted Veras in favor of southpaw Drew Smyly. Ellsbury fell behind in the count 1-2 before battling back to draw a walk. That brought up Victorino, which prompted Leyland to make yet another pitching change. Al Alburquerque registered a strikeout to get the Tigers within one out of escaping the inning and remained in the game to face Pedroia, who slapped a single to right to load the bases.

For all of their hitting woes to this point, the Red Sox were a swing away from possibly tying up the game. And if the team's hopes for remaining competitive in the series hinged on the outcome of the next at-bat, it couldn't have asked for a better situation. Ortiz, among the all-time postseason leaders in a slew of offensive categories, walked out of the on-deck circle to take his hacks against the latest arm out of the Detroit bullpen, righty Joaquin Benoit. In 26 previous plate appearances against Benoit, Ortiz had zero extra-base hits. But none of what took place in the past really mattered on this night. His team needed him, and with two outs and the bases loaded, Big Papi wasn't about to let the Red Sox down.

Ortiz didn't wait for the drama to build any more than it already had. He swung at Benoit's first-pitch changeup and hit it on a line toward the right-field alley. Tigers right fielder Torii Hunter, an able defender if there ever was one, gave chase toward the wall and appeared to have a play on the ball. In what later became a highlight for the ages, Hunter, on a dead run, reached up to snare the ball and, in the process, went hurtling over the short outfield fence. The ball barely eluded his grasp as he fell head over heels into the bullpen. Grand slam. Tie game. Even the Boston police officer stationed in the Red Sox bullpen couldn't help but join in the bedlam that broke out at Fenway.

The Red Sox capped the epic comeback with a run in the bottom of the ninth to tie the series at one game apiece. Following Jarrod Saltalamacchia's walk-off single, Victorino and his teammates swarmed the field and rejoiced in the moment.

"That was the turning point for us," Victorino said after the postseason. "It catapulted us to where we ended up."

A split of the first two games at Fenway normally wouldn't have offered cause for celebration, but the particulars of the situation dramatically altered the dynamics of the series. The Red Sox were back from the brink. But they still had a lot of work to do, not the least of which involved trying to get the upper hand against Verlander in a game that would decide which team was going to take control of the series.

Would Ortiz's dramatic grand slam jump start the flagging Red Sox offense? And if Boston continued to struggle offensively, could Game 3 starter John Lackey keep them competitive? Since signing a lucrative contract with the Red Sox after the 2009 season, Lackey had failed to make a positive impression on fans or a significant contribution to the team. The 2013 regular season was his best to date in a Boston uniform, and now he had a chance to put the disappointment from previous years behind him.

Only one run crossed the plate in Game 3—and it came on a seventh-inning homer by Mike Napoli. In keeping with the emerging theme of timely hitting, Napoli's blast was only the team's third hit of the afternoon off Verlander. Lackey kept the Tigers off the board for 6⅔ innings, and the Red Sox bullpen blanked the home team the rest of the way.

A series that was on the verge of getting away from the Red Sox a couple days earlier had become theirs to lose. With two games remaining at Comerica Park, the Tigers had no chance of winning the series at home. And if the Red Sox managed to split Games 4 and 5, they would return to Fenway having to win just one more time.

That is the position the Red Sox wound up in. In Game 5, a Red Sox win that gave them a series lead, Victorino tried to hit left-handed. But his 0-for-5 night at the plate convinced him to put switch-hitting on hiatus again, at least until 2014.

Struggling at the plate and in pain, it was Victorino's turn to play hero.

Up against Scherzer in Game 6, the Red Sox trailed the Tigers by a run going into the bottom of the seventh inning. Gomes started a rally with a leadoff double. An out later, Scherzer walked Xander Bogaerts. As he did in Game 2, Leyland brought in Smyly to face Ellsbury, who hit a ground ball that the Tigers might have turned for an inning-ending double play. But Detroit shortstop Jose Iglesias, a defensive ace who had played much of the season with the Red Sox, booted the grounder. The bases were loaded.

Having earlier in the game failed to drop down a sacrifice bunt that would have advanced runners into scoring position, Victorino came to the plate with a chance to earn major redemption. As Leyland replaced Smyly with Veras, the capacity crowd serenaded Victorino with Bob Marley's "Three Little Birds," his walk-up music for the 2013 season. He fell behind in the count 0-2 before lifting a Veras curveball high into the Boston night and over the Green Monster. The blast propelled Boston to a 5–2 win, and Victorino joined Thome as the only players in major league history with multiple postseason grand slams.

Baseball, especially its postseason, is all about moments and pictures, both moving and still. The 2013 American League Championship Series featured a pair of iconic visual moments: Ortiz's Game 2 grand slam, with its enduring image of a jubilant police officer and a tumbling outfielder, qualifies as one of the most memorable postseason plays ever. And in terms of dramatic flair and guaranteed posterity, Victorino's seventh-inning shot over the Green Monster in Game 6 rivaled Ortiz's blast. It was an antidote to Bucky Bleepin' Dent, who broke the hearts of Red Sox Nation in 1978 with a similar Monster-clearing blast.

"Boston Strong!" Victorino exclaimed after the game in a televised on-the-field interview that was simulcast in Fenway Park. "People counted me out, people said last year I was done. No. When I came here, there was 'rejubilation.' There was something inside of me that said I wanted to prove something."

Back in the "rejubilant" clubhouse, Victorino reflected on his clutch hit: "My thought was to just get something in the air and get us back into the game. When I hit it, I started to think maybe it could hit the wall or go out. It was a big moment. I was excited. I started to pound my chest going around the bases. I hope [the Tigers] understand. It was a special moment. I meant no disrespect to them."

A few weeks after the World Series, Victorino reflected again on his gigantic hit: "I was struggling at the plate. People were questioning whether I should be moved down in the lineup or benched. A moment like that makes people forget what happened before it."

The momentous hit got Victorino some quality time after the game with U.S. Secretary of State John Kerry, a former Massachusetts senator. More importantly, it got the Red Sox to the World Series.

FOR THE FIRST TIME SINCE 1999, the World Series featured a matchup between the two teams with the best records in their respective leagues. The Red Sox and St. Louis Cardinals had for the past decade established themselves as baseball elites. The Cardinals were appearing in their fourth World Series in 10 years, and the Red Sox were back in the Fall Classic for the third time since 2004, the year they swept St. Louis for their first World Series victory since 1918.

On the strength of pitching and key hits by Ortiz, Victorino, and Napoli, the Red Sox got past the Tigers. It was doubtful, however, that they could win another series without showing some consistency on offense.

During the regular season, the Cardinals had been the best clutch-hitting team in baseball, posting a remarkable .330 average with runners in scoring position. And their pitching was peaking at the right time, too. In the NLCS, St. Louis held the Dodgers to just 13 runs in six games. Adam Wainwright was the undisputed ace of the staff, but a 22-year-old rookie named Michael Wacha had emerged as the postseason's biggest revelation, winning three games and posting a 0.43 ERA to help St. Louis win the National League pennant.

The opening game of the World Series combined the best of what the Red Sox had to offer: they knocked Wainwright around and got help from a porous Cardinals defense that committed three errors. Lester, meanwhile, dominated the opposing lineup, pitching 7⅔ innings of scoreless ball. Behind two hits each from Ortiz and Pedroia, the Red Sox cruised to an 8–1 victory in a game that would have been even more lopsided had Carlos Beltran not robbed Ortiz of a grand slam in the second inning.

The Cardinals drew even in the series the next night, scoring three times in the seventh inning to secure a 4–2 win.

After a pedestrian start, the 2013 World Series was about to get extremely peculiar. In Game 3, the Red Sox erased an early two-run deficit to tie the game, only to see the Cardinals plate two more runs to take a 4–2 lead. Boston rallied in the eighth to draw even again.

The game remained tied entering the bottom of the ninth. Brandon Workman fanned Matt Adams but then gave up a single to Yadier Molina. Uehara, the MVP of the American League Championship Series, entered the game to try and preserve the tie. Allen Craig greeted Uehara with a double that put runners on second and third with one out, paving the way for one of the oddest finishes in postseason history.

It started with a sharp grounder to Pedroia at second. If the ball had slipped through the infield, the Cardinals would have registered a routine walk-off win. But Pedroia snared the ball, sprung to his feet, and threw home to nail Molina at the plate. Meanwhile, Craig was on his way to third base. Saltalamacchia's throw to third baseman Will Middlebrooks soared wide and into foul territory as Craig slid into the bag. Middlebrooks, sprawled out on his stomach, lifted his legs in the air and tripped Craig, who had gotten to his feet and was heading for home. The play continued, with Daniel Nava appearing to throw out Craig at the plate. But third-base umpire Jim Joyce ruled that Middlebrooks had interfered with Craig. The Cardinals swarmed the field, victory theirs on the walk-off obstruction call, a postseason first.

Victorino and his teammates were dumbfounded. "You go from watching your second baseman make a great play in a pressure situation to asking yourself, 'What just happened?'" he said. "It was a shock. We went into the clubhouse and were arguing amongst each other, just trying to figure out what had happened. You never want to see a game end that way, but it turned out it was the right call."

Through three games of the World Series, Victorino was 0-for-10. His body wasn't feeling right, and his manager knew it. Shortly before Game 4, Victorino was scratched from the lineup with the same lower back tightness that had plagued him during the season.

"I was hoping my World Series wasn't over. I was going to do whatever I needed to get back out there," Victorino said later. "It was one of the most difficult decisions I've ever had to make, but what made it easier was knowing that we had guys on the team who were prepared to step in."

Farrell moved Nava from left field to right field and inserted Gomes into the lineup as the left fielder. Gomes, who entered the game hitless in his eight at-bats during the series, took advantage of his unexpected start.

With the score tied at 1–1 in the top of the sixth inning, Cardinals starting pitcher Lance Lynn yielded a two-out single to Pedroia. When Ortiz followed with a walk, Matheny replaced Lynn with Seth Maness, who had yet to yield an earned run in seven postseason relief appearances. The odds appeared in St. Louis' favor. But this postseason was all about the unusual. Gomes blasted a 2-2 pitch from Maness over the left-field wall for a three-run home run.

The Cardinals cut the lead to 4–2, but their attempt to stage a late-inning comeback came to a crashing halt when, with Beltran at the plate, Uehara picked pinch runner Kolten Wong off first base with two outs in the bottom of the ninth. Yet again, a World Series game ended in a way none ever had before, this time on a pick-off play.

"It's great to see what happened tonight," Victorino said after the game. "Sometimes you don't play and you see someone go in for you at your position and they make a mistake, or don't have a good night, you feel worse. But with Jonny, I know every day he's thinking he's playing. Every day he's 'game on.'"

Wong, a former first-round pick out of the University of Hawaii, played the role of the goat. If Victorino was the Flyin' Hawaiian, then the rookie Wong was the Cryin' Hawaiian when he tearfully spoke to reporters after the game. Victorino and Wong, whose shared background sparked a friendship, traded text messages and enjoyed a meal together during the postseason. Following Wong's enormous World Series gaffe, Victorino reached out to comfort his friend: "I texted him after the game and told him how I respected the way he stood up in front of the media and answered questions. I told him that everything that happens in the game is part of the learning curve."

Victorino sat out the final game in St. Louis and watched from the bench as Lester capped his masterful postseason with 7⅔ innings of one-run ball. Uehara retired the Cardinals in order in the ninth to record his seventh save of the postseason.

Boston now faced the same scenario it had in the ALCS, needing to win one of two games at Fenway. On the off-day before Game 6, Victorino got what Dennis Eckersley and many others believed he so richly deserved: his fourth Gold Glove Award.

With his team a victory away from clinching a World Series championship at Fenway for the first time since 1918, Victorino willed himself back into action. Dropped to sixth in the batting order, his first hit of the World Series ended up being a decisive one. His two-out, three-run double off Wacha in the third inning staked the Red Sox to a lead they never surrendered. As Ortiz walked back to the dugout after crossing home plate, he pointed at Victorino and rubbed his fingers together, a gesture signifying that Victorino was a "money player." It was also an indication of the growing kinship between the massive Dominican and the compact Hawaiian.

"Papi is one of those guys who make you want to be better," Victorino said. "People doubted him and questioned him a few years ago, too. I felt I was kind of in the same boat. He's a special individual, and I'm lucky to call him a teammate."

Following four straight close battles, the outcome of Game 6 was never really in question after Victorino knocked in a trio of runs. Junichi Tazawa got his sixth hold of the postseason, and Uehara came on in the ninth inning to finish off Boston's 6–1 victory.

The celebration near home plate at Fenway Park featured a sight almost identical to the one that took place five years and three days earlier. Back then, Victorino leaped onto a pile of joyous Philadelphia Phillies, who were celebrating the second championship in franchise history. This time, with equal aplomb, the former high school sprinter dashed in and perfectly timed his vault onto the top of a group of frenzied teammates. He later conducted postgame interviews with his son, Kingston, in his arms. Soon joined by his wife and daughter, Victorino enjoyed the festivities well into the early morning hours.

"The moment itself and thinking back to April 15 and what happened to the city amplified the excitement," Victorino said. "To be part of a team that could bring happiness back to the city and to win the final game at Fenway, talk about special! It still hasn't sunk in."

On the day of the victory parade, which included the team escorting the World Series trophy to the finish line of the Boston Marathon, an estimated 2 million people joined the revelry. Photos of a shirtless Mike Napoli roaming the streets of chilly Boston circulated on the Internet. Another set of photos featuring Victorino buying groceries at a local supermarket also surfaced online. The following week started with Ortiz, Victorino, and bullpen police officer Steve Horgan participating in a nationally televised shaving of their beards. It continued with Gomes and Victorino appearing on Boston native Conan O'Brien's late-night talk show.

ONLY A SELECT GROUP OF PLAYERS can say they played an instrumental role in helping two different teams achieve World Series glory. Even fewer can lay claim to having done so in two baseball-crazed cities like Boston and Philadelphia.

The 2013 Red Sox were a memorable bunch. The clutch hitting of Victorino and Ortiz, the steady play of Ellsbury and Pedroia, a pitching staff that outperformed its more touted counterparts in the playoffs, a pair of Japanese imports making an impact out of the bullpen, and the flowing beards worn by nearly everyone on the team. Big Papi, Salty, the Muddy Chicken, and the Flyin' Hawaiian. The team constructed by Ben Cherington, who was honored with the Executive of the Year Award, and led by John Farrell had personality, and more importantly, got winning results.

The 2013 season represented another chapter in Victorino's incredible baseball journey. Left unprotected by the Dodgers, cut loose by the Padres, cast aside again by the Dodgers, embraced in Philadelphia, and then faced with another period of uncertainty. Now this. And more change was on the horizon. Ellsbury's move to the Yankees after the season paved the way for a possible return to center field for Victorino.

The festive ending to the 2013 season left little doubt that Shane Victorino had found another home.

ACKNOWLEDGMENTS

WHEN THE FIRST EDITION OF THIS BOOK came out in 2011, Shane Victorino and the Philadelphia Phillies were enjoying a period of unprecedented success. Shane had overcome myriad personal and professional obstacles to establish himself as a fixture in the Phillies outfield. A lot can change in a few years, however. And I thank Triumph Books for the opportunity to update readers on the significant developments in Shane's career. Tom Bast and Adam Motin were great to work with on both editions of the book.

Chuck Myron, a trusted friend and supremely talented writer and editor, was an invaluable source of support and guidance from the time I first proposed a Victorino book in 2009 to the publication of this second edition.

I wouldn't have been able to fully tell Shane's story without the wonderful anecdotes and reminiscences of the Victorino family.

Perry Rogers believed in this project from day one, and Shane's agent, John Boggs, showed equal enthusiasm for the book's second edition.

Thanks to Jim McCloskey, Kate Germond, and everyone at Centurion Ministries. It's a pleasure to work with such dedicated and talented people.

Several articles and columns that appeared in the Boston press helped me gain better perspective on the 2013 Red Sox, just as the Philadelphia media's coverage of Shane and the Phillies aided the writing of the first edition. In both editions, I relied heavily on the trove of information available at baseball-reference.com.

Thanks to my sister, Gill, and parents, Mort and Elaine, all of whom know writing, baseball, and how to provide copious amounts of love and encouragement.

I'm grateful to my wife, Angela, for her love and unwavering support. The newest addition to our family, Lisette, came off the bench just in time to see the Red Sox win the 2013 World Series. Her older sisters, Dasia, Madison, and Annabelle, look forward to going to her first baseball game with her.

Thanks finally to Shane Victorino for sharing his own story with humor, candor, and incredible detail.

ABOUT THE AUTHOR

Alan Maimon is an award-winning journalist, author, and researcher. As a newspaper reporter, he was a finalist for the 2004 Pulitzer Prize in Public Service. He is the co-author of *If You Love This Game: An MVP's Life in Baseball* (with Andre Dawson) and *The Mouth that Roared: My Six Outspoken Decades in Baseball* (with Dallas Green). He started his professional writing career as a news assistant and sportswriter in the Berlin bureau of *The New York Times*. He is currently a staff investigator for Centurion Ministries, a nonprofit based in Princeton, New Jersey, that works to vindicate and free wrongfully convicted prisoners. He is a Philadelphia native and a graduate of Brown University.